BATMAN AND THE OUTSIDERS

The CHRYSALIS

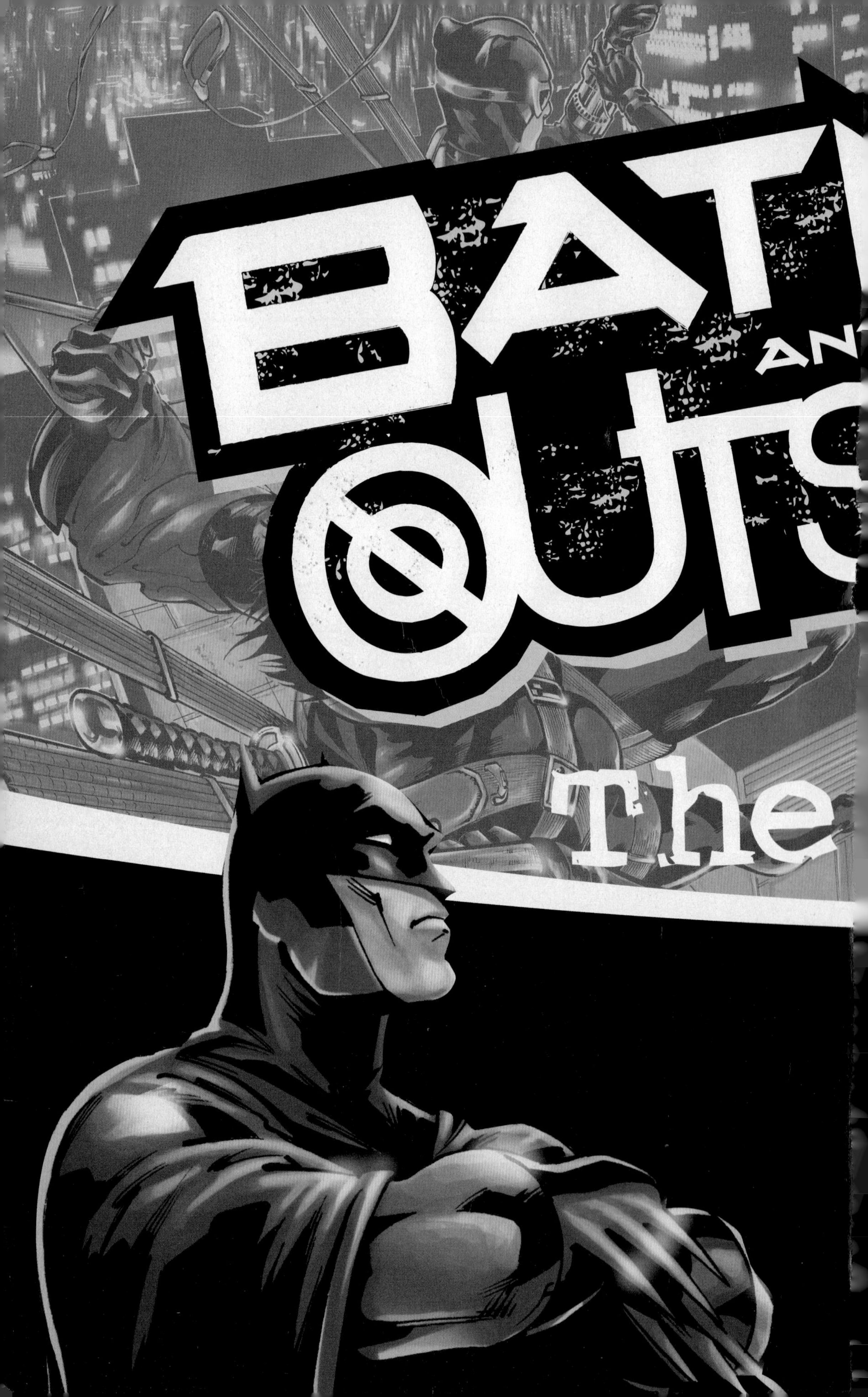
BAT
AN
OUTS
The

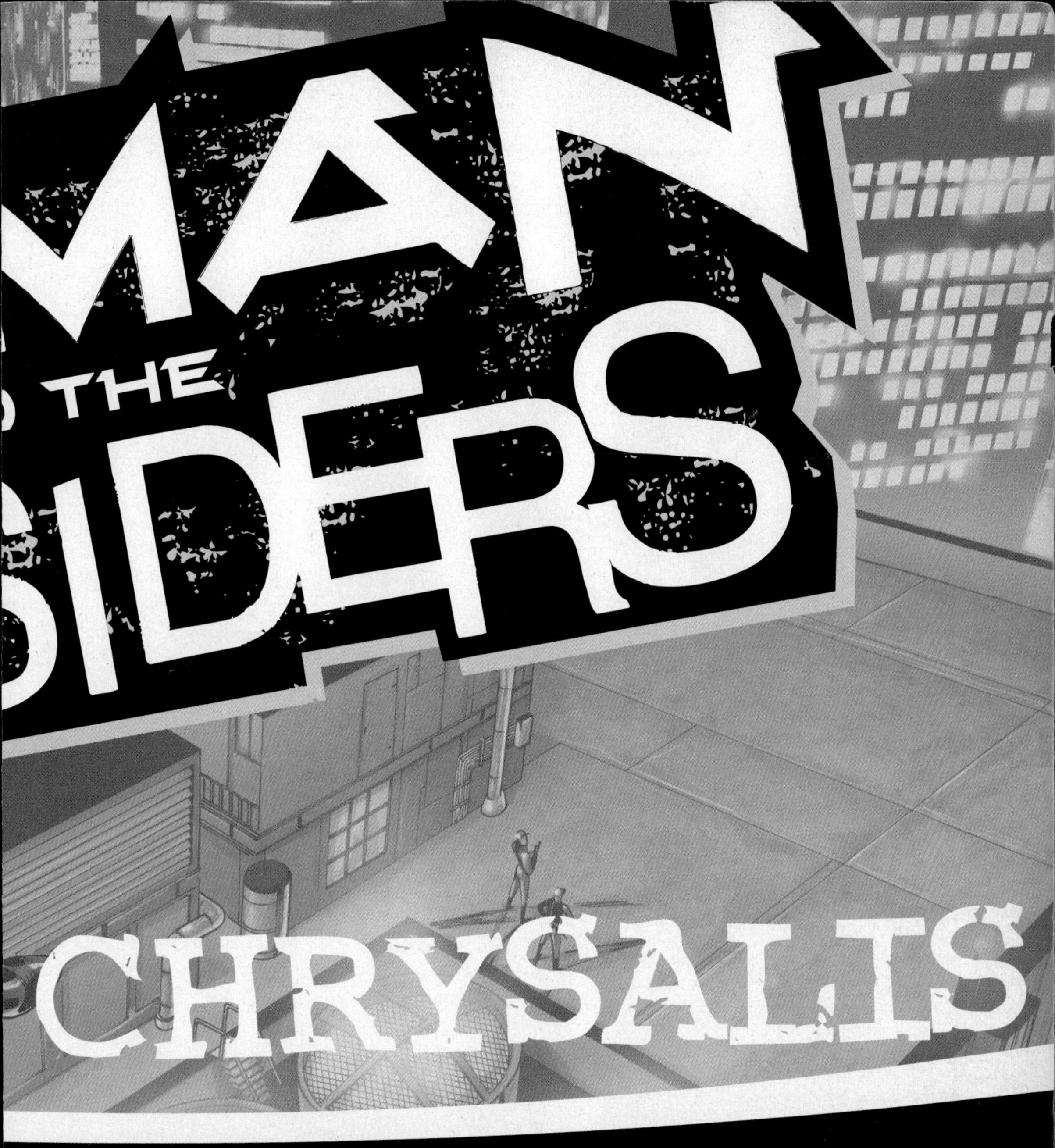
MAN
THE
SIDERS
CHRYSALIS

WRITTEN BY
CHUCK DIXON

PENCILS BY
JULIAN LOPEZ
CARLOS RODRIGUEZ

INKS BY
BIT

COLORS BY
MARTA MARTINEZ
with JAVIER MENA

LETTERED BY
TRAVIS LANHAM
KEN LOPEZ
NICK J. NAPOLITANO
STEVE WANDS

ORIGINAL SERIES COVERS BY
DOUG BRAITHWAITE
RYAN SOOK
ERIC BATTLE
ART THIBERT

BATMAN CREATED BY BOB KANE

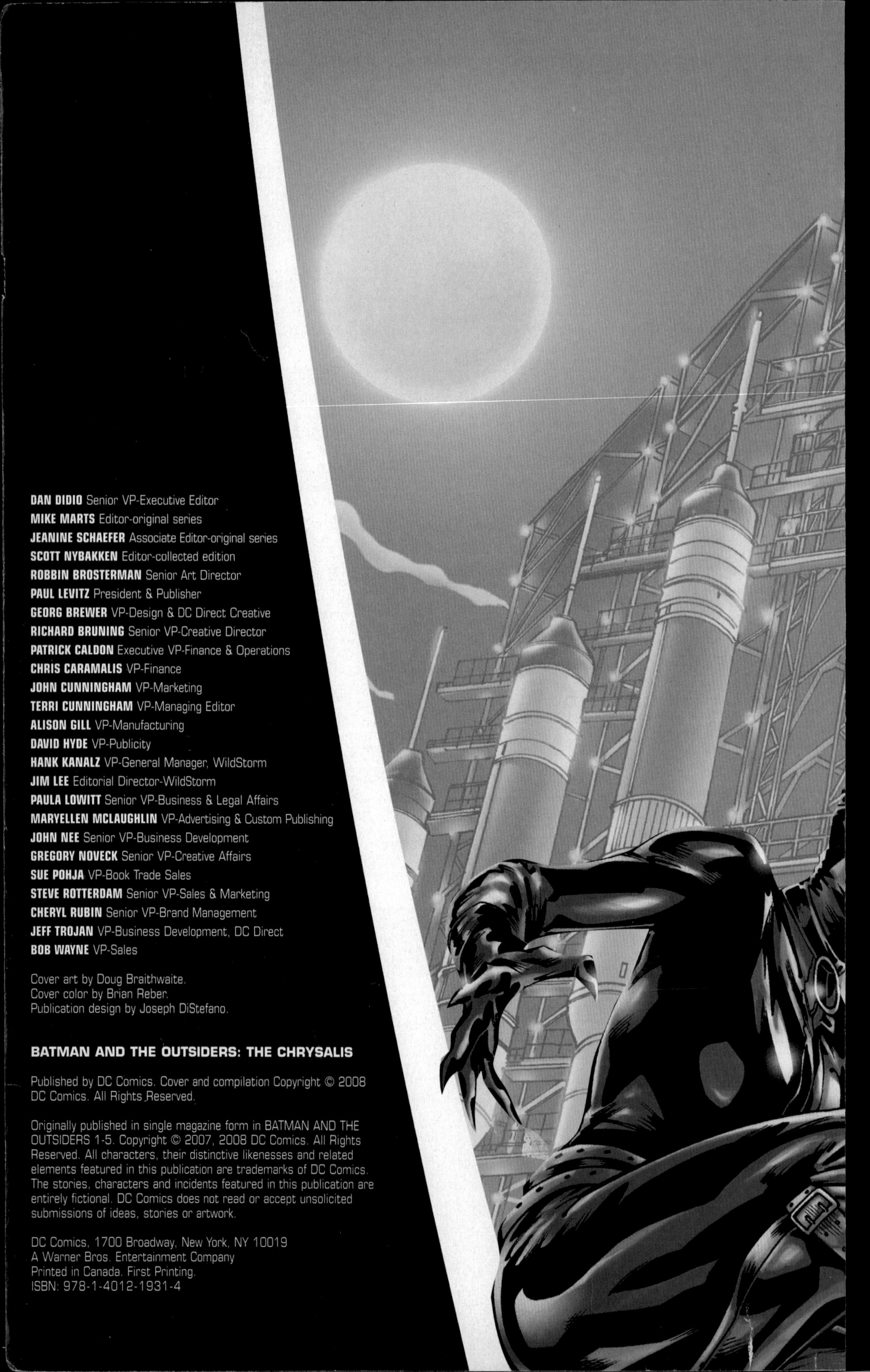

Cover art by Doug Braithwaite.
Cover color by Brian Reber.
Publication design by Joseph DiStefano.

BATMAN AND THE OUTSIDERS: THE CHRYSALIS

DC Comics, 1700 Broadway, New York, NY 10019
A Warner Bros. Entertainment Company
Printed in Canada. First Printing.
ISBN: 978-1-4012-1931-4

Contents

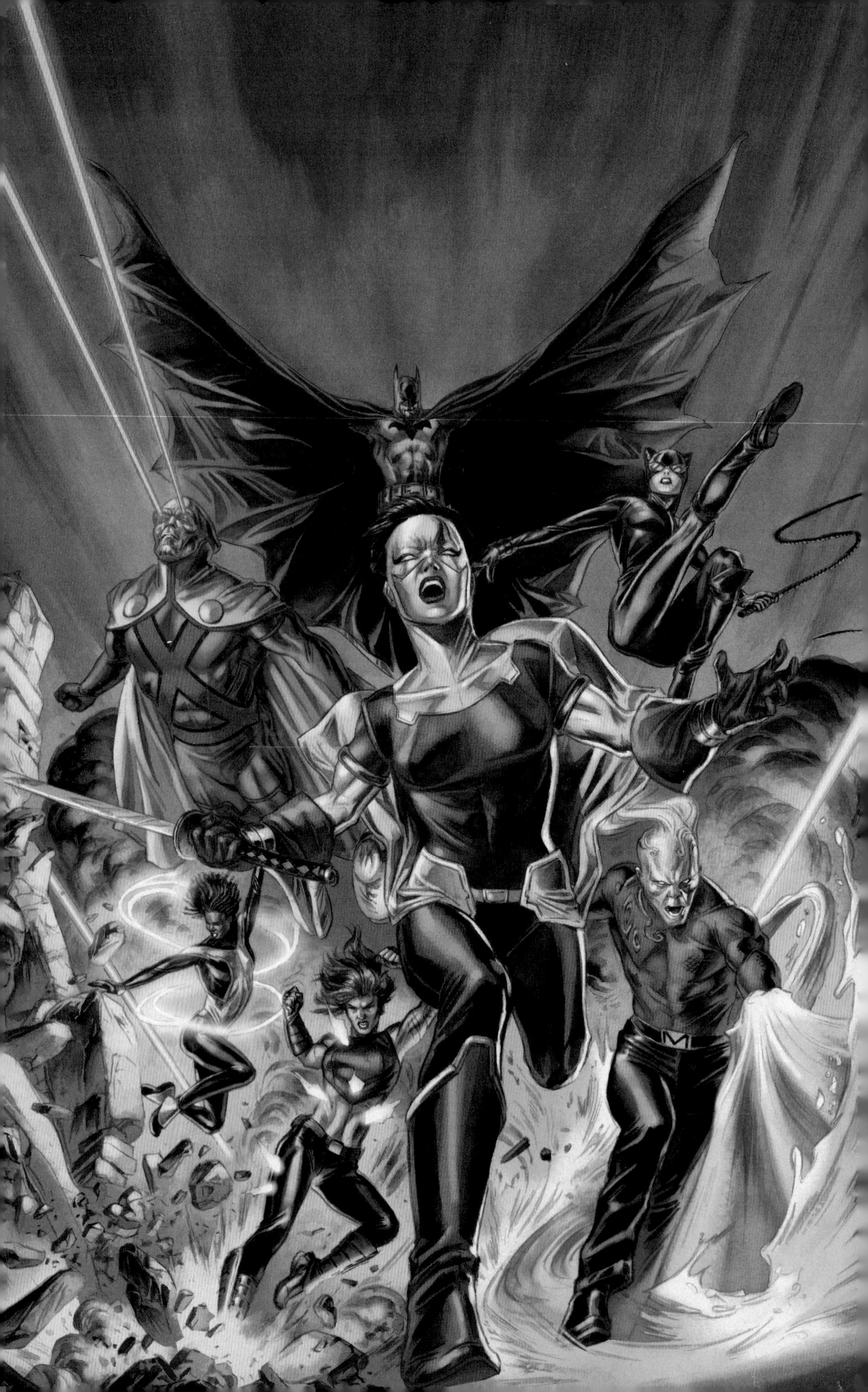

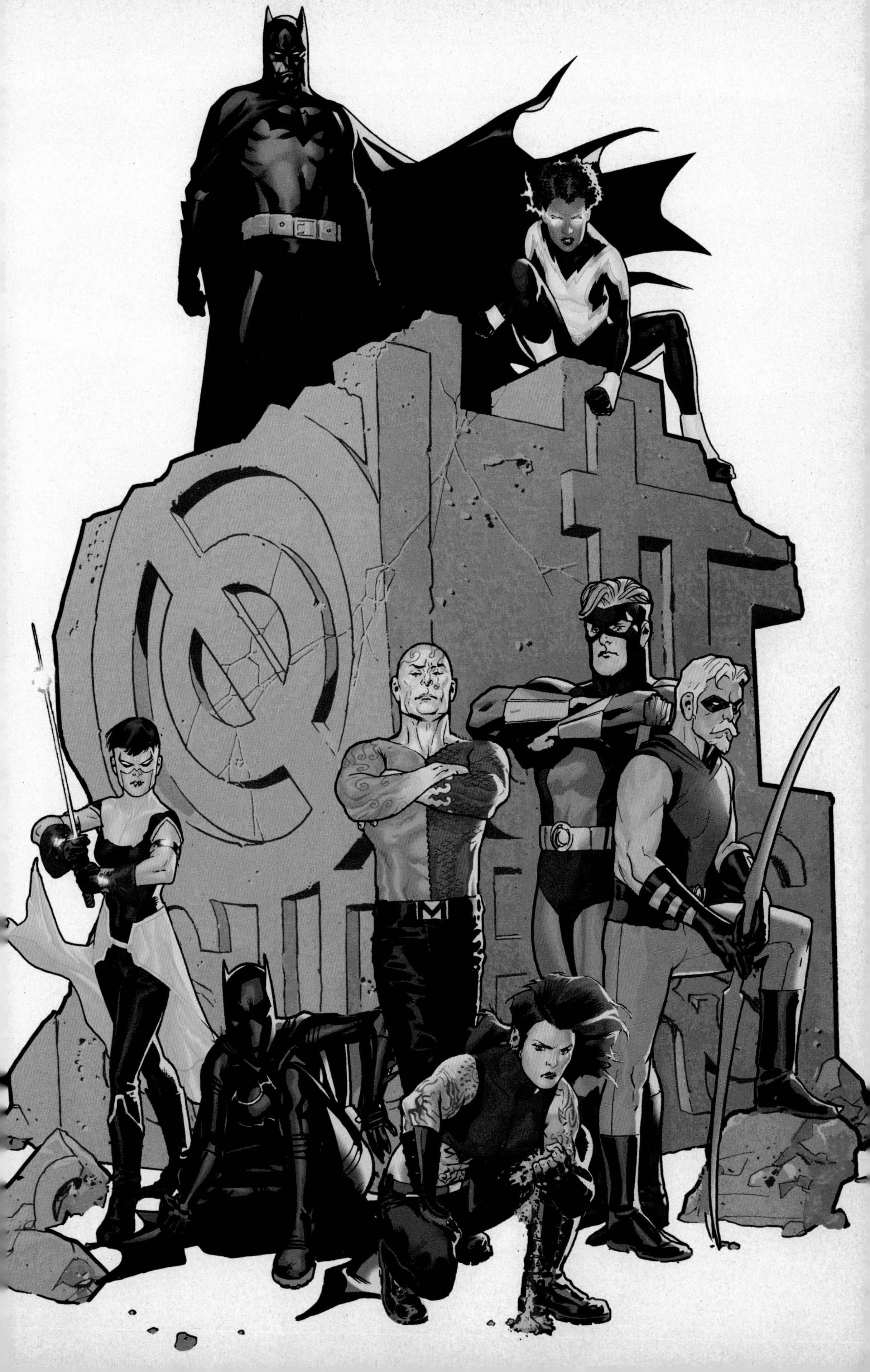

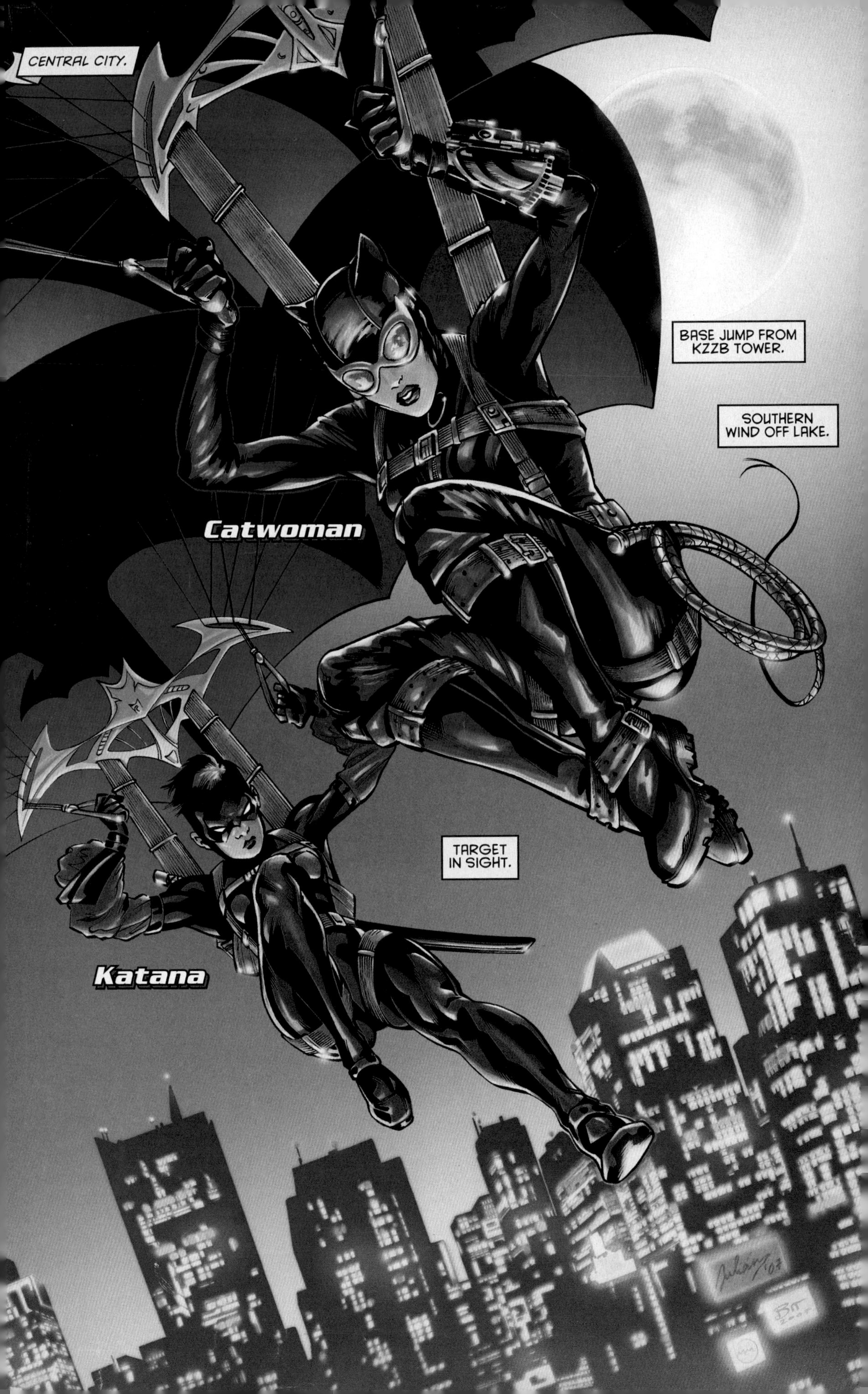
CENTRAL CITY.
BASE JUMP FROM KZZB TOWER.
SOUTHERN WIND OFF LAKE.
Catwoman
TARGET IN SIGHT.
Katana

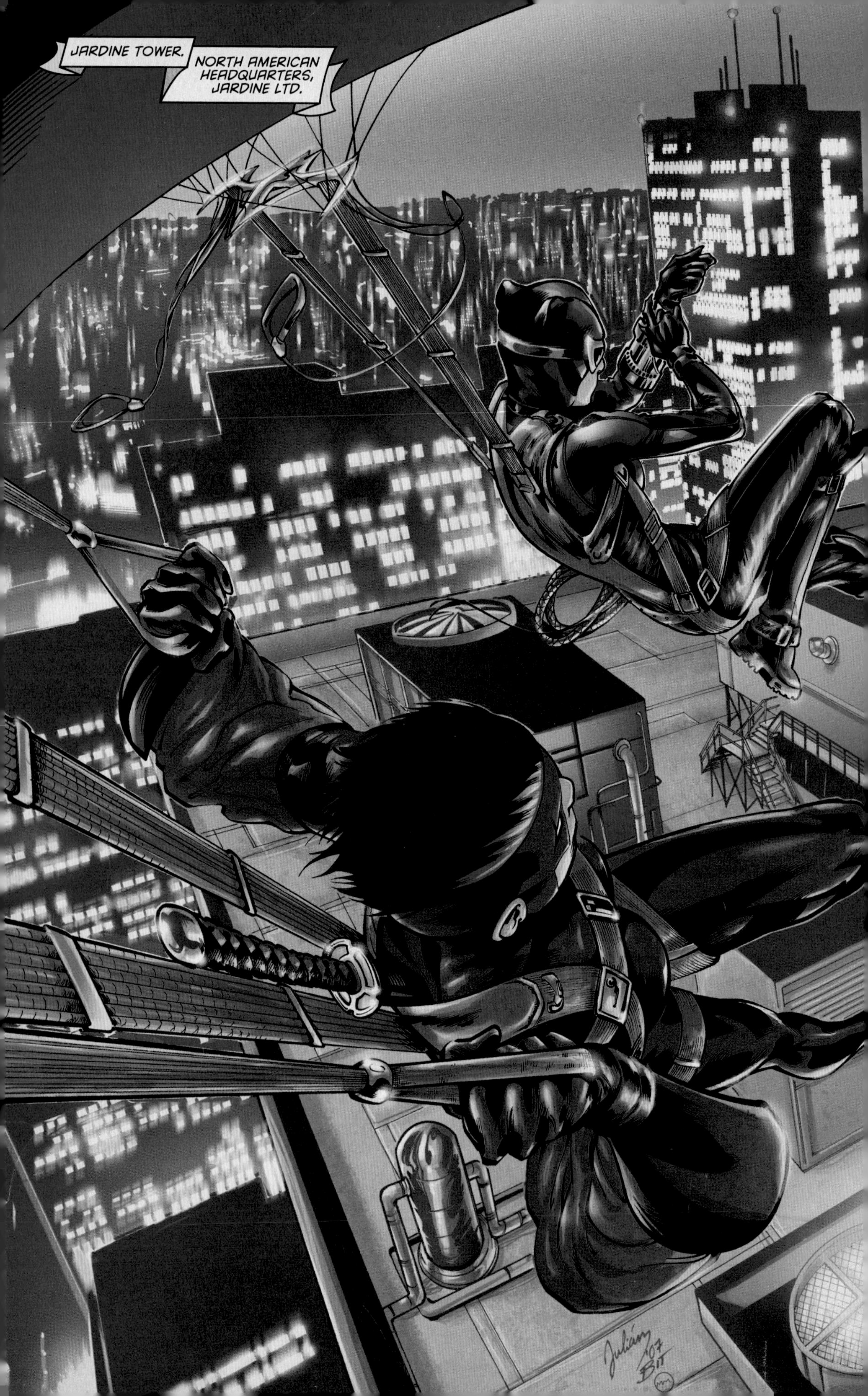
JARDINE TOWER.
NORTH AMERICAN HEADQUARTERS, JARDINE LTD.

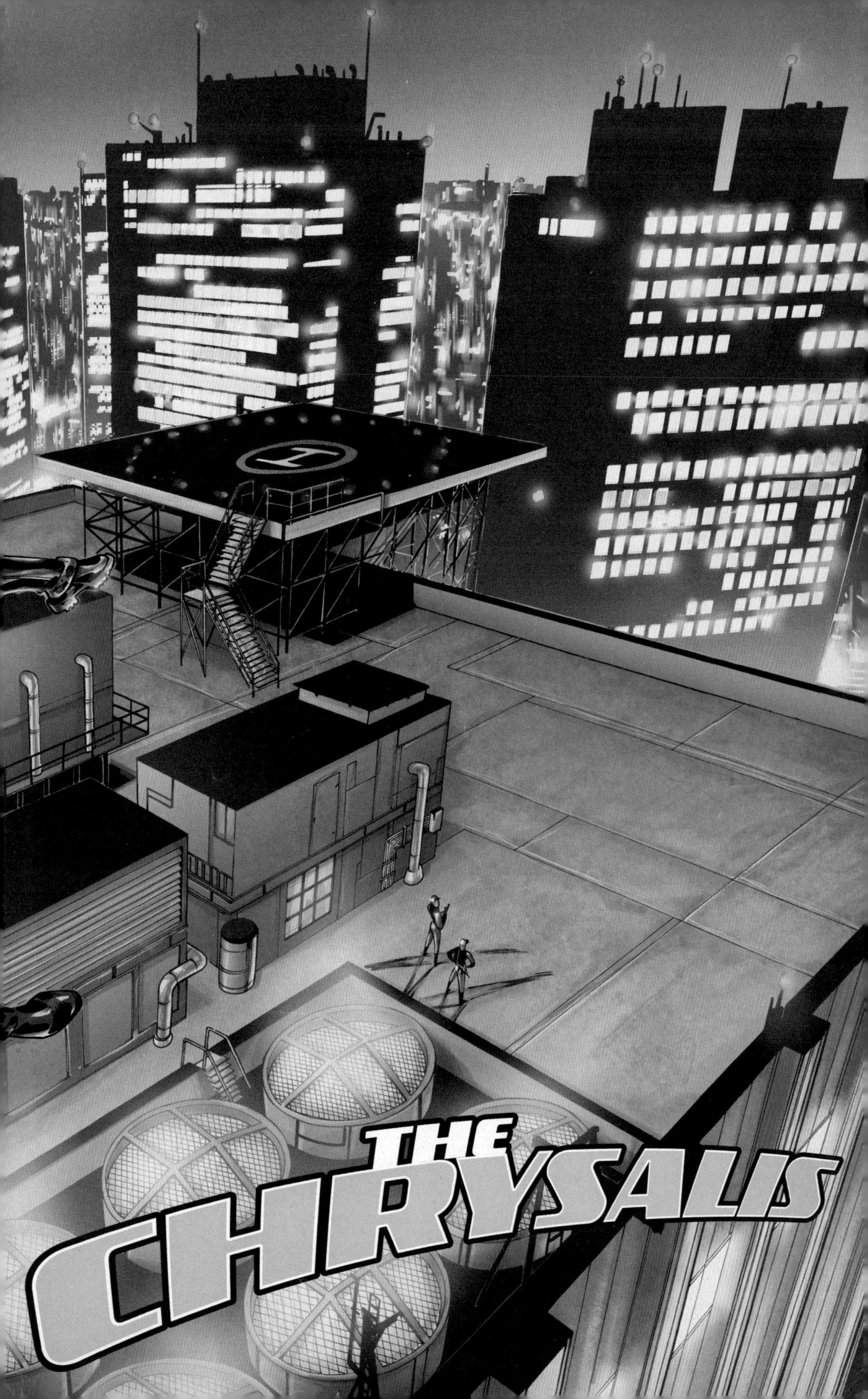
THE
CHRYSALIS

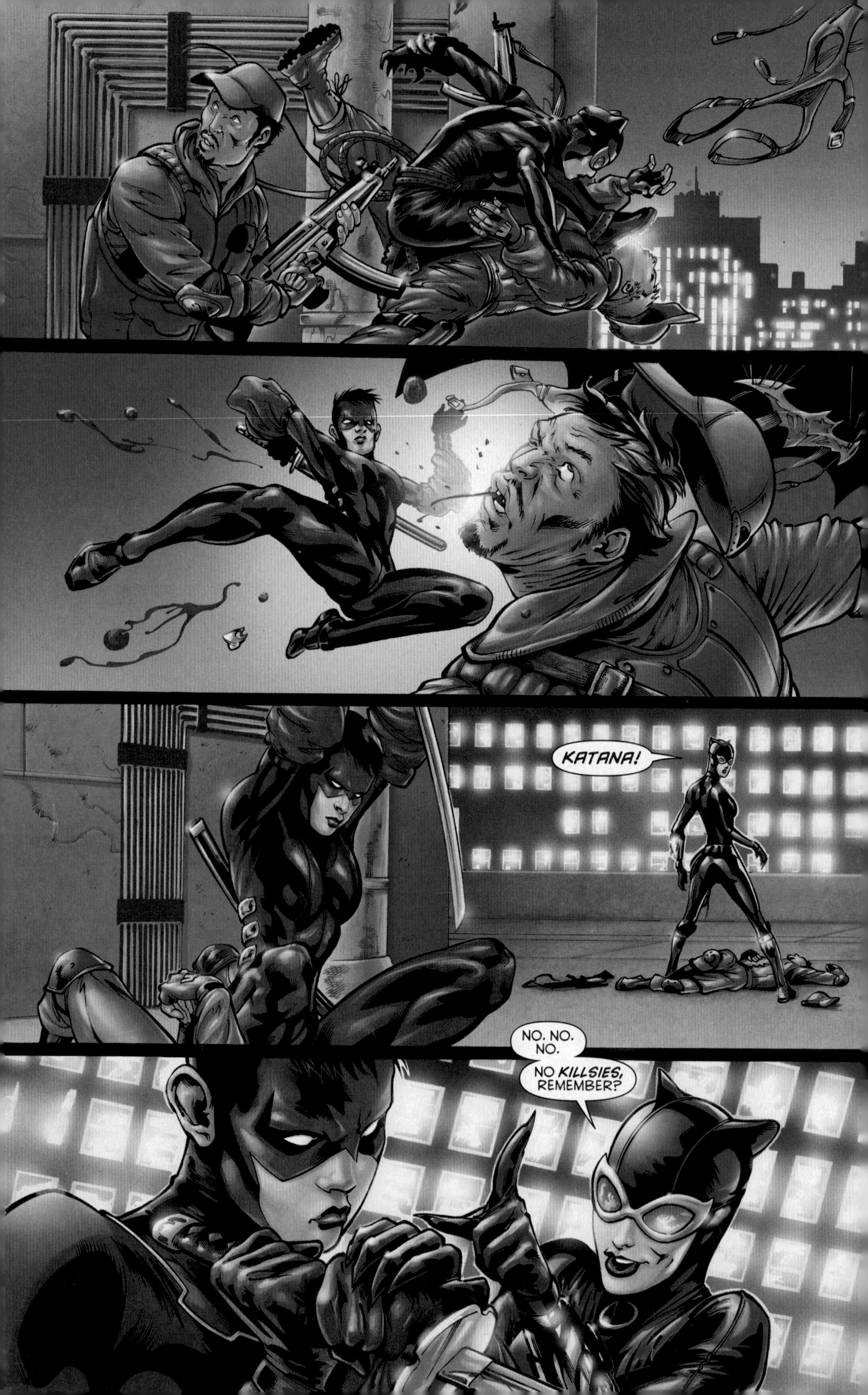
KATANA!
NO. NO. NO.
NO KILLSIES, REMEMBER?

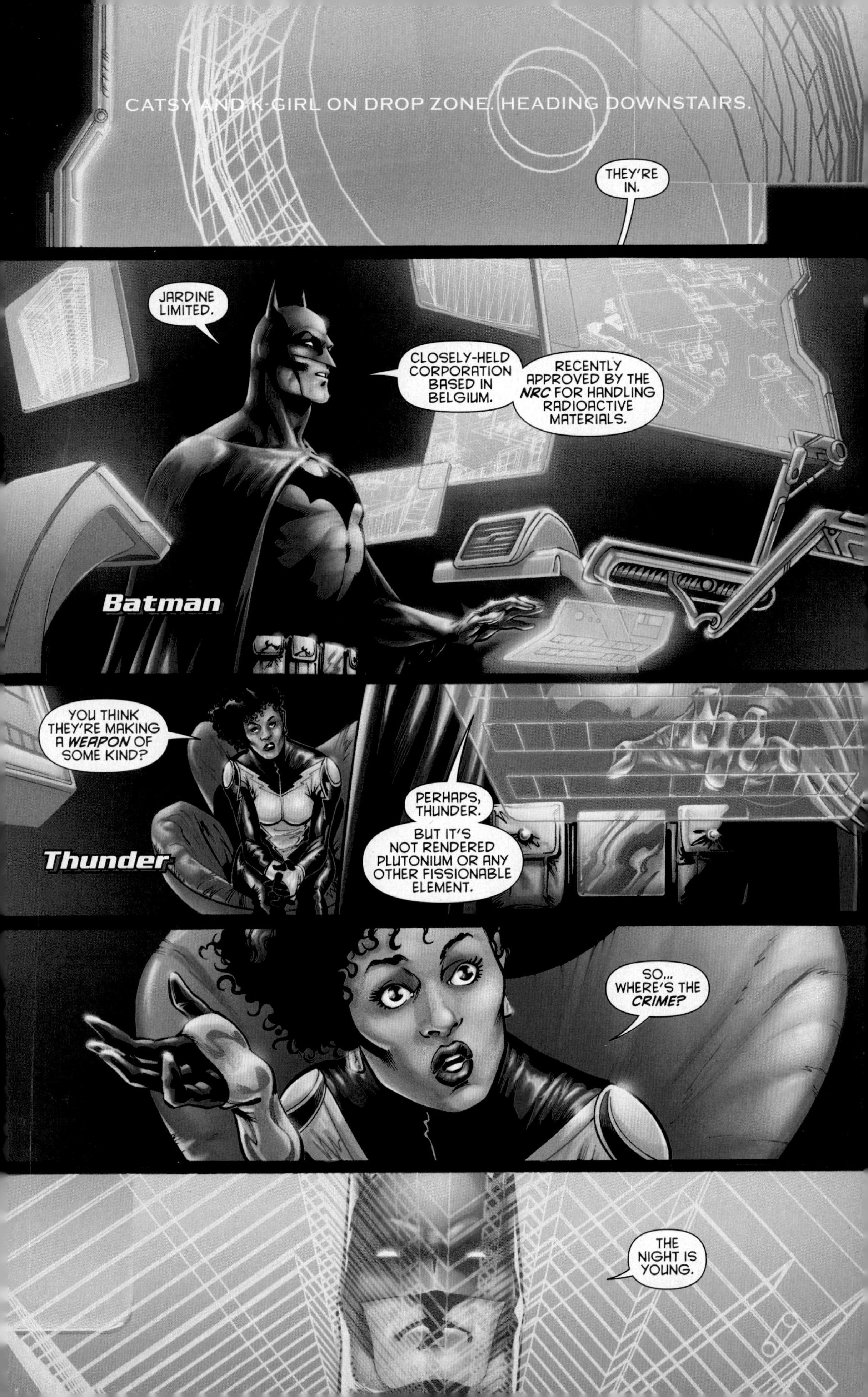
CATSY AND K-GIRL ON DROP ZONE. HEADING DOWNSTAIRS.
THEY'RE IN.
JARDINE LIMITED.
CLOSELY-HELD CORPORATION BASED IN BELGIUM.
RECENTLY APPROVED BY THE NRC FOR HANDLING RADIOACTIVE MATERIALS.
Batman
YOU THINK THEY'RE MAKING A WEAPON OF SOME KIND?
PERHAPS, THUNDER.
BUT IT'S NOT RENDERED PLUTONIUM OR ANY OTHER FISSIONABLE ELEMENT.
Thunder
SO... WHERE'S THE CRIME?
THE NIGHT IS YOUNG.

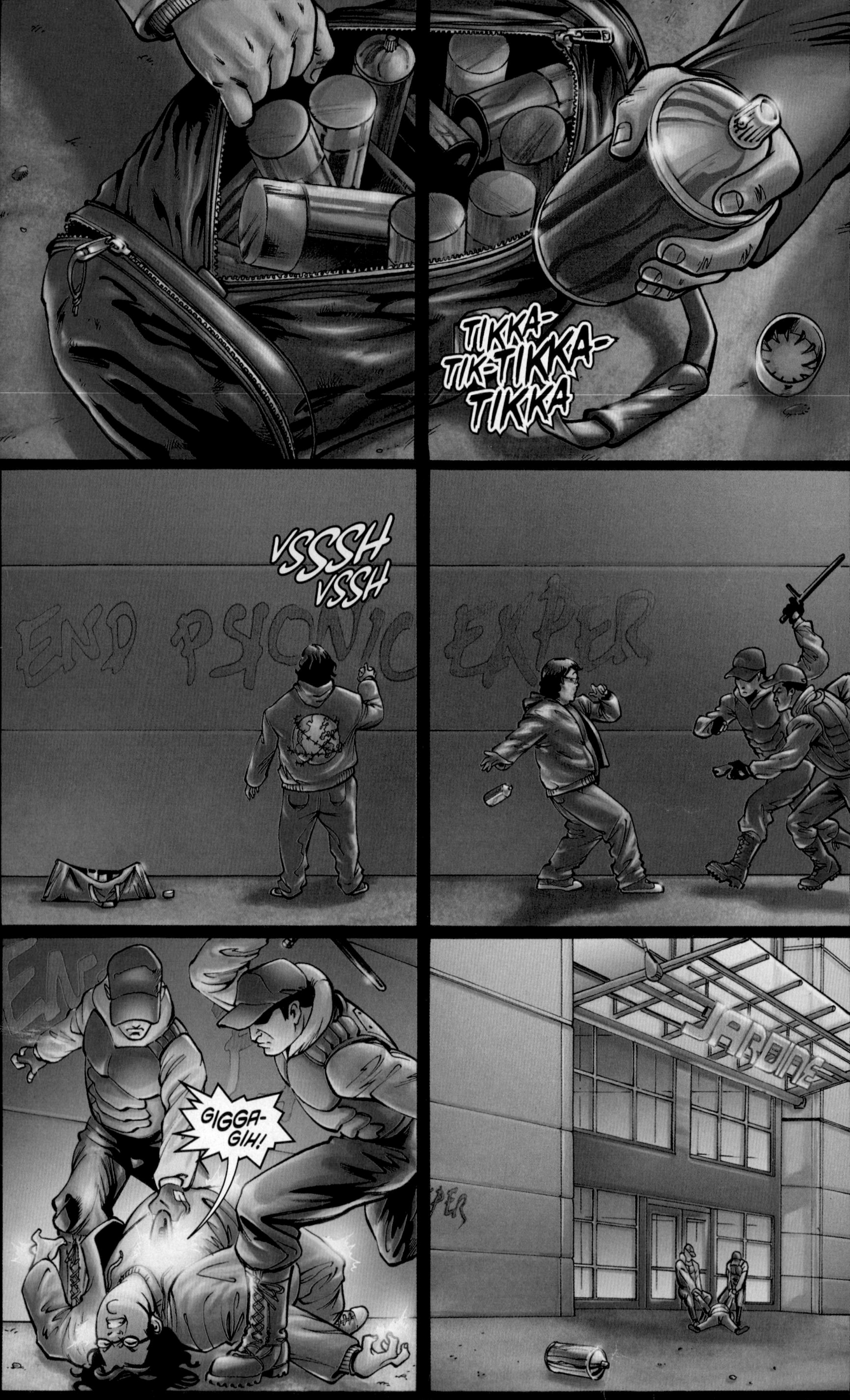
TIKKA-
TIK-TIKKA-
TIKKA
VSSSH
VSSH
END PSYONIC EXPER
GIGGA-
GIH!

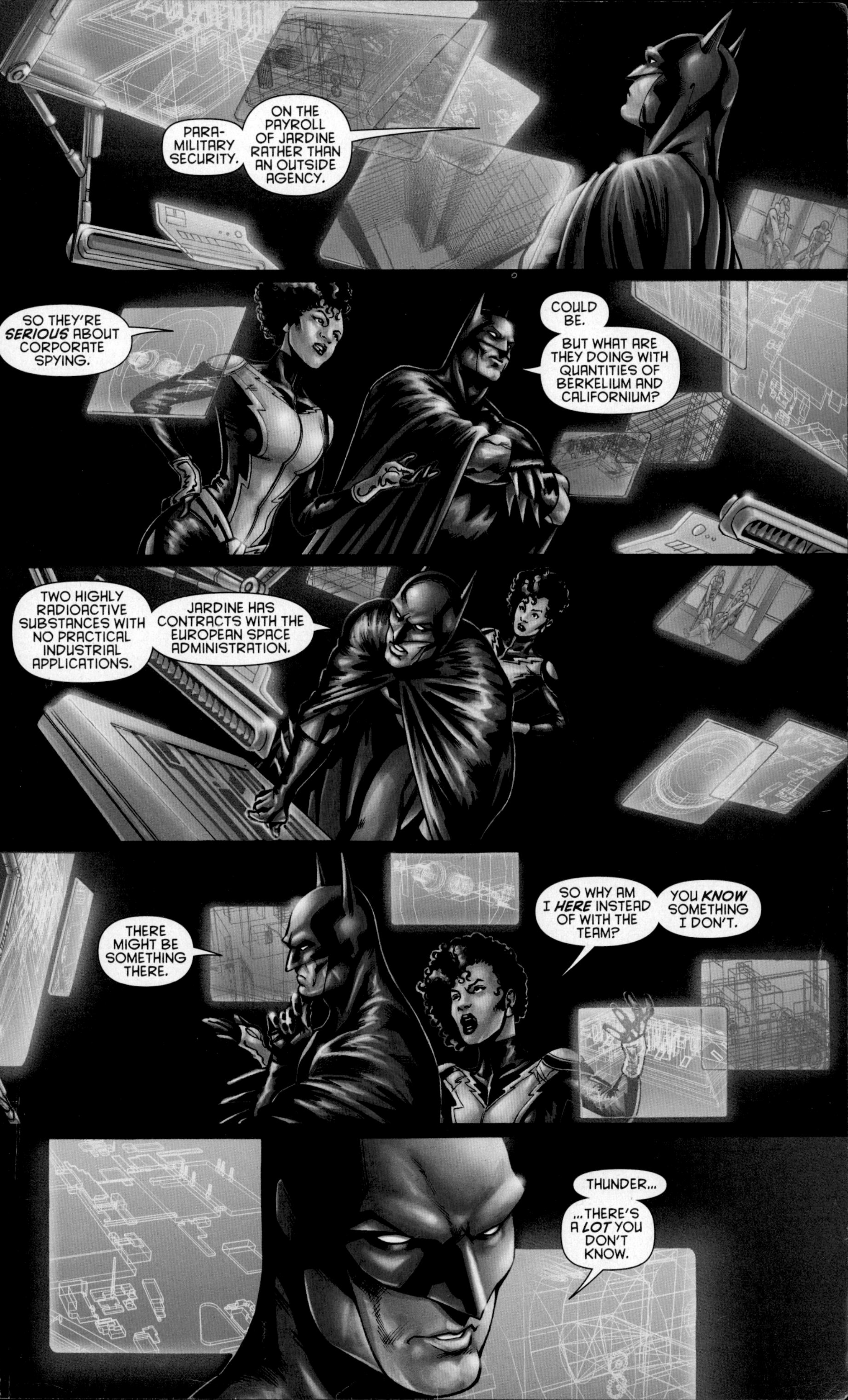
PARA-MILITARY SECURITY.
ON THE PAYROLL OF JARDINE RATHER THAN AN OUTSIDE AGENCY.
SO THEY'RE SERIOUS ABOUT CORPORATE SPYING.
COULD BE.
BUT WHAT ARE THEY DOING WITH QUANTITIES OF BERKELIUM AND CALIFORNIUM?
TWO HIGHLY RADIOACTIVE SUBSTANCES WITH NO PRACTICAL INDUSTRIAL APPLICATIONS.
JARDINE HAS CONTRACTS WITH THE EUROPEAN SPACE ADMINISTRATION.
THERE MIGHT BE SOMETHING THERE.
SO WHY AM I HERE INSTEAD OF WITH THE TEAM?
YOU KNOW SOMETHING I DON'T.
THUNDER...
...THERE'S A LOT YOU DON'T KNOW.

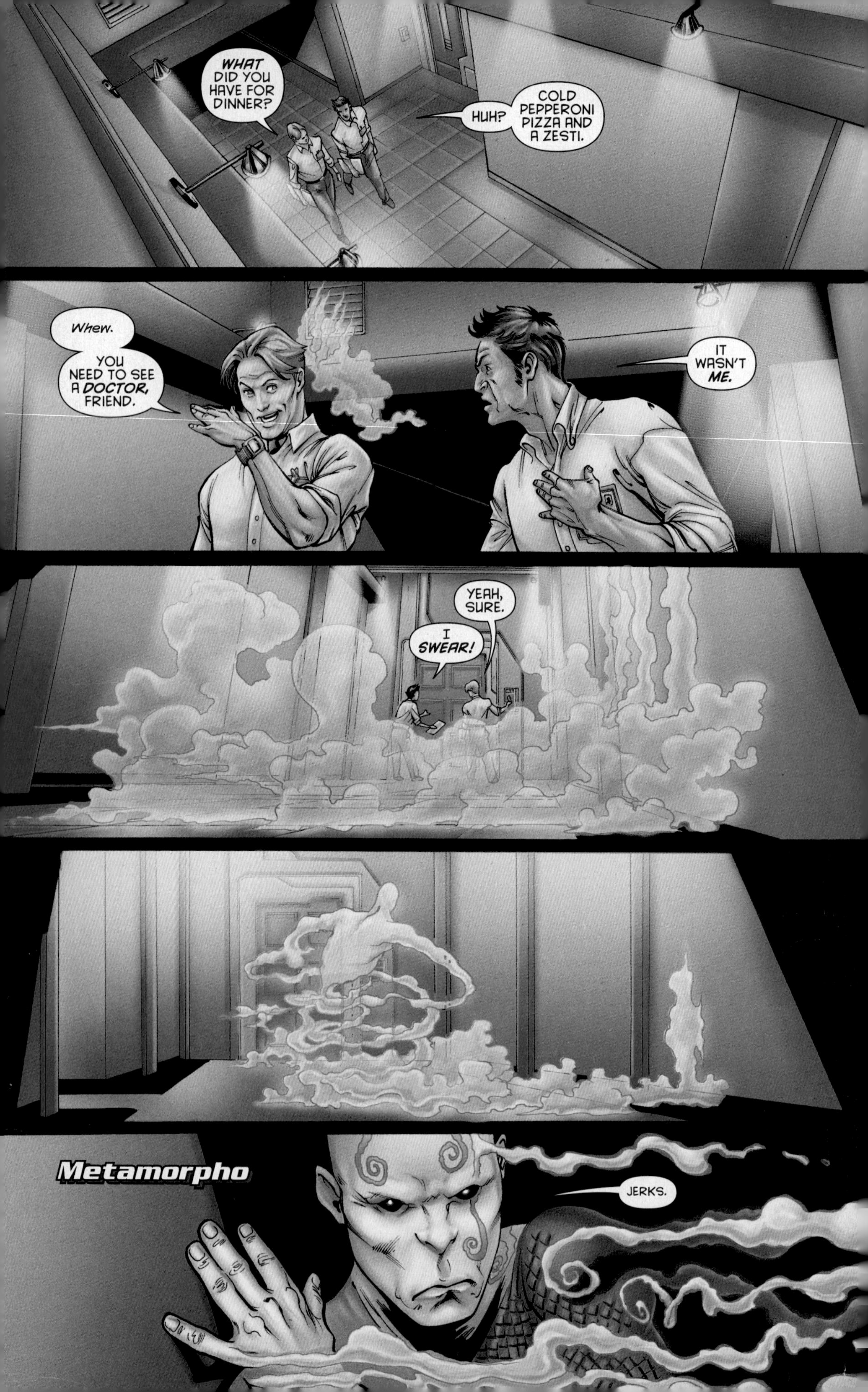
WHAT DID YOU HAVE FOR DINNER?
HUH?
COLD PEPPERONI PIZZA AND A ZESTI.
Whew.
YOU NEED TO SEE A DOCTOR, FRIEND.
IT WASN'T ME.
YEAH, SURE.
I SWEAR!
Metamorpho
JERKS.

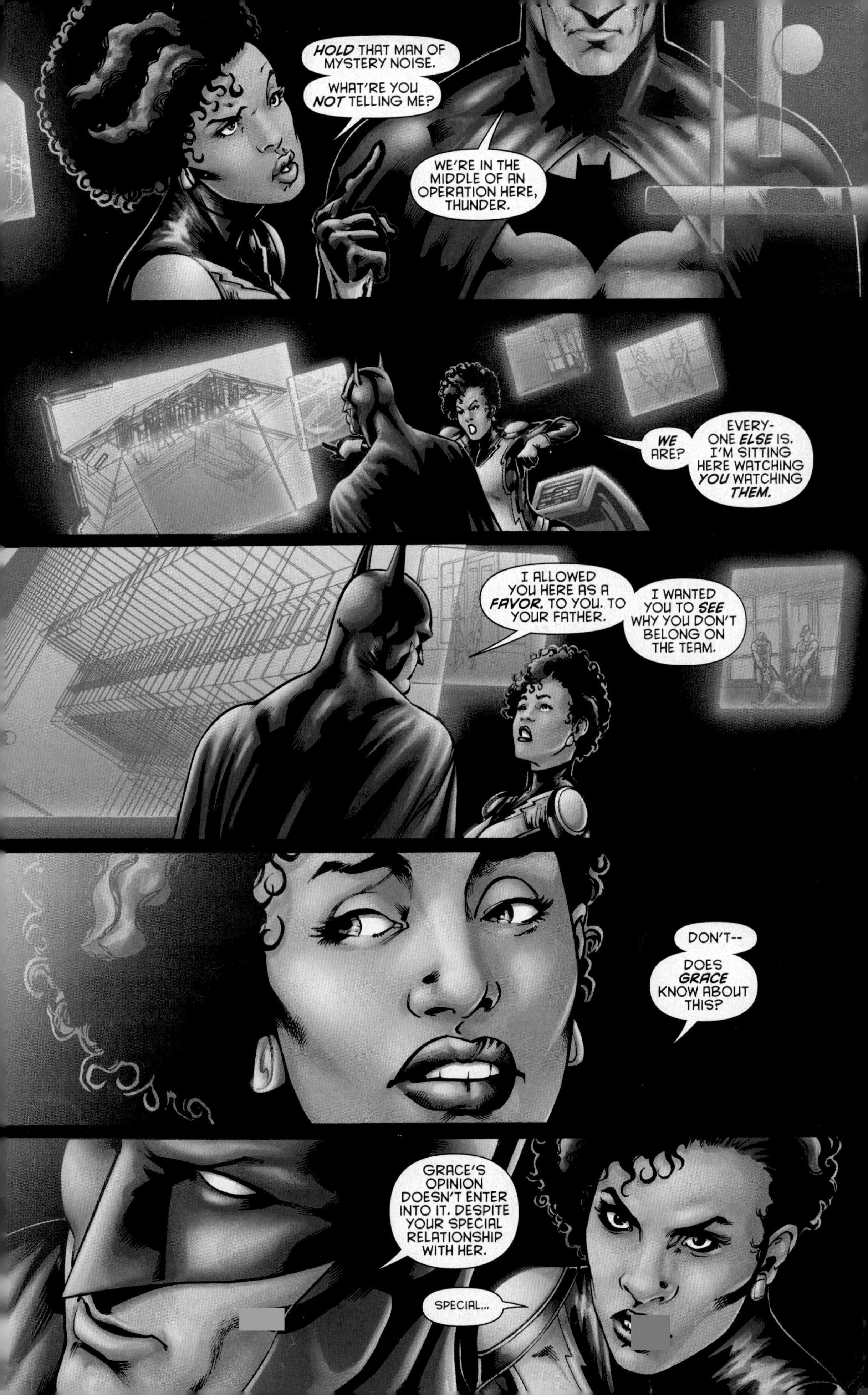
HOLD THAT MAN OF MYSTERY NOISE.
WHAT'RE YOU NOT TELLING ME?
WE'RE IN THE MIDDLE OF AN OPERATION HERE, THUNDER.
WE ARE?
EVERY-ONE ELSE IS. I'M SITTING HERE WATCHING YOU WATCHING THEM.
I ALLOWED YOU HERE AS A FAVOR. TO YOU. TO YOUR FATHER.
I WANTED YOU TO SEE WHY YOU DON'T BELONG ON THE TEAM.
DON'T--
DOES GRACE KNOW ABOUT THIS?
GRACE'S OPINION DOESN'T ENTER INTO IT. DESPITE YOUR SPECIAL RELATIONSHIP WITH HER.
SPECIAL...

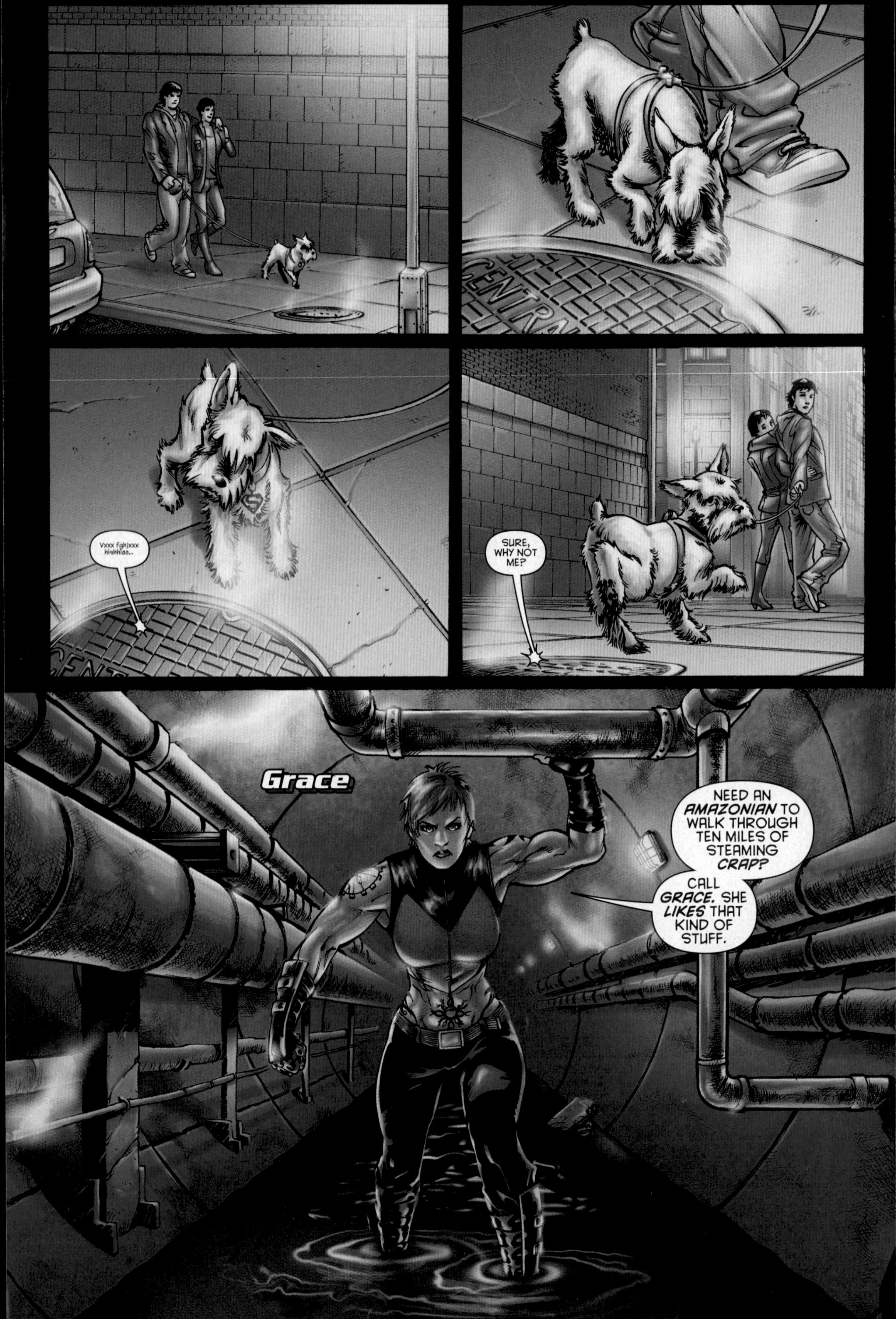
CENTRAL
Vxxx fghjxxx hishhiaa...
SURE, WHY NOT ME?
Grace
NEED AN AMAZONIAN TO WALK THROUGH TEN MILES OF STEAMING CRAP?
CALL GRACE. SHE LIKES THAT KIND OF STUFF.

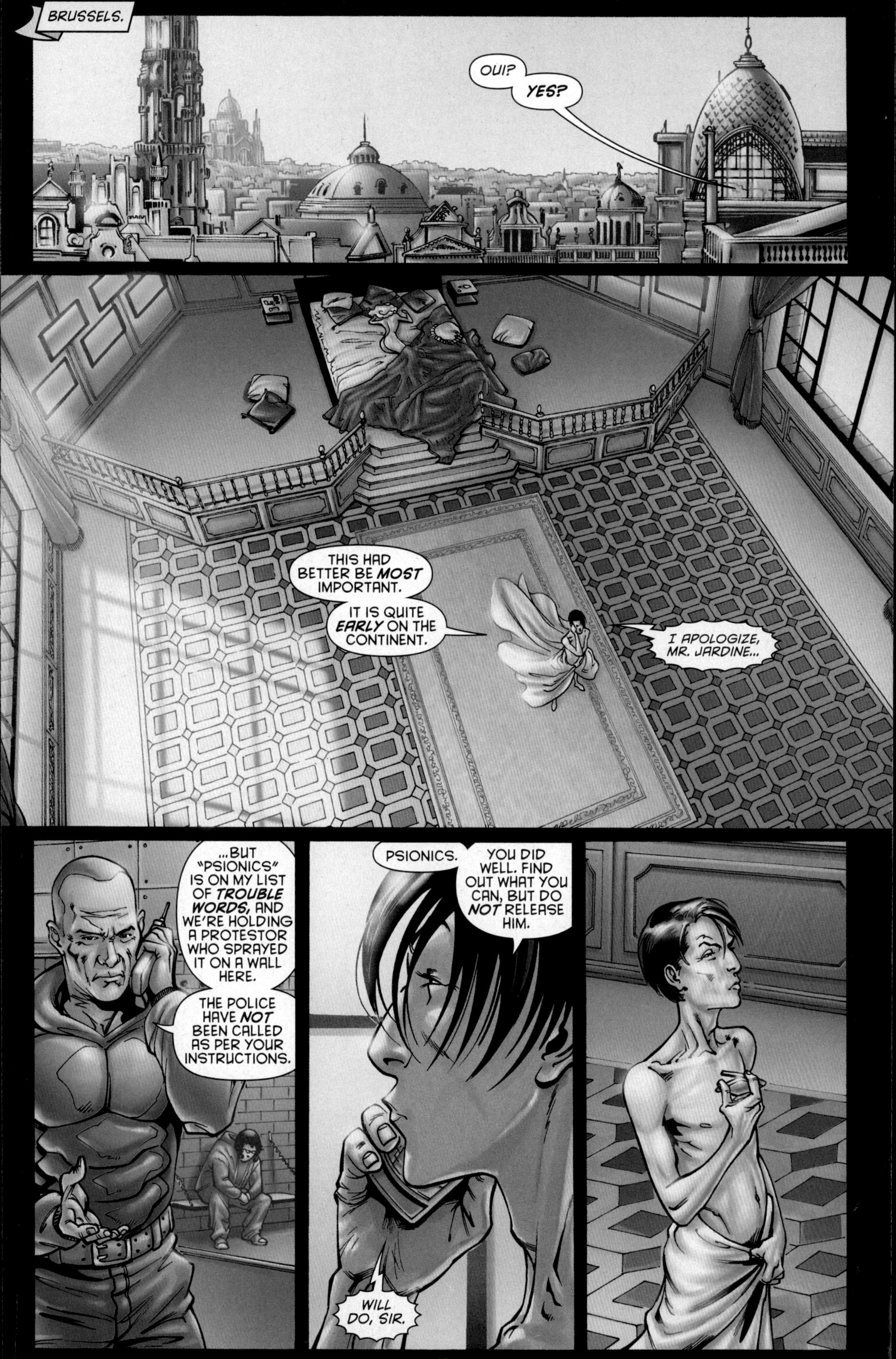
BRUSSELS.
OUI?
YES?
THIS HAD BETTER BE MOST IMPORTANT.
IT IS QUITE EARLY ON THE CONTINENT.
I APOLOGIZE, MR. JARDINE...
...BUT "PSIONICS" IS ON MY LIST OF TROUBLE WORDS, AND WE'RE HOLDING A PROTESTOR WHO SPRAYED IT ON A WALL HERE.
THE POLICE HAVE NOT BEEN CALLED AS PER YOUR INSTRUCTIONS.
PSIONICS.
YOU DID WELL. FIND OUT WHAT YOU CAN, BUT DO NOT RELEASE HIM.
WILL DO, SIR.

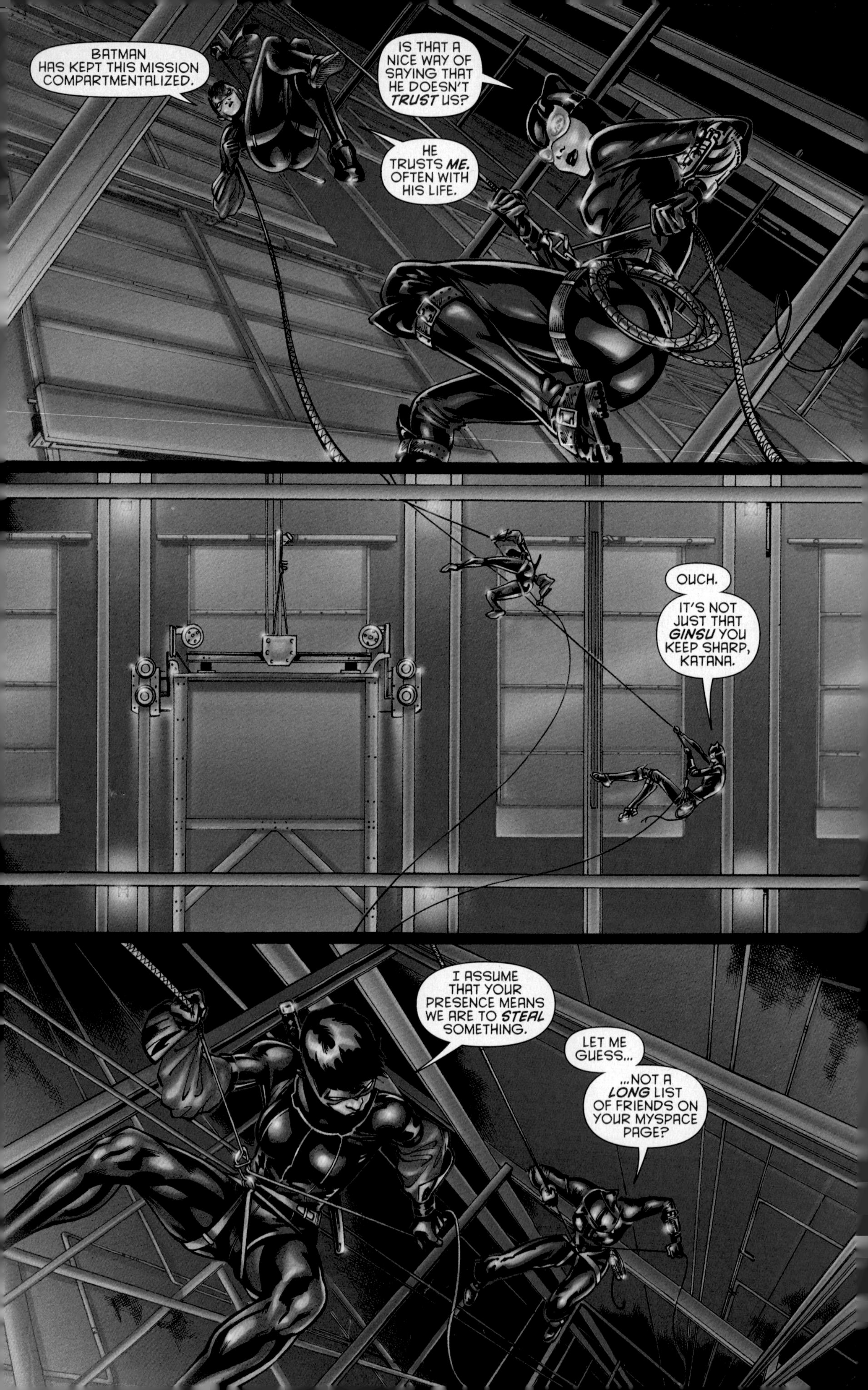

BATMAN HAS KEPT THIS MISSION COMPARTMENTALIZED.
IS THAT A NICE WAY OF SAYING THAT HE DOESN'T TRUST US?
HE TRUSTS ME. OFTEN WITH HIS LIFE.
OUCH.
IT'S NOT JUST THAT GINSU YOU KEEP SHARP, KATANA.
I ASSUME THAT YOUR PRESENCE MEANS WE ARE TO STEAL SOMETHING.
LET ME GUESS...
...NOT A LONG LIST OF FRIENDS ON YOUR MYSPACE PAGE?

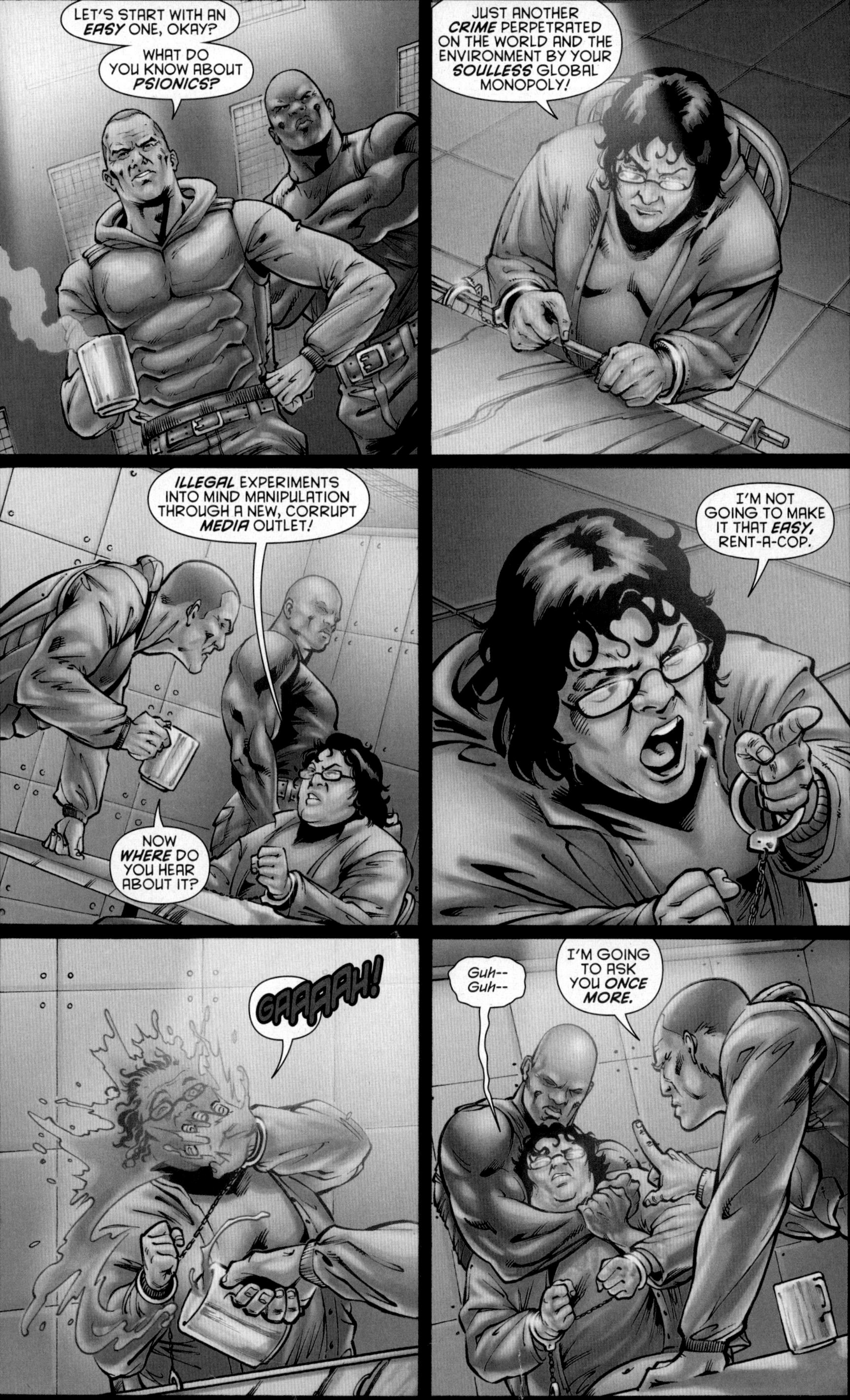

LET'S START WITH AN EASY ONE, OKAY?
WHAT DO YOU KNOW ABOUT PSIONICS?
JUST ANOTHER CRIME PERPETRATED ON THE WORLD AND THE ENVIRONMENT BY YOUR SOULLESS GLOBAL MONOPOLY!
ILLEGAL EXPERIMENTS INTO MIND MANIPULATION THROUGH A NEW, CORRUPT MEDIA OUTLET!
NOW WHERE DO YOU HEAR ABOUT IT?
I'M NOT GOING TO MAKE IT THAT EASY, RENT-A-COP.
GAAAAH!
Guh-- Guh--
I'M GOING TO ASK YOU ONCE MORE.

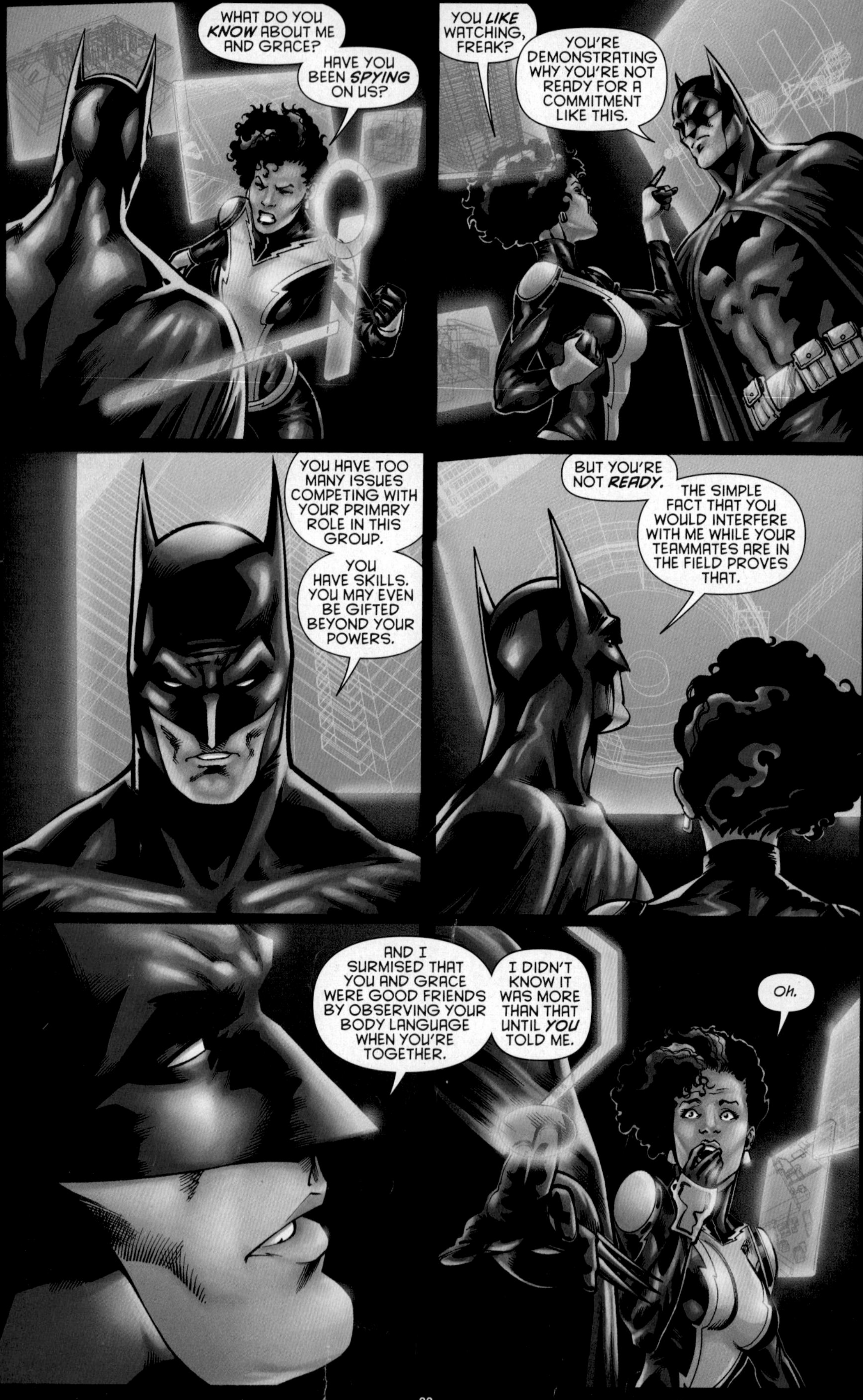
WHAT DO YOU *KNOW* ABOUT ME AND GRACE?
HAVE YOU BEEN *SPYING* ON US?
YOU *LIKE* WATCHING, FREAK?
YOU'RE DEMONSTRATING WHY YOU'RE NOT READY FOR A COMMITMENT LIKE THIS.
YOU HAVE TOO MANY ISSUES COMPETING WITH YOUR PRIMARY ROLE IN THIS GROUP.
YOU HAVE SKILLS. YOU MAY EVEN BE GIFTED BEYOND YOUR POWERS.
BUT YOU'RE NOT *READY.*
THE SIMPLE FACT THAT YOU WOULD INTERFERE WITH ME WHILE YOUR TEAMMATES ARE IN THE FIELD PROVES THAT.
AND I SURMISED THAT YOU AND GRACE WERE GOOD FRIENDS BY OBSERVING YOUR BODY LANGUAGE WHEN YOU'RE TOGETHER.
I DIDN'T KNOW IT WAS MORE THAN THAT UNTIL *YOU* TOLD ME.
Oh.

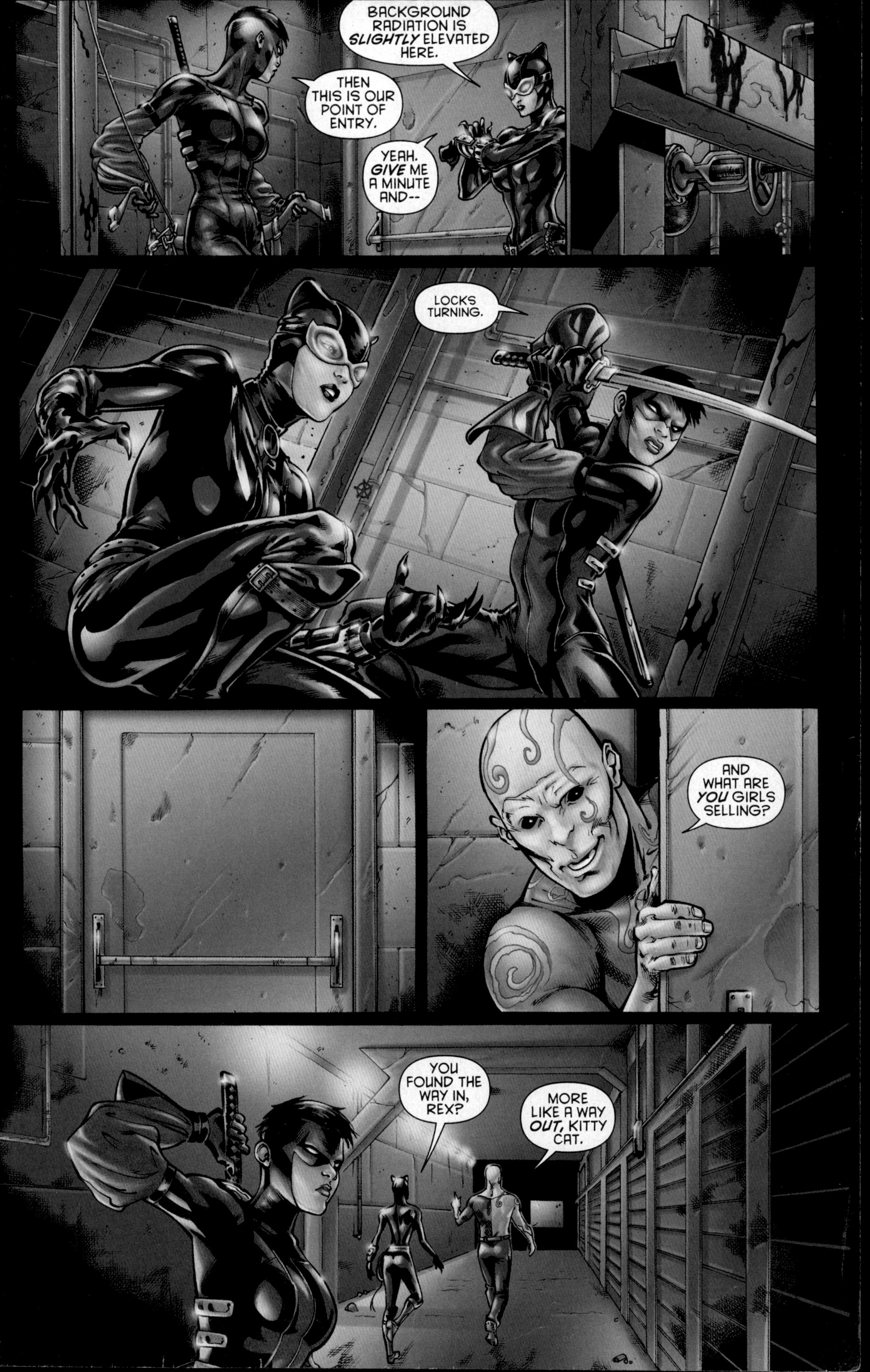
BACKGROUND RADIATION IS SLIGHTLY ELEVATED HERE.
THEN THIS IS OUR POINT OF ENTRY.
YEAH. GIVE ME A MINUTE AND--
LOCKS TURNING.
AND WHAT ARE YOU GIRLS SELLING?
YOU FOUND THE WAY IN, REX?
MORE LIKE A WAY OUT, KITTY CAT.

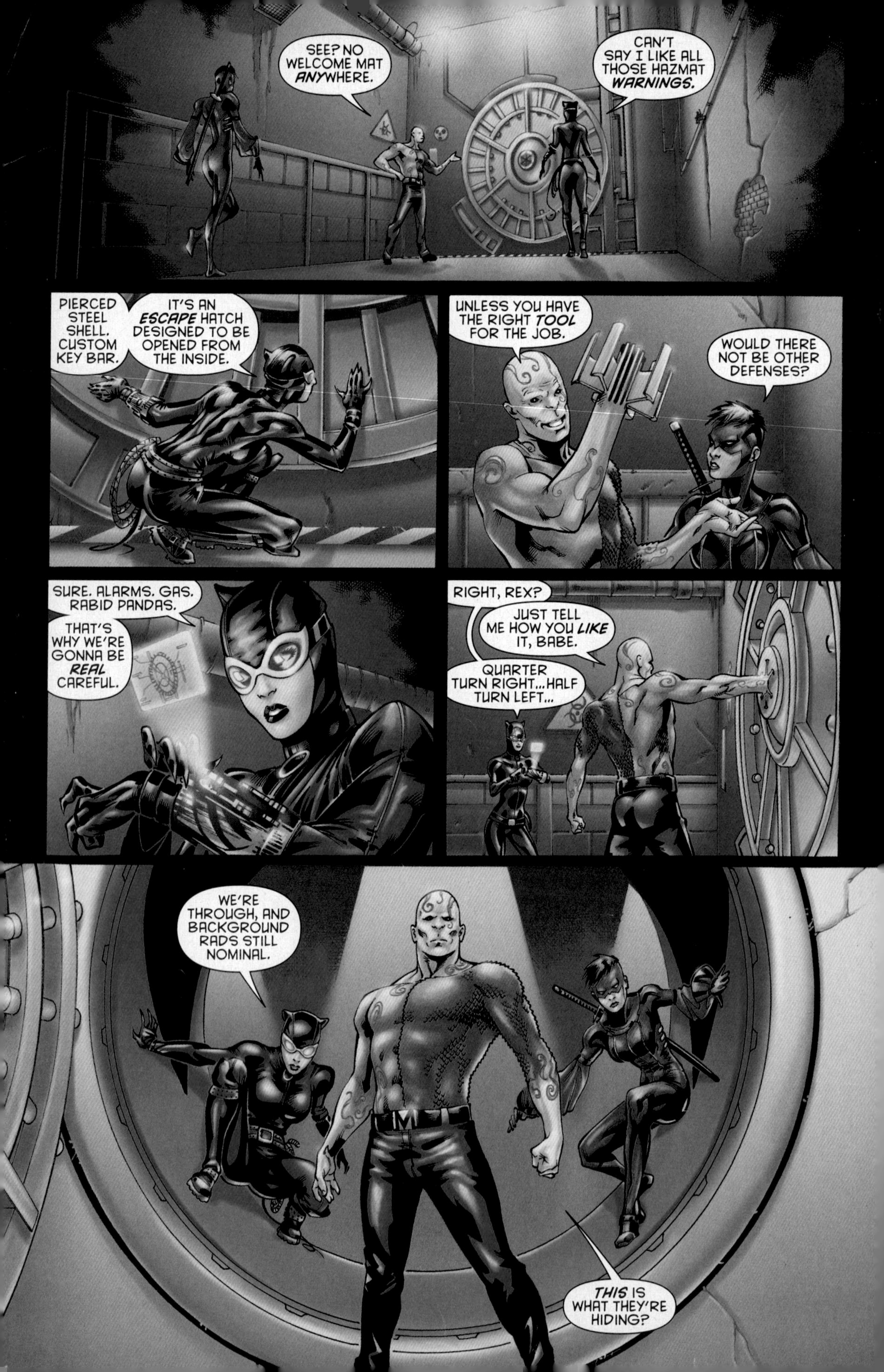
SEE? NO WELCOME MAT *ANY*WHERE.
CAN'T SAY I LIKE ALL THOSE HAZMAT *WARNINGS.*
PIERCED STEEL SHELL. CUSTOM KEY BAR.
IT'S AN *ESCAPE* HATCH DESIGNED TO BE OPENED FROM THE INSIDE.
UNLESS YOU HAVE THE RIGHT *TOOL* FOR THE JOB.
WOULD THERE NOT BE OTHER DEFENSES?
SURE. ALARMS. GAS. RABID PANDAS.
THAT'S WHY WE'RE GONNA BE *REAL* CAREFUL.
RIGHT, REX?
JUST TELL ME HOW YOU *LIKE* IT, BABE.
QUARTER TURN RIGHT...HALF TURN LEFT...
WE'RE THROUGH, AND BACKGROUND RADS STILL NOMINAL.
THIS IS WHAT THEY'RE HIDING?

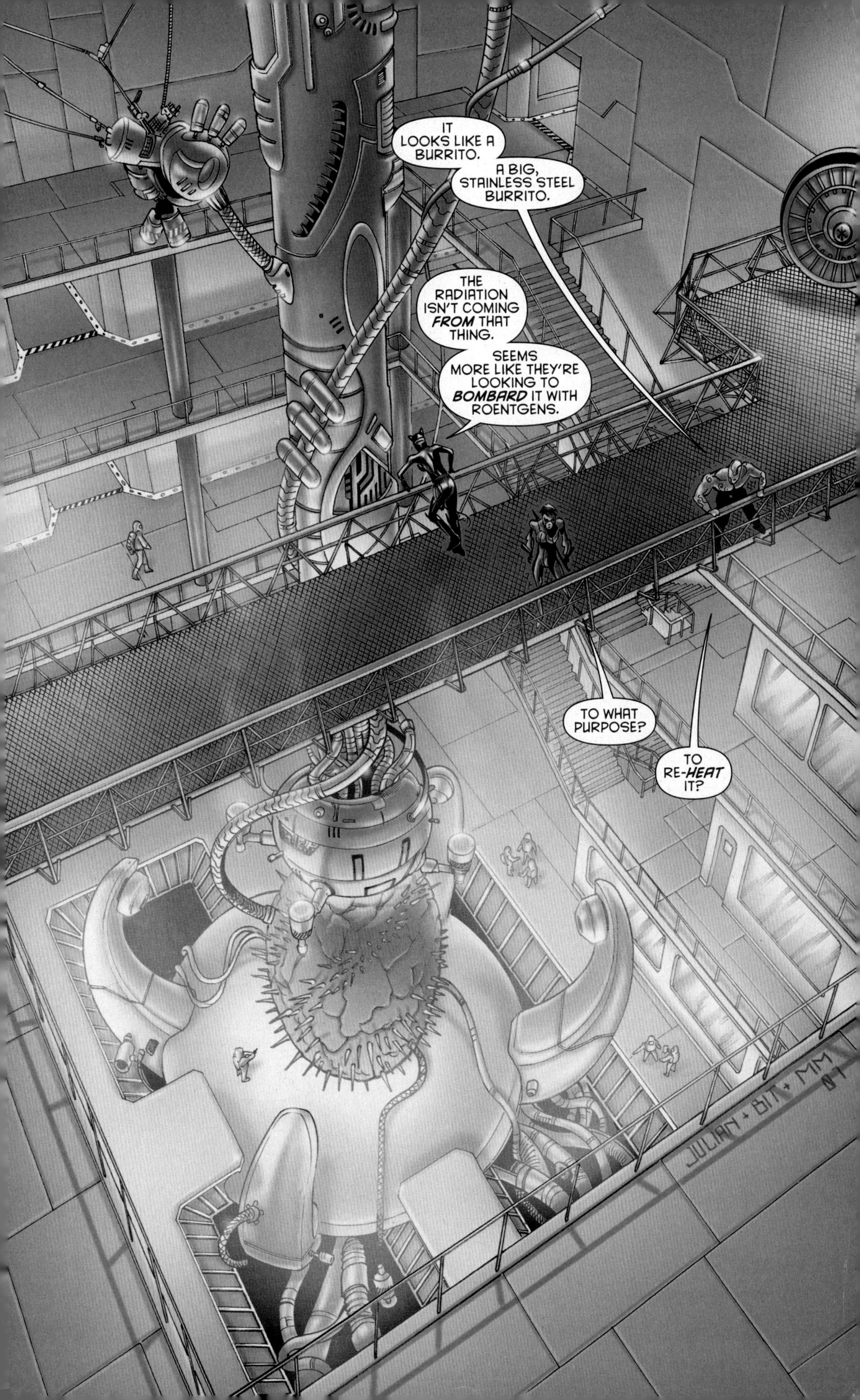
IT LOOKS LIKE A BURRITO.
A BIG, STAINLESS STEEL BURRITO.
THE RADIATION ISN'T COMING FROM THAT THING.
SEEMS MORE LIKE THEY'RE LOOKING TO BOMBARD IT WITH ROENTGENS.
TO WHAT PURPOSE?
TO RE-HEAT IT?
JULIAN + BIT + MM 01

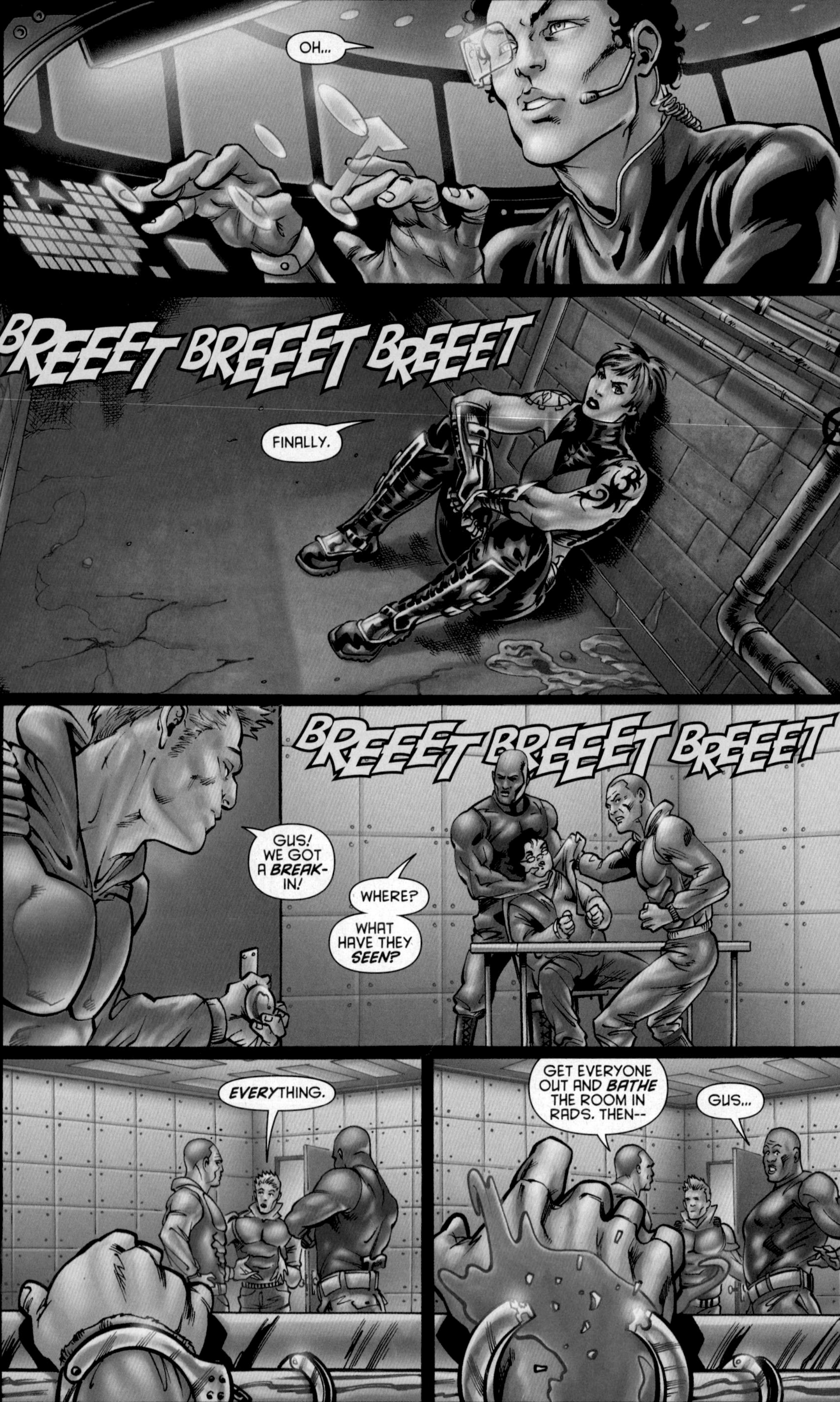

OH...
BREEEET BREEEET BREEEET
FINALLY.
BREEEET BREEEET BREEEET
GUS! WE GOT A *BREAK-IN!*
WHERE?
WHAT HAVE THEY *SEEN?*
*EVERY*THING.
GET EVERYONE OUT AND *BATHE* THE ROOM IN RADS. THEN--
GUS...

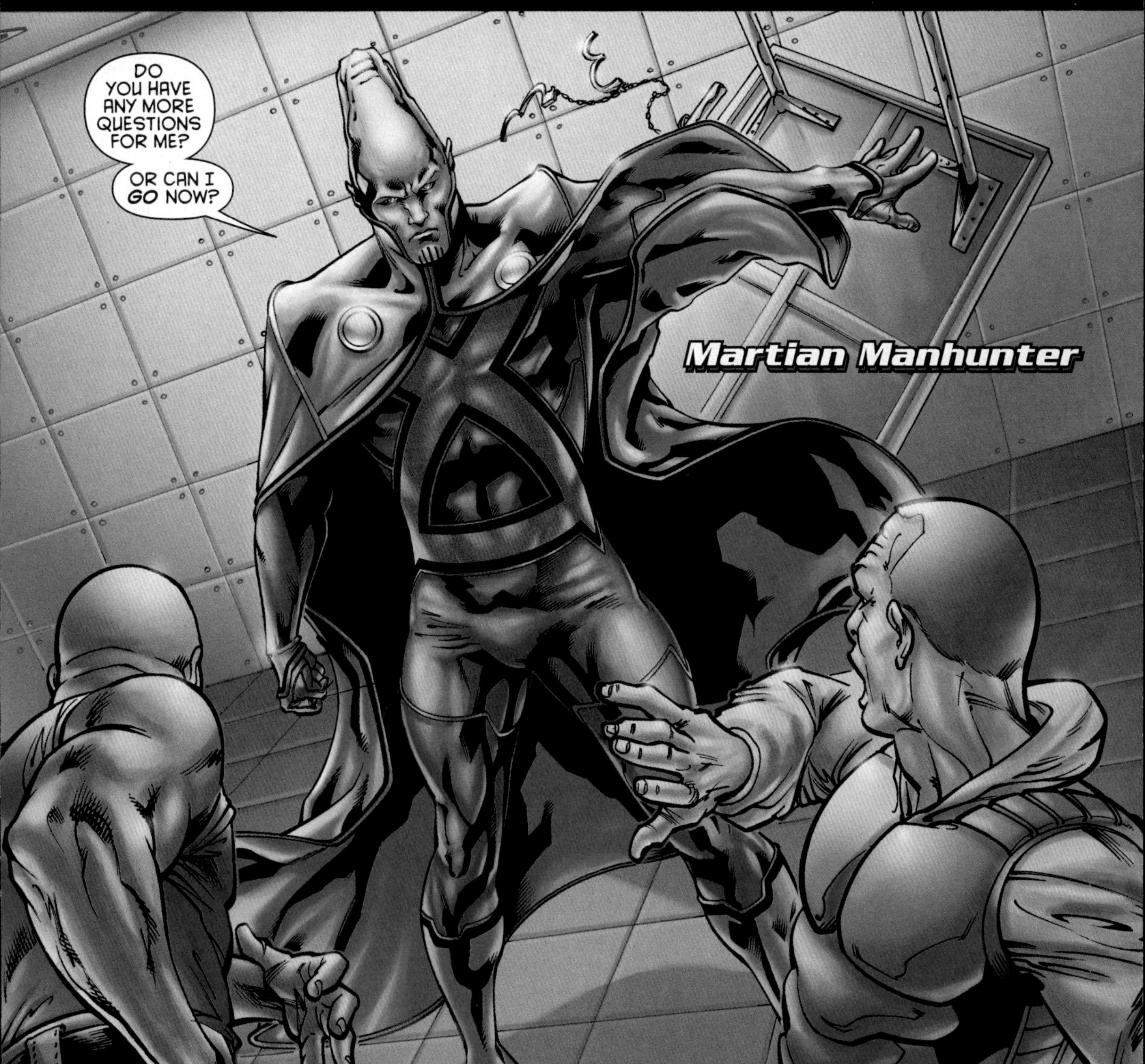
DO YOU HAVE ANY MORE QUESTIONS FOR ME?
OR CAN I GO NOW?
Martian Manhunter

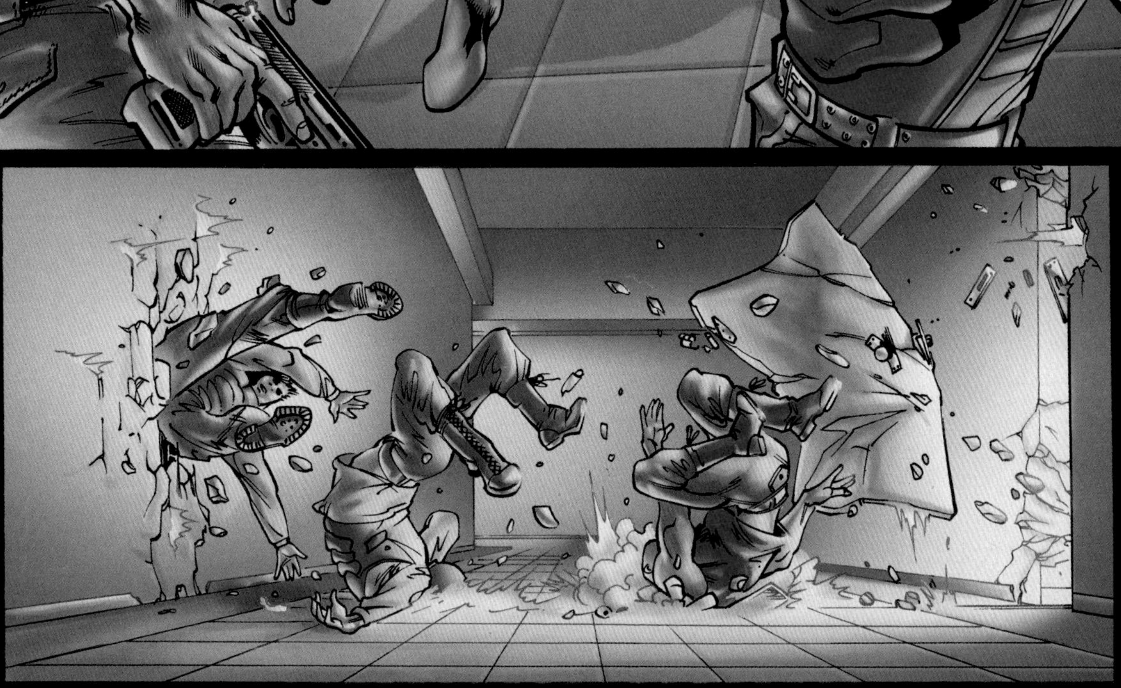

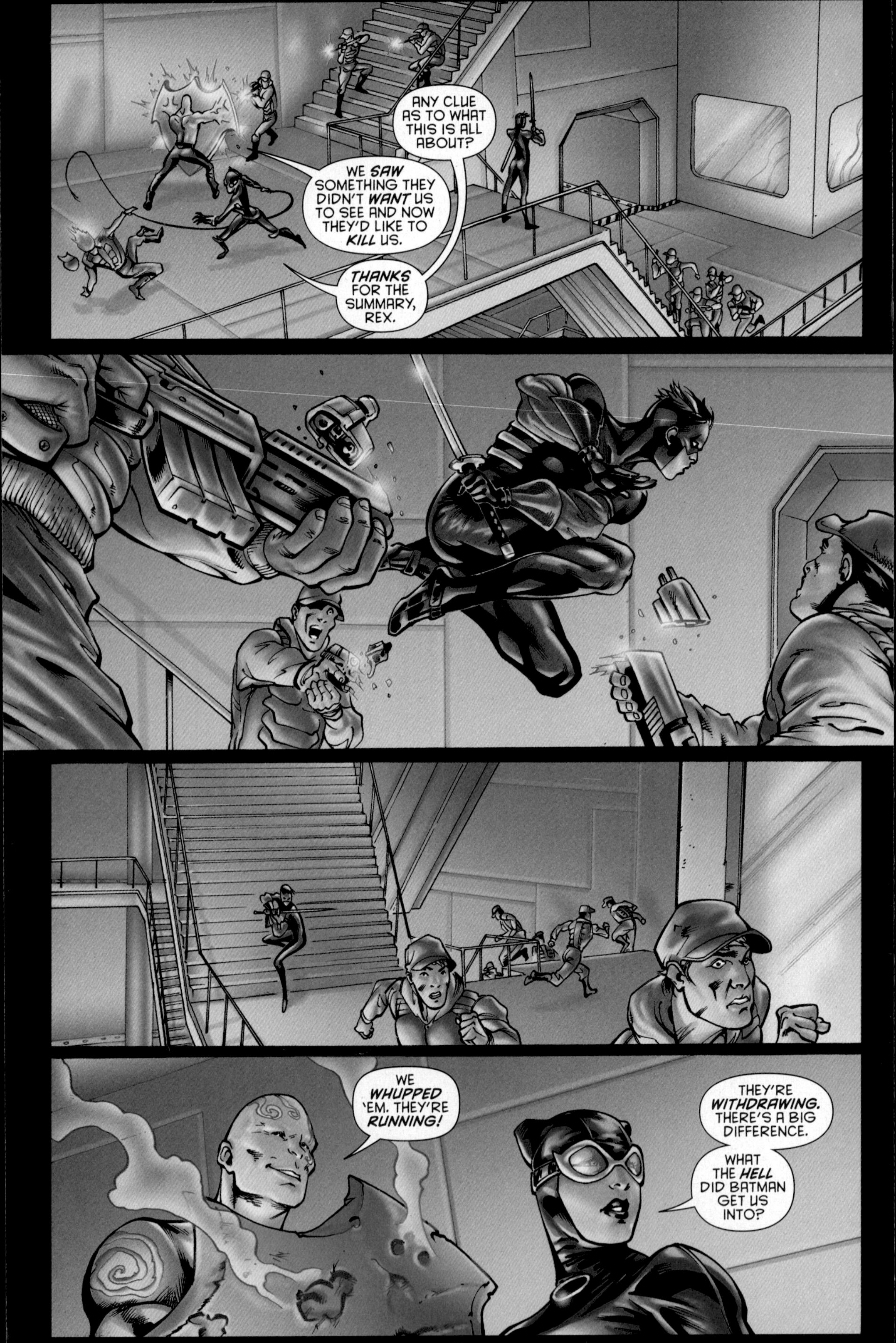
ANY CLUE AS TO WHAT THIS IS ALL ABOUT?
WE *SAW* SOMETHING THEY DIDN'T *WANT* US TO SEE AND NOW THEY'D LIKE TO *KILL* US.
THANKS FOR THE SUMMARY, REX.
WE *WHUPPED* 'EM. THEY'RE *RUNNING!*
THEY'RE *WITHDRAWING.* THERE'S A BIG DIFFERENCE.
WHAT THE *HELL* DID BATMAN GET US INTO?

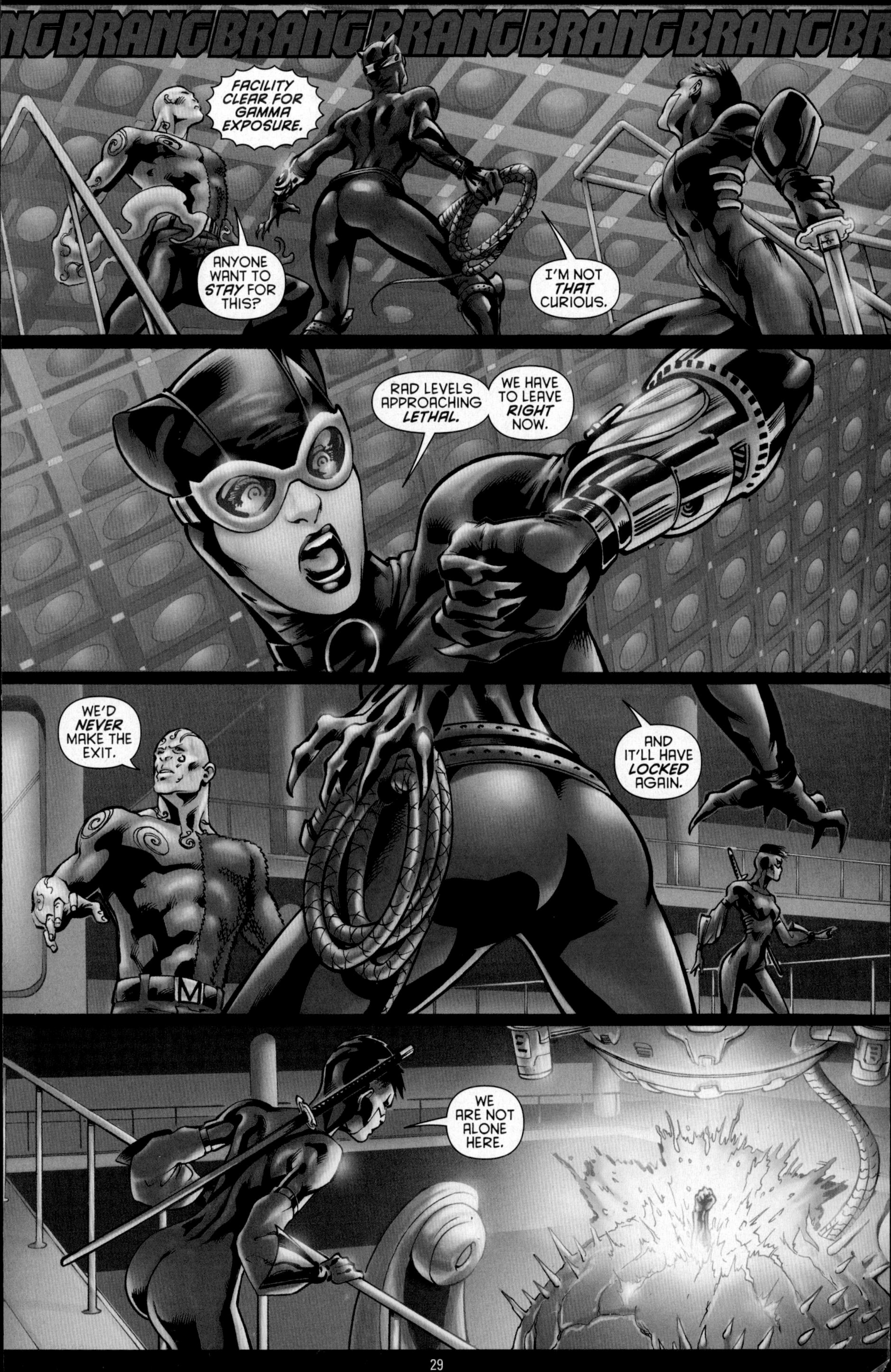
BRANG BRANG BRANG BRANG BRANG
FACILITY CLEAR FOR GAMMA EXPOSURE.
ANYONE WANT TO STAY FOR THIS?
I'M NOT THAT CURIOUS.
RAD LEVELS APPROACHING LETHAL.
WE HAVE TO LEAVE RIGHT NOW.
WE'D NEVER MAKE THE EXIT.
AND IT'LL HAVE LOCKED AGAIN.
WE ARE NOT ALONE HERE.

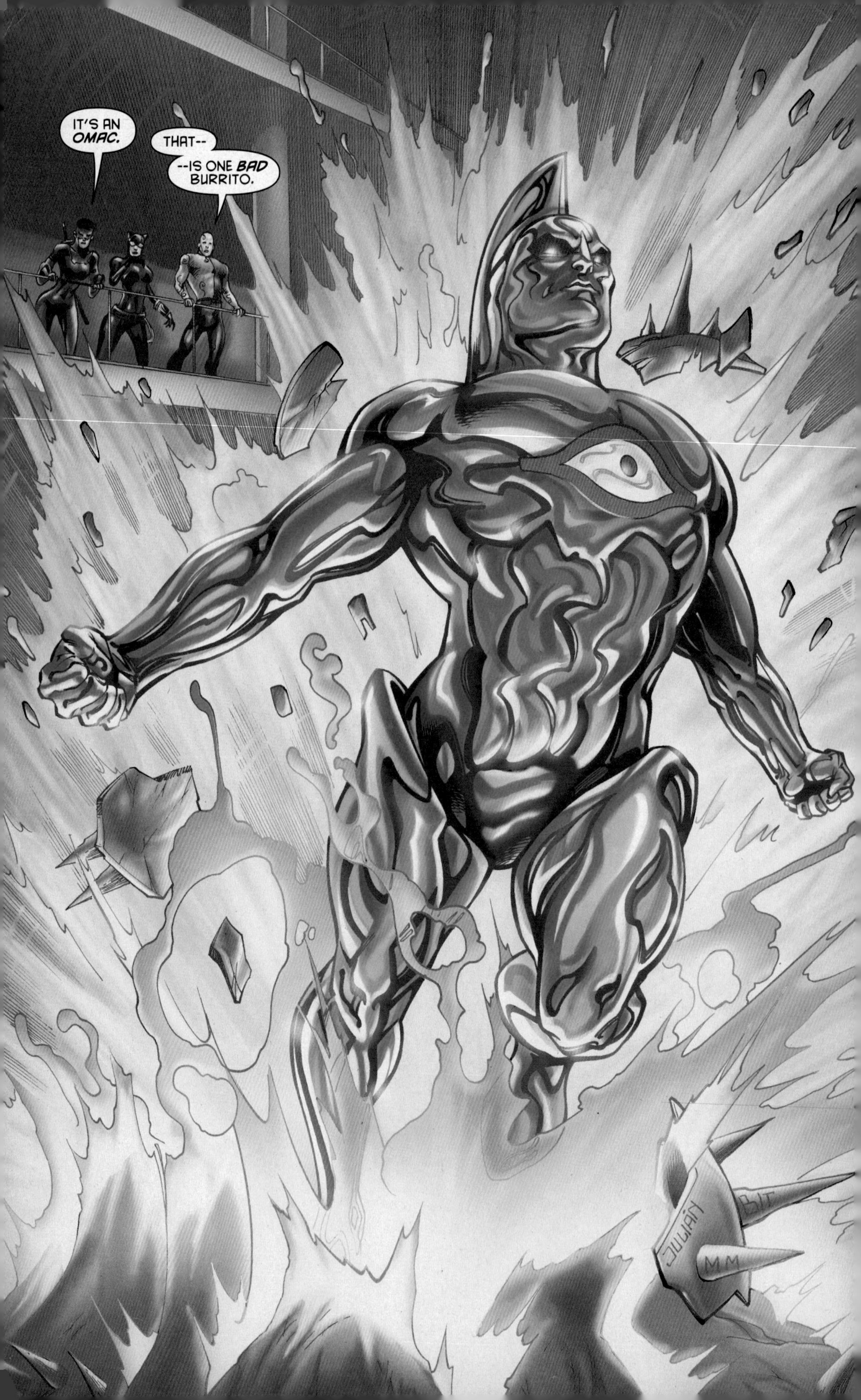
IT'S AN OMAC.
THAT--
--IS ONE BAD BURRITO.

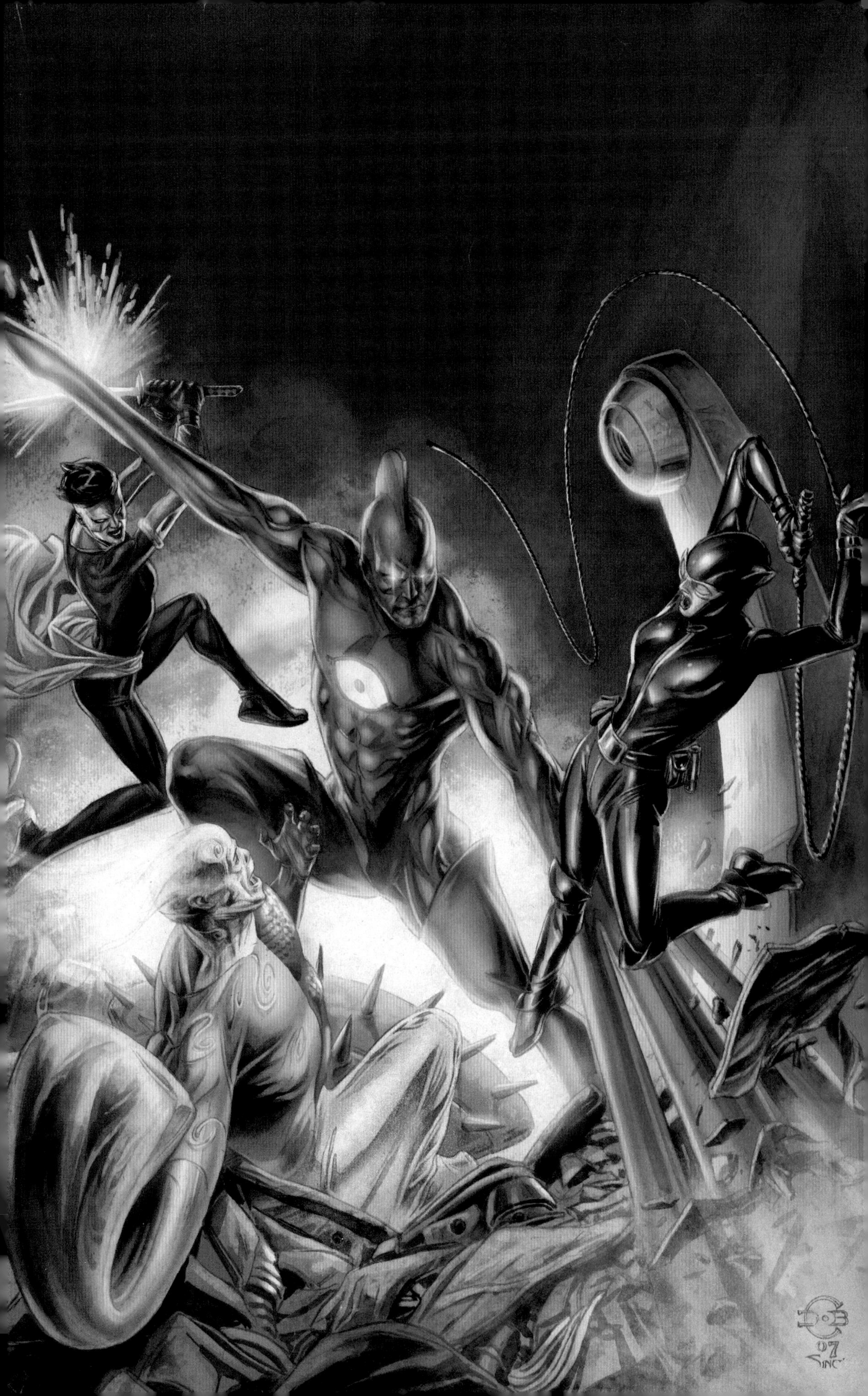

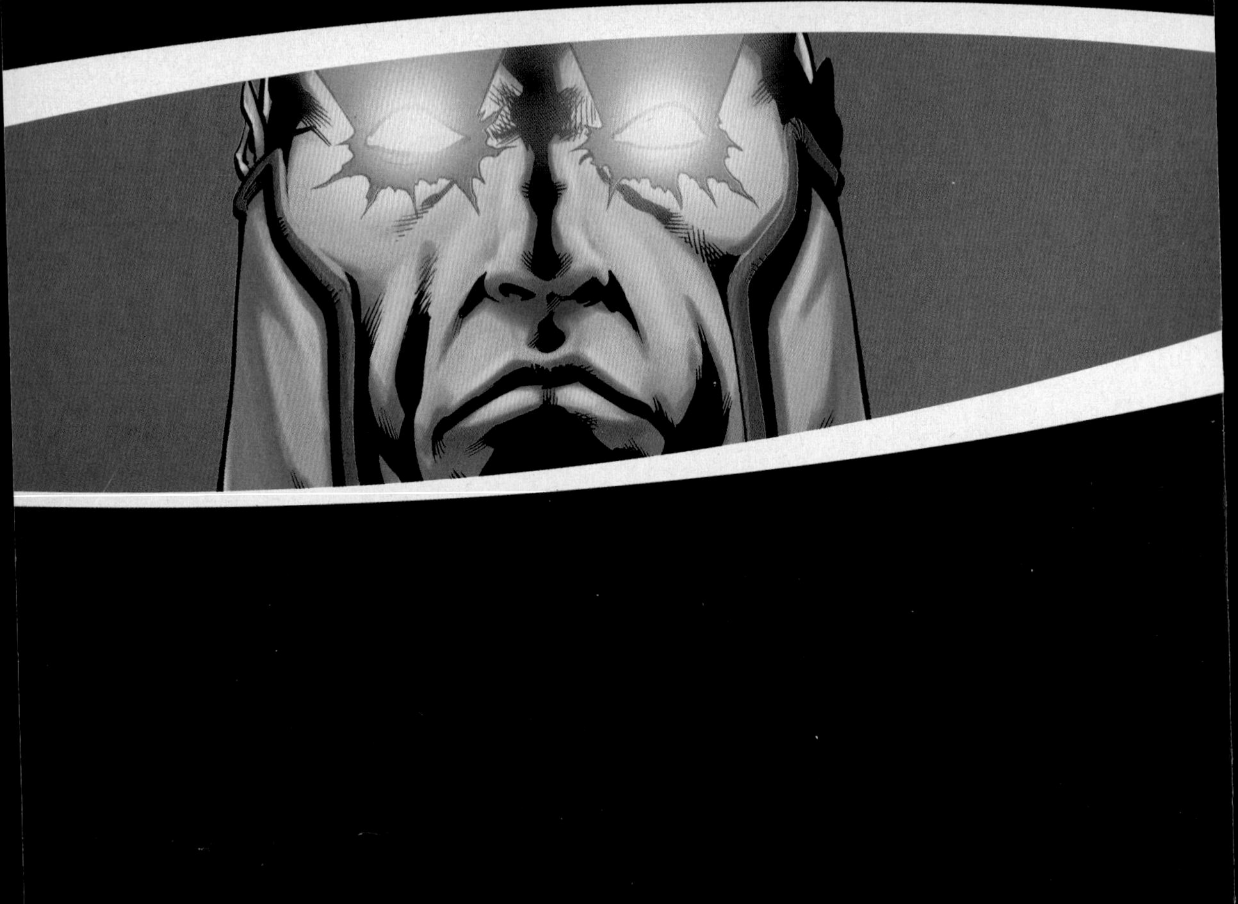

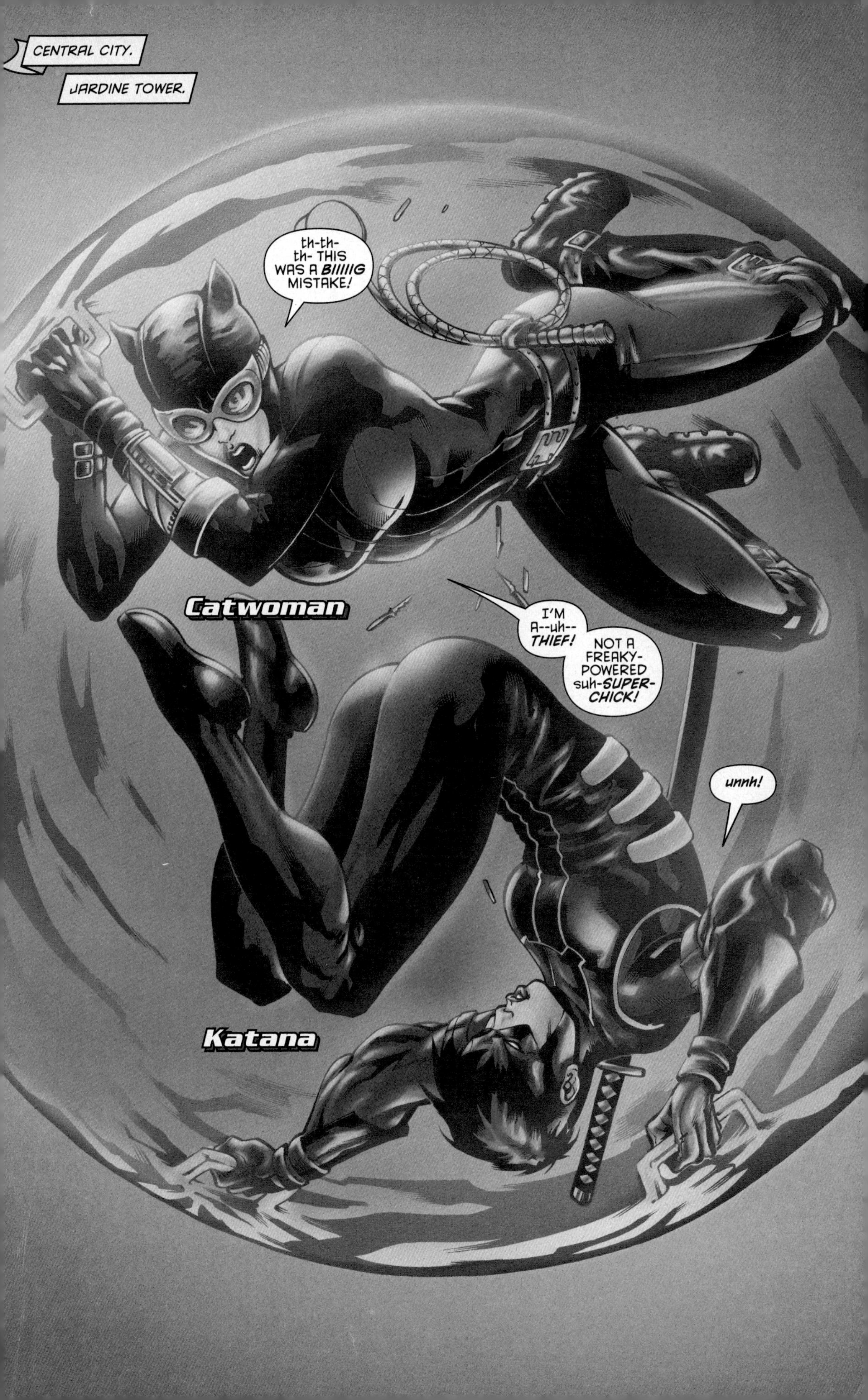
CENTRAL CITY.
JARDINE TOWER.
th-th-th- THIS WAS A BIIIIIG MISTAKE!
Catwoman
I'M A--uh-- THIEF!
NOT A FREAKY-POWERED suh-SUPER-CHICK!
unnh!
Katana

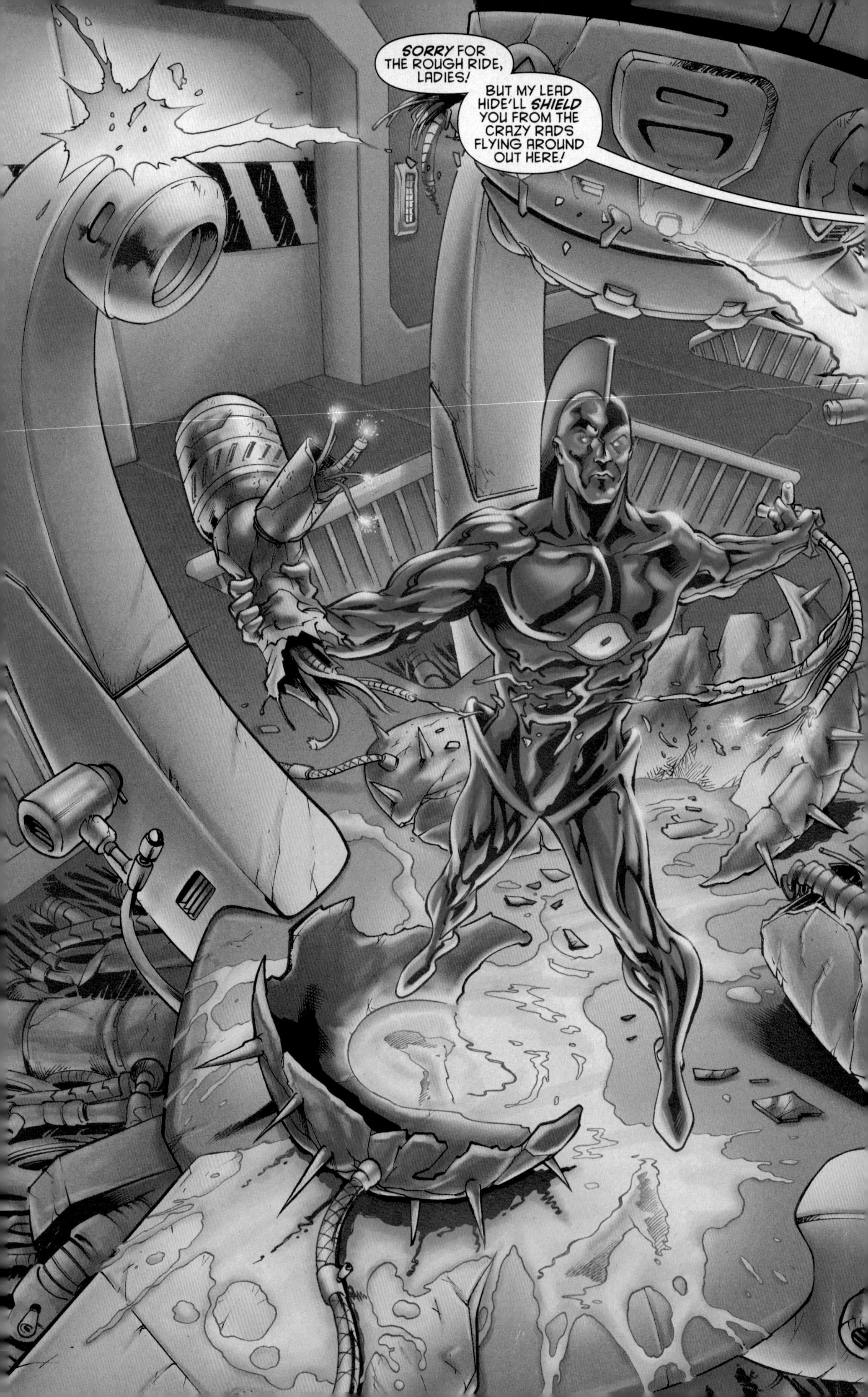
SORRY FOR THE ROUGH RIDE, LADIES!
BUT MY LEAD HIDE'LL SHIELD YOU FROM THE CRAZY RADS FLYING AROUND OUT HERE!

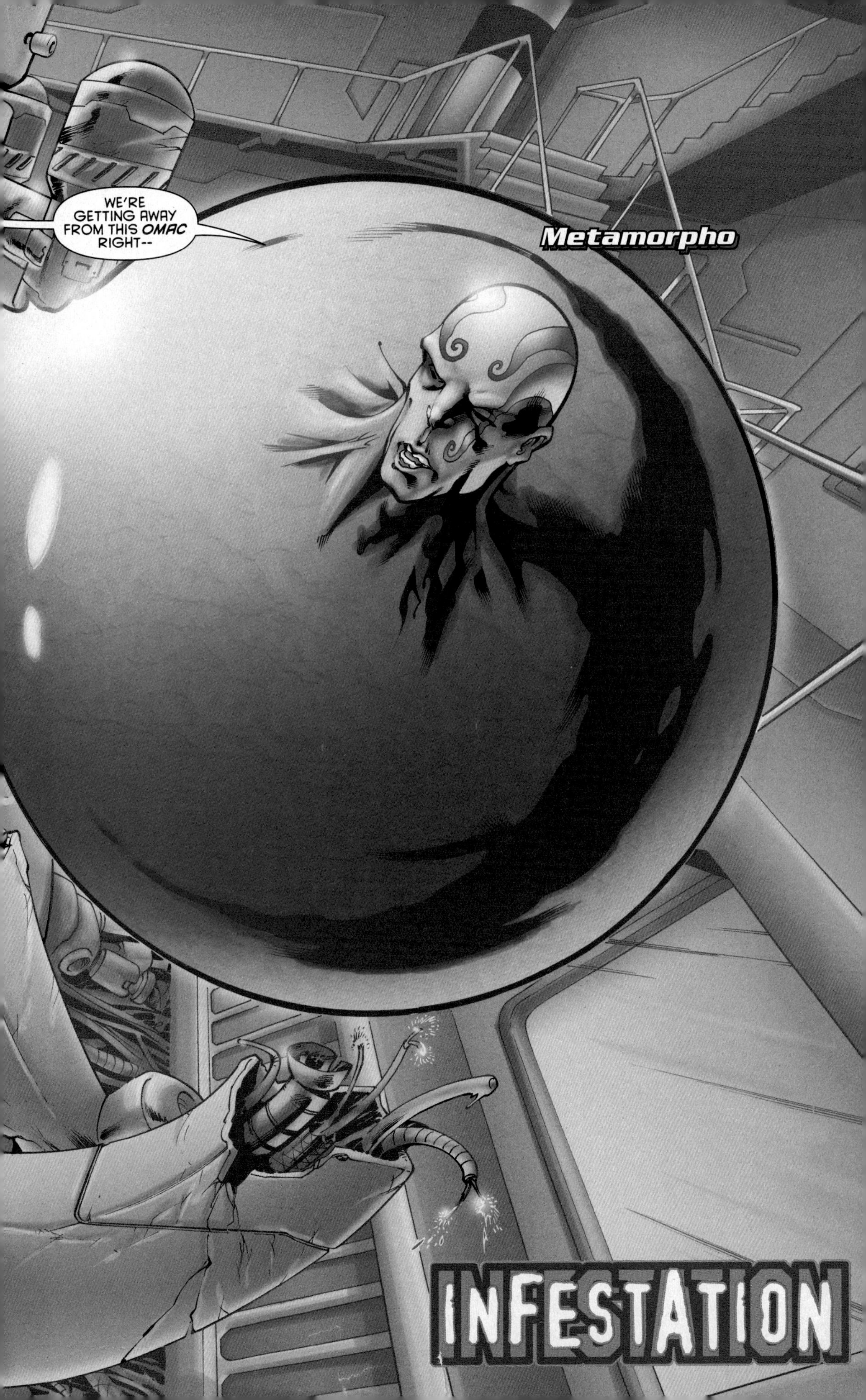
WE'RE GETTING AWAY FROM THIS OMAC RIGHT--
Metamorpho
INFESTATION

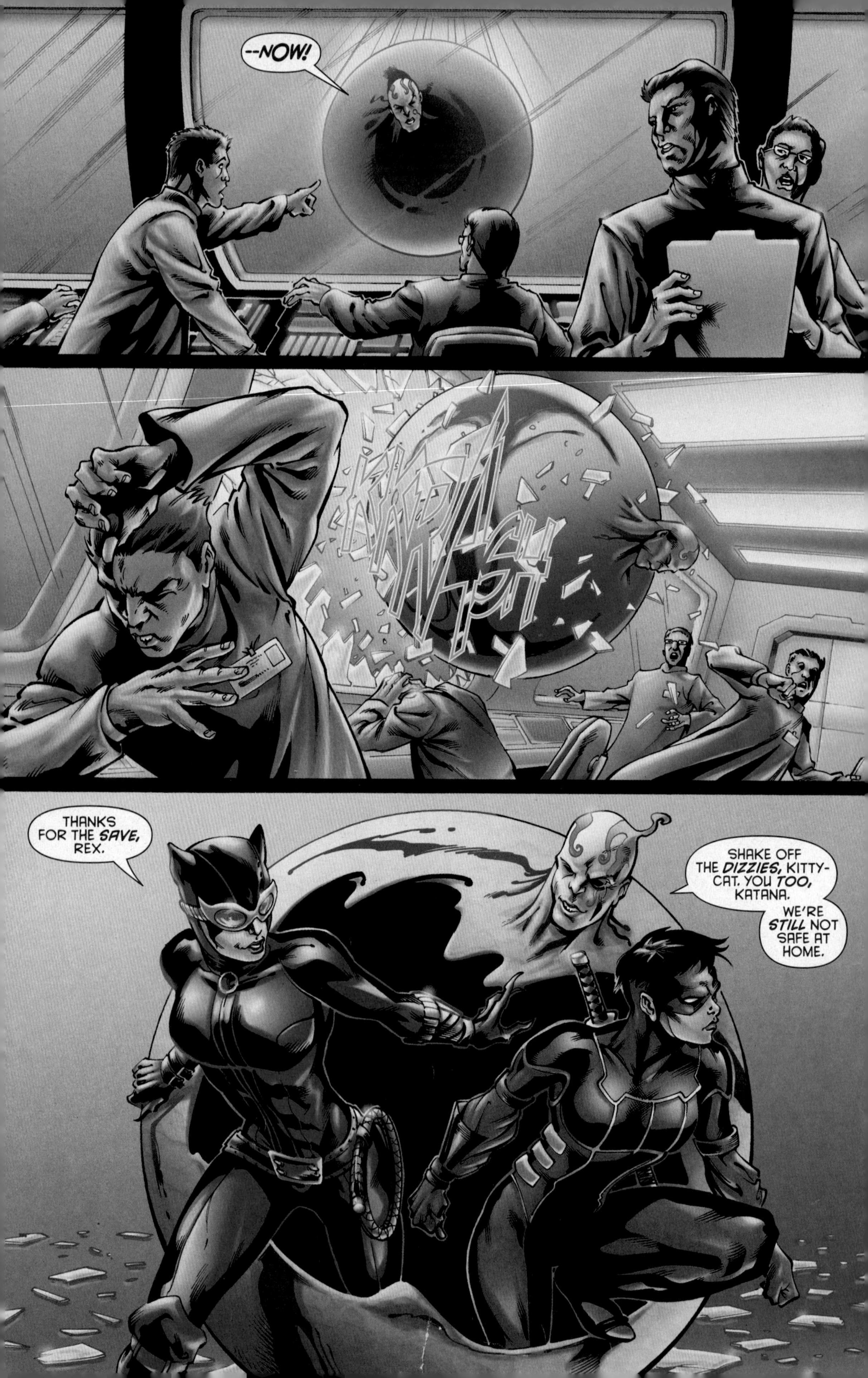
--NOW!
KRAASH
THANKS FOR THE SAVE, REX.
SHAKE OFF THE DIZZIES, KITTY-CAT. YOU TOO, KATANA.
WE'RE STILL NOT SAFE AT HOME.

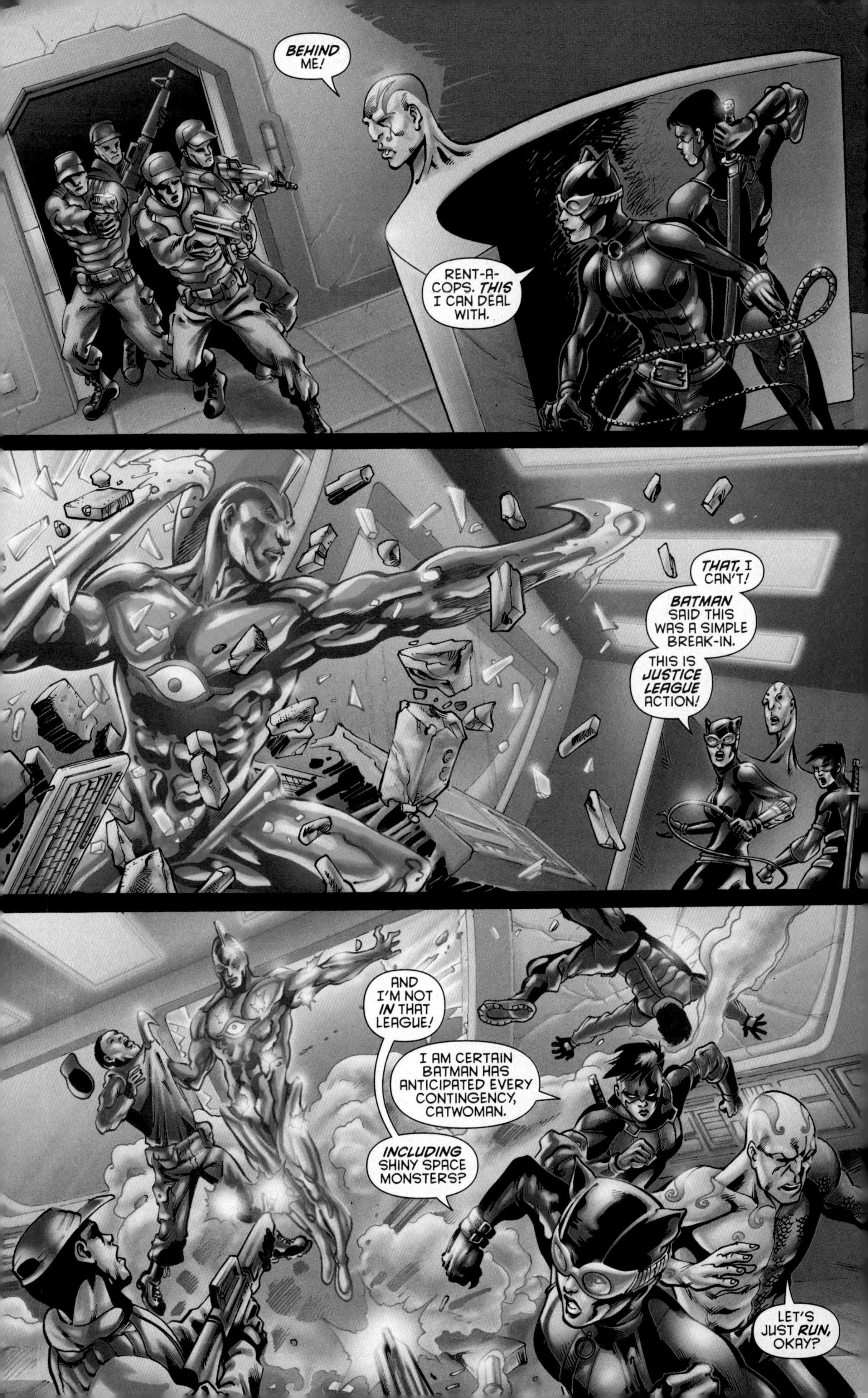
BEHIND ME!
RENT-A-COPS. THIS I CAN DEAL WITH.
THAT, I CAN'T!
BATMAN SAID THIS WAS A SIMPLE BREAK-IN.
THIS IS JUSTICE LEAGUE ACTION!
AND I'M NOT IN THAT LEAGUE!
I AM CERTAIN BATMAN HAS ANTICIPATED EVERY CONTINGENCY, CATWOMAN.
INCLUDING SHINY SPACE MONSTERS?
LET'S JUST RUN, OKAY?

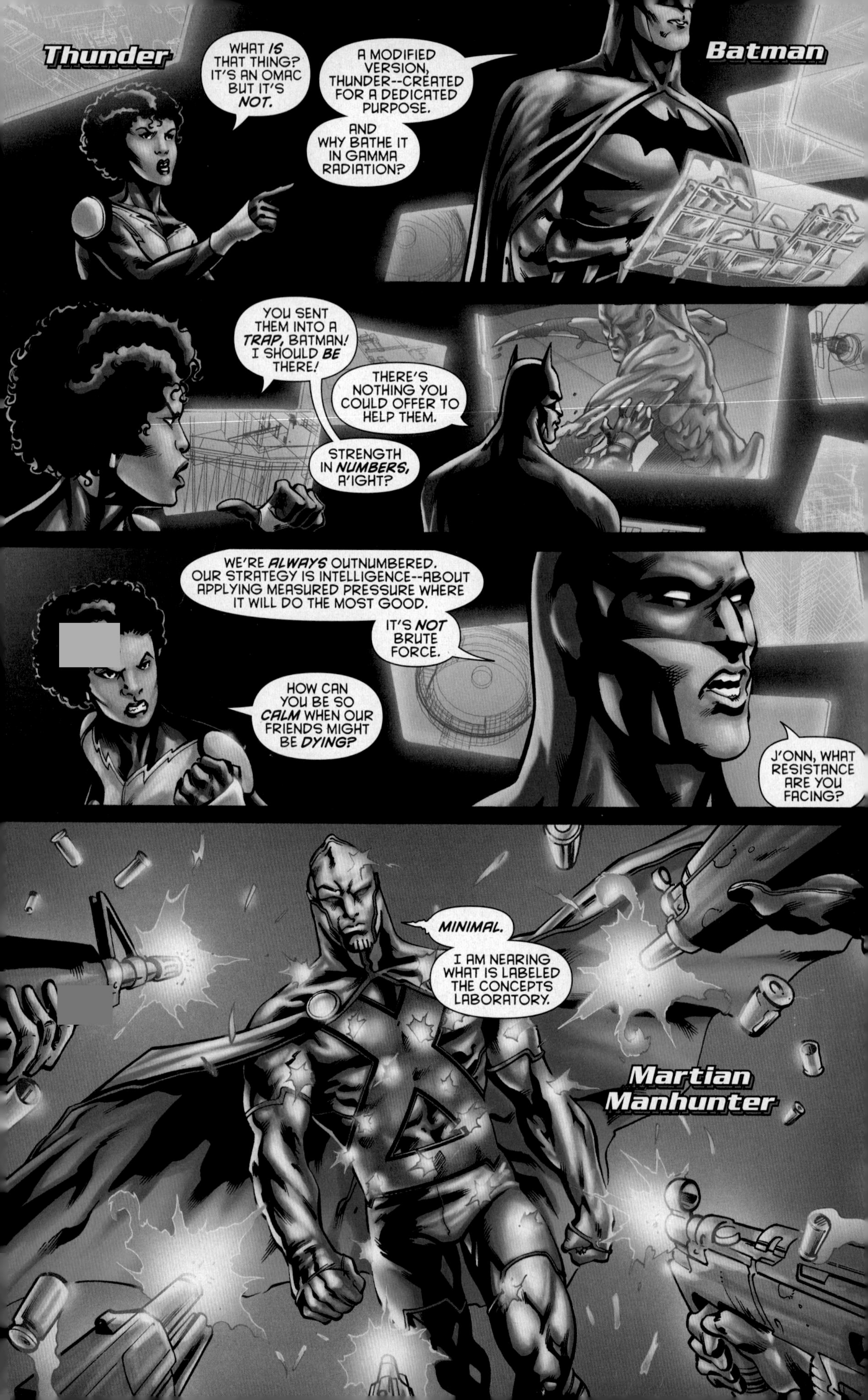
Thunder
WHAT *IS* THAT THING? IT'S AN OMAC BUT IT'S *NOT.*
A MODIFIED VERSION, THUNDER--CREATED FOR A DEDICATED PURPOSE.
AND WHY BATHE IT IN GAMMA RADIATION?
Batman
YOU SENT THEM INTO A *TRAP,* BATMAN! I SHOULD *BE* THERE!
THERE'S NOTHING YOU COULD OFFER TO HELP THEM.
STRENGTH IN *NUMBERS,* A'IGHT?
WE'RE *ALWAYS* OUTNUMBERED. OUR STRATEGY IS INTELLIGENCE--ABOUT APPLYING MEASURED PRESSURE WHERE IT WILL DO THE MOST GOOD.
IT'S *NOT* BRUTE FORCE.
HOW CAN YOU BE SO *CALM* WHEN OUR FRIENDS MIGHT BE *DYING?*
J'ONN, WHAT RESISTANCE ARE YOU FACING?
MINIMAL.
I AM NEARING WHAT IS LABELED THE CONCEPTS LABORATORY.
Martian Manhunter

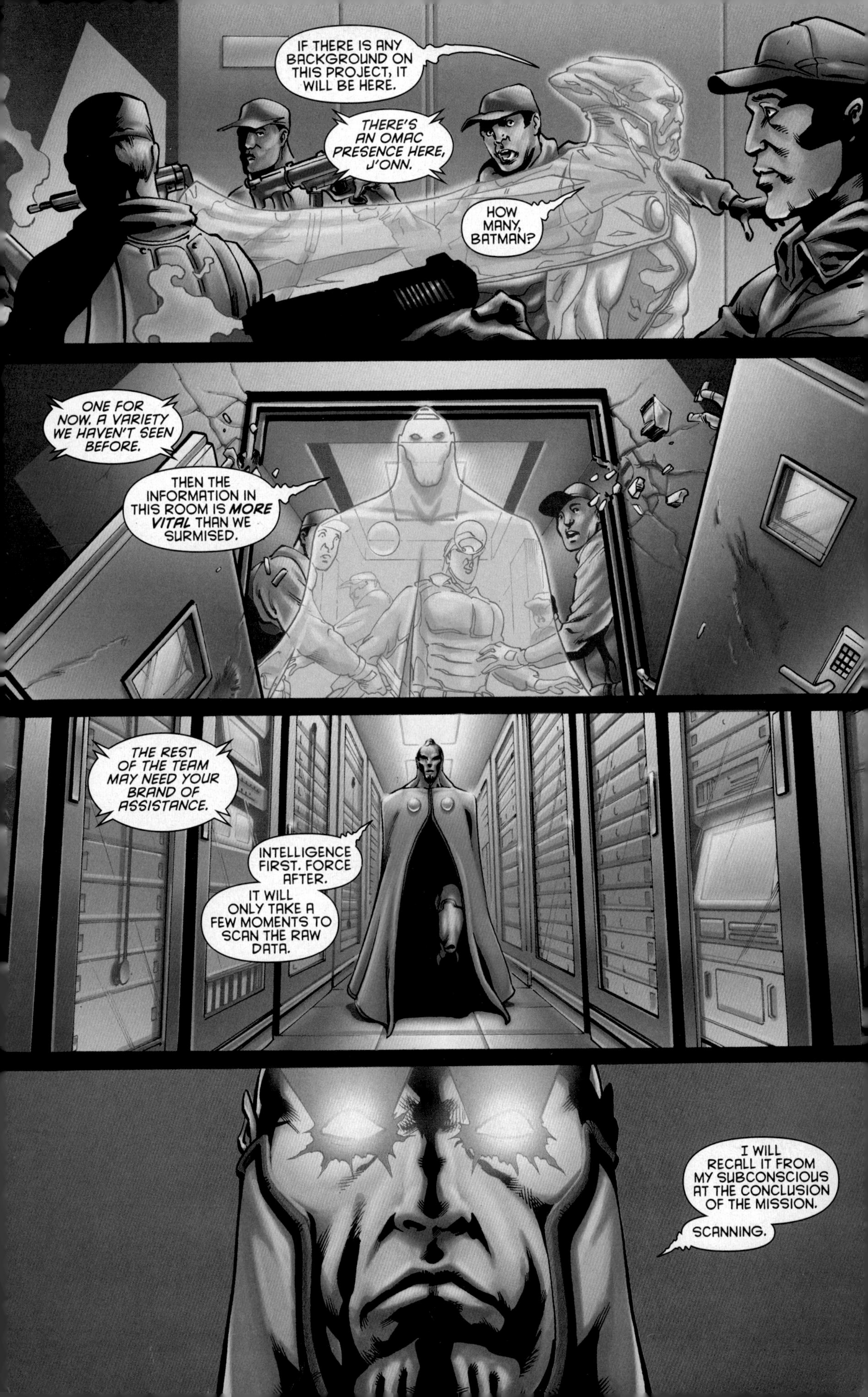
IF THERE IS ANY BACKGROUND ON THIS PROJECT, IT WILL BE HERE.
THERE'S AN OMAC PRESENCE HERE, J'ONN.
HOW MANY, BATMAN?
ONE FOR NOW. A VARIETY WE HAVEN'T SEEN BEFORE.
THEN THE INFORMATION IN THIS ROOM IS MORE VITAL THAN WE SURMISED.
THE REST OF THE TEAM MAY NEED YOUR BRAND OF ASSISTANCE.
INTELLIGENCE FIRST. FORCE AFTER.
IT WILL ONLY TAKE A FEW MOMENTS TO SCAN THE RAW DATA.
I WILL RECALL IT FROM MY SUBCONSCIOUS AT THE CONCLUSION OF THE MISSION.
SCANNING.

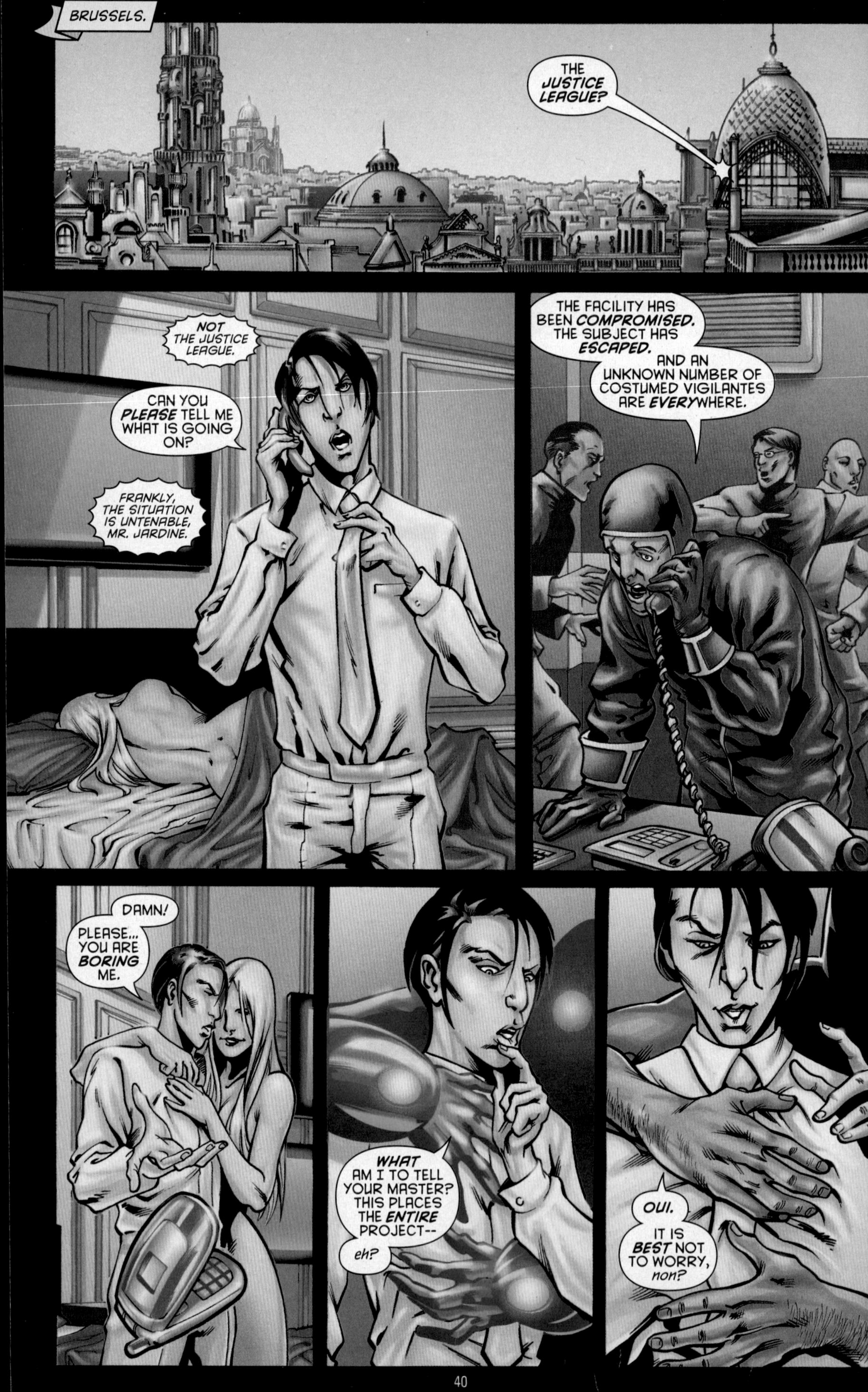
BRUSSELS.
THE JUSTICE LEAGUE?
NOT THE JUSTICE LEAGUE.
CAN YOU PLEASE TELL ME WHAT IS GOING ON?
FRANKLY, THE SITUATION IS UNTENABLE, MR. JARDINE.
THE FACILITY HAS BEEN COMPROMISED. THE SUBJECT HAS ESCAPED.
AND AN UNKNOWN NUMBER OF COSTUMED VIGILANTES ARE EVERYWHERE.
DAMN!
PLEASE... YOU ARE BORING ME.
WHAT AM I TO TELL YOUR MASTER? THIS PLACES THE ENTIRE PROJECT--
eh?
OUI.
IT IS BEST NOT TO WORRY, non?

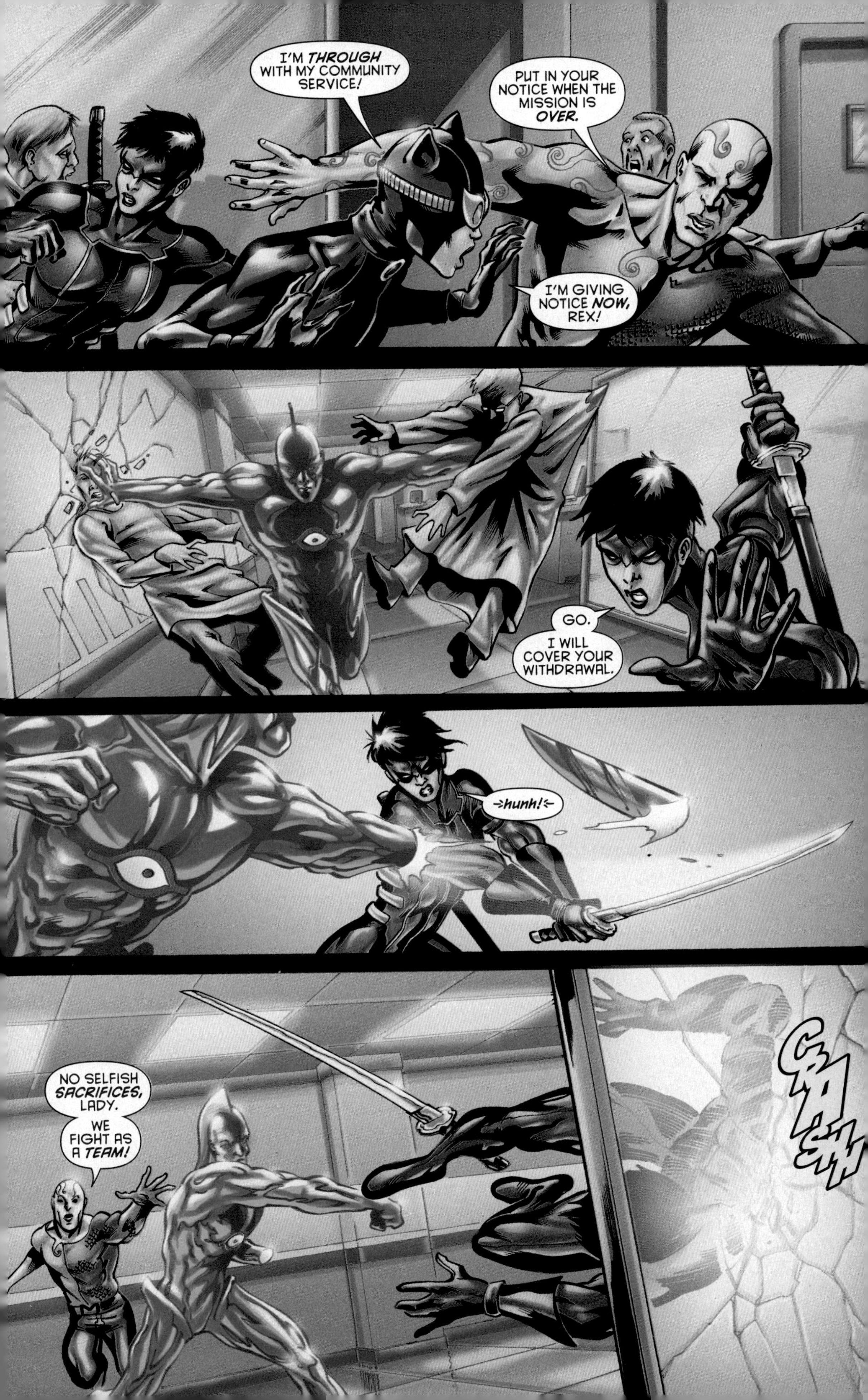
I'M THROUGH WITH MY COMMUNITY SERVICE!
PUT IN YOUR NOTICE WHEN THE MISSION IS OVER.
I'M GIVING NOTICE NOW, REX!
GO. I WILL COVER YOUR WITHDRAWAL.
hunh!
NO SELFISH SACRIFICES, LADY.
WE FIGHT AS A TEAM!
CRASH

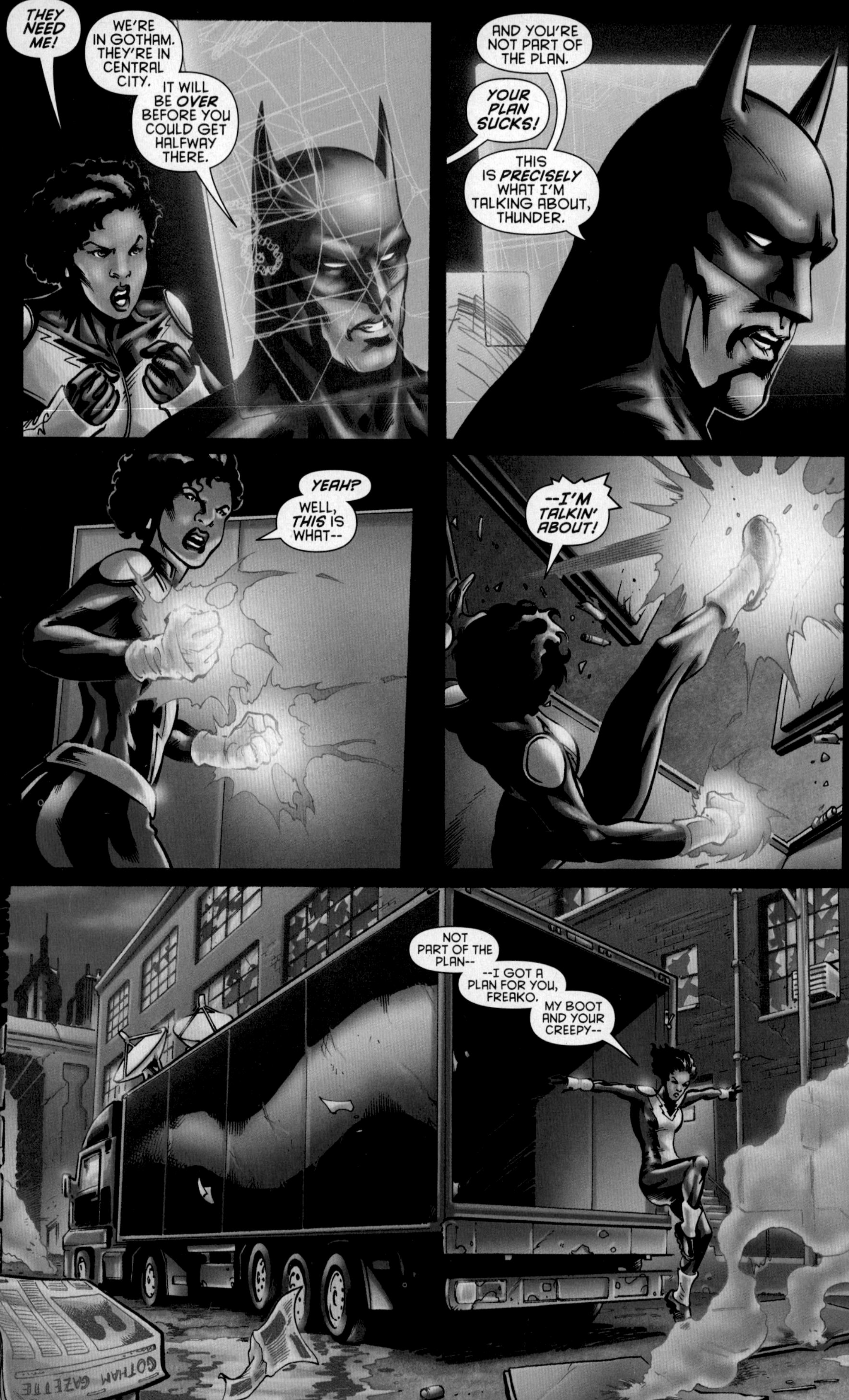
THEY NEED ME!
WE'RE IN GOTHAM. THEY'RE IN CENTRAL CITY.
IT WILL BE OVER BEFORE YOU COULD GET HALFWAY THERE.
AND YOU'RE NOT PART OF THE PLAN.
YOUR PLAN SUCKS!
THIS IS PRECISELY WHAT I'M TALKING ABOUT, THUNDER.
YEAH?
WELL, THIS IS WHAT--
--I'M TALKIN' ABOUT!
NOT PART OF THE PLAN--
--I GOT A PLAN FOR YOU, FREAKO.
MY BOOT AND YOUR CREEPY--
GOTHAM GAZETTE

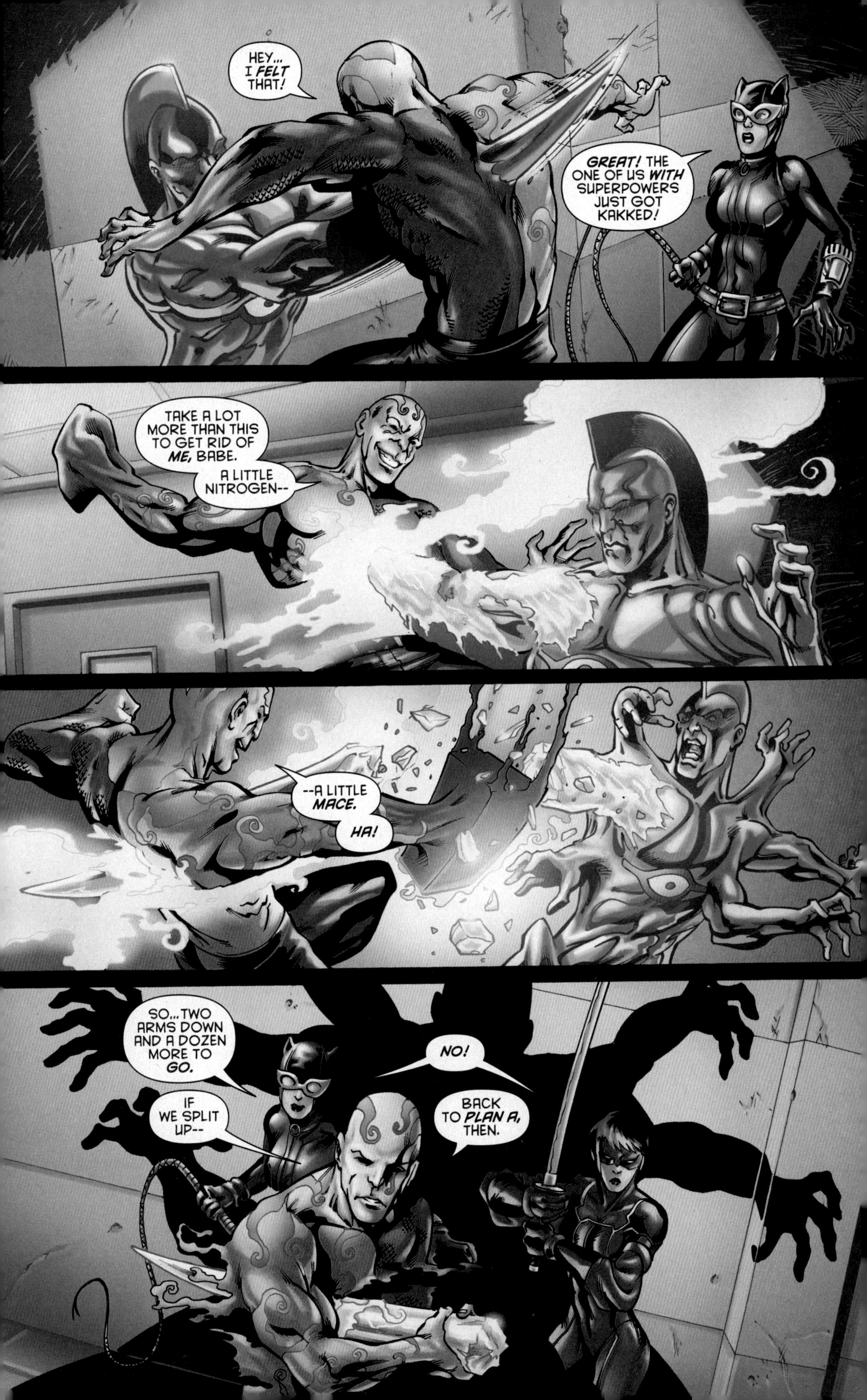
HEY... I FELT THAT!
GREAT! THE ONE OF US WITH SUPERPOWERS JUST GOT KAKKED!
TAKE A LOT MORE THAN THIS TO GET RID OF ME, BABE.
A LITTLE NITROGEN--
--A LITTLE MACE.
HA!
SO... TWO ARMS DOWN AND A DOZEN MORE TO GO.
IF WE SPLIT UP--
NO!
BACK TO PLAN A, THEN.

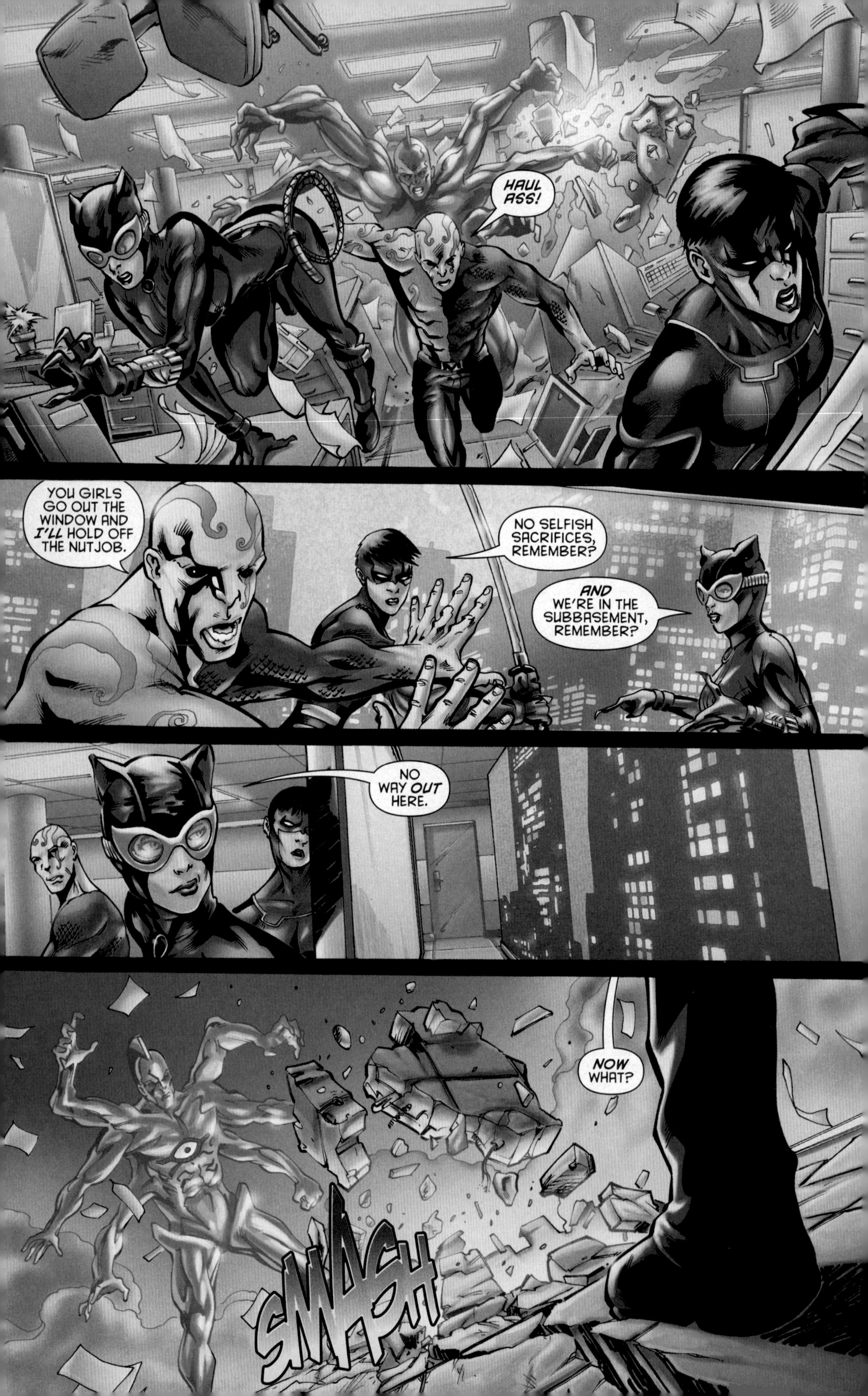
HAUL ASS!
YOU GIRLS GO OUT THE WINDOW AND I'LL HOLD OFF THE NUTJOB.
NO SELFISH SACRIFICES, REMEMBER?
AND WE'RE IN THE SUBBASEMENT, REMEMBER?
NO WAY OUT HERE.
NOW WHAT?
SMASH

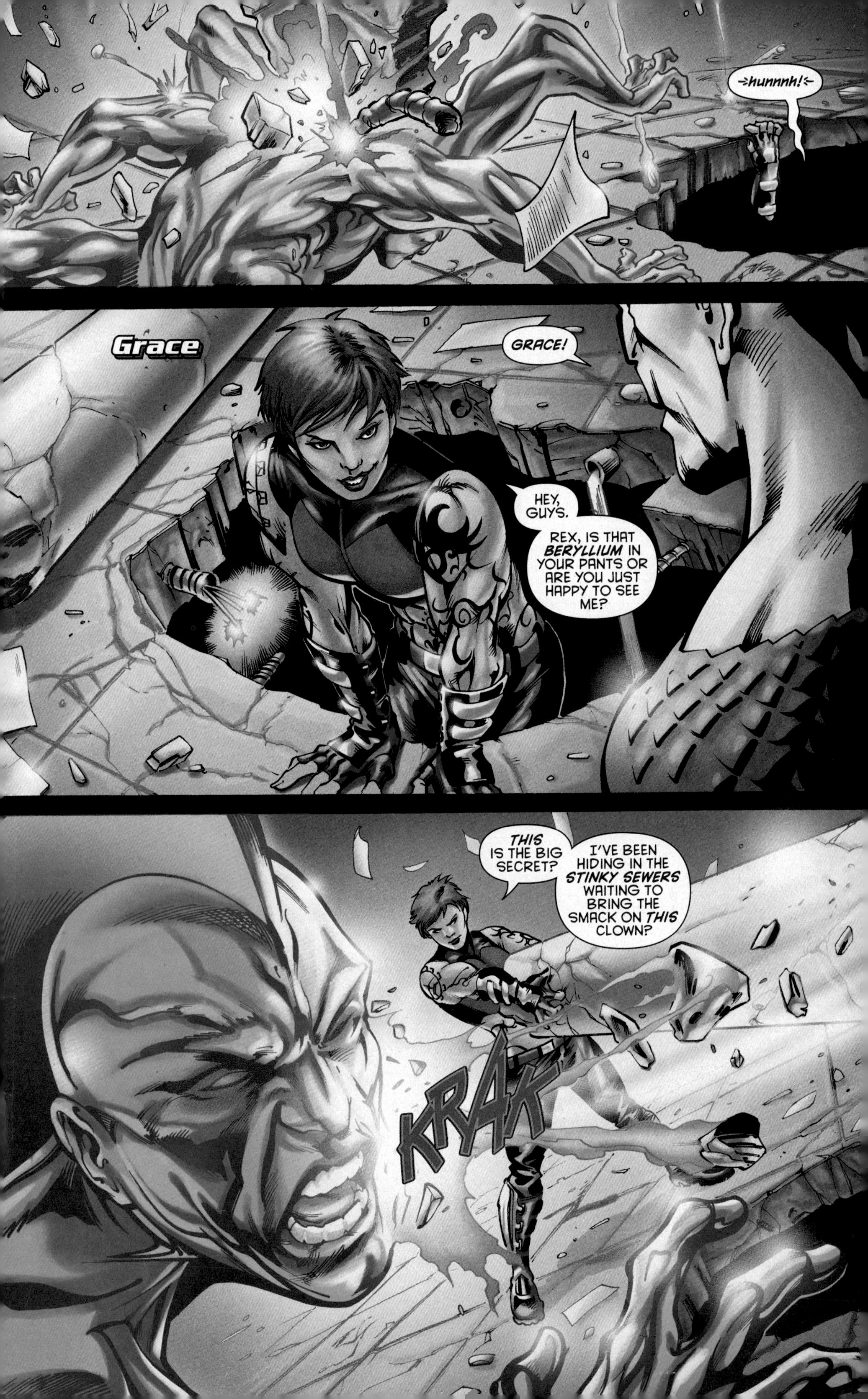
-hunnnh!-
Grace
GRACE!
HEY, GUYS.
REX, IS THAT BERYLLIUM IN YOUR PANTS OR ARE YOU JUST HAPPY TO SEE ME?
THIS IS THE BIG SECRET?
I'VE BEEN HIDING IN THE STINKY SEWERS WAITING TO BRING THE SMACK ON THIS CLOWN?
KRAK

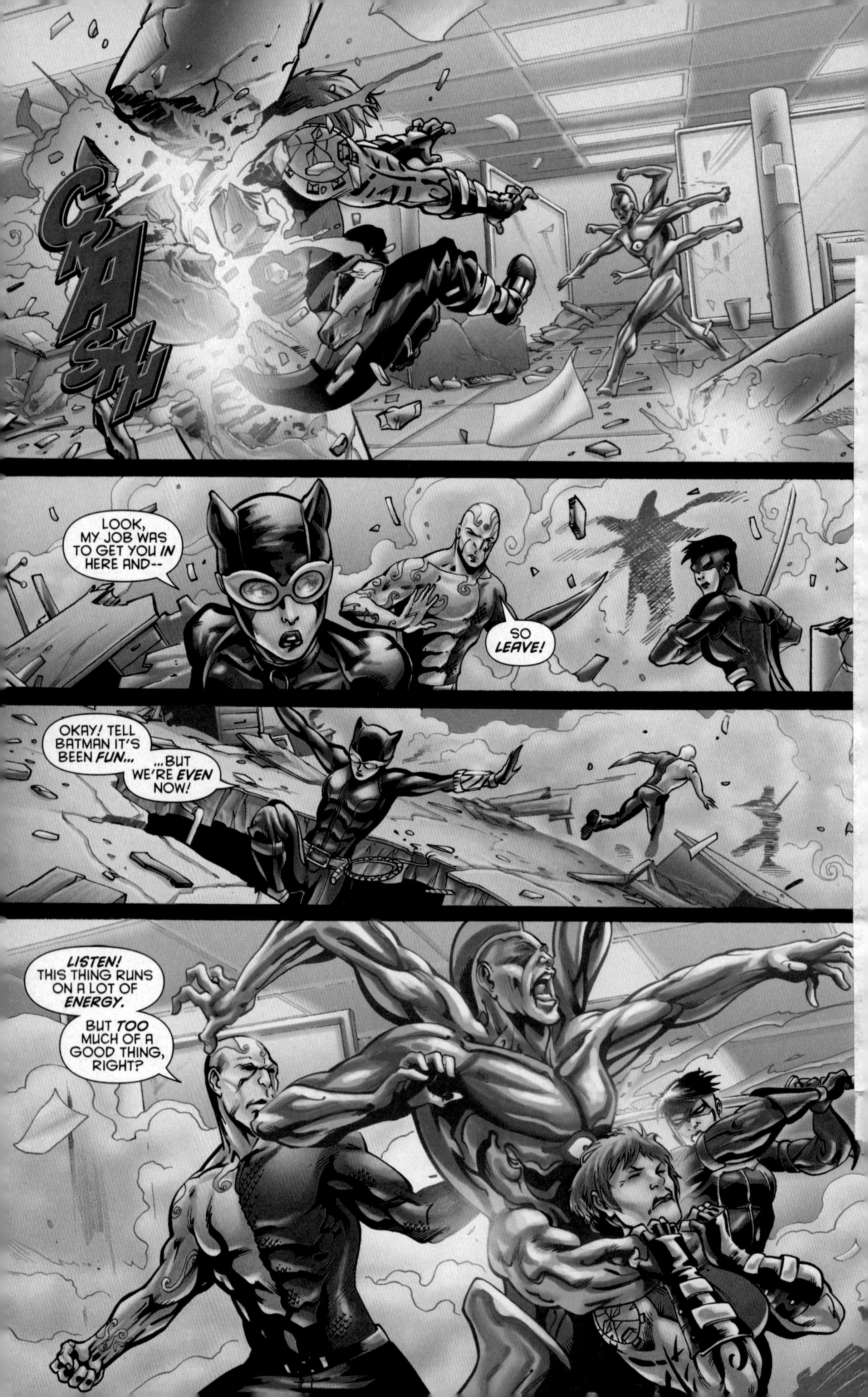
CRASSH
LOOK, MY JOB WAS TO GET YOU *IN* HERE AND--
SO *LEAVE!*
OKAY! TELL BATMAN IT'S BEEN *FUN...*
...BUT WE'RE *EVEN* NOW!
LISTEN! THIS THING RUNS ON A LOT OF *ENERGY.*
BUT *TOO* MUCH OF A GOOD THING, RIGHT?

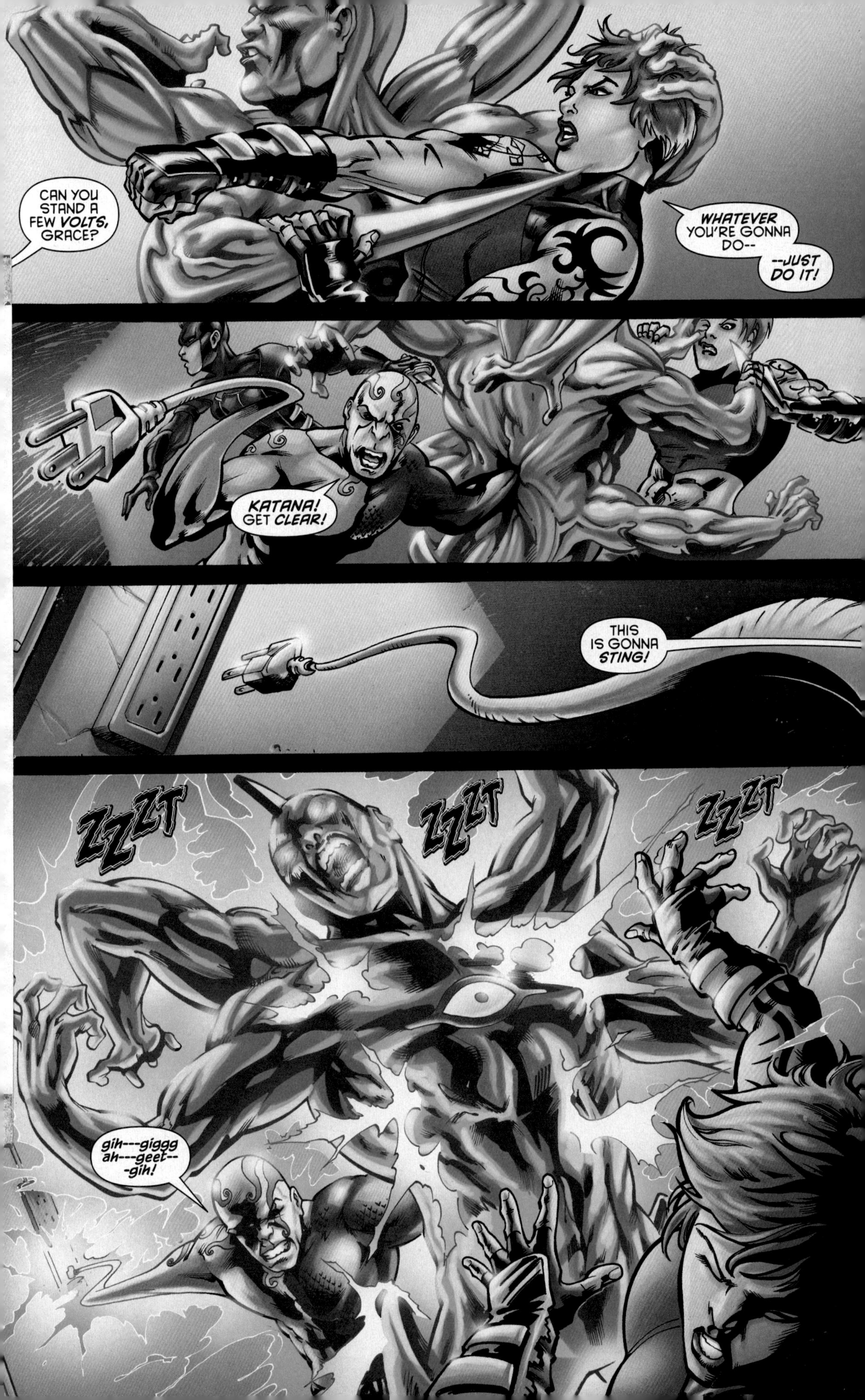
CAN YOU STAND A FEW VOLTS, GRACE?
WHATEVER YOU'RE GONNA DO--
--JUST DO IT!
KATANA! GET CLEAR!
THIS IS GONNA STING!
ZZZZT
ZZZZT
ZZZZT
gih---giggg ah---geet-- -gih!

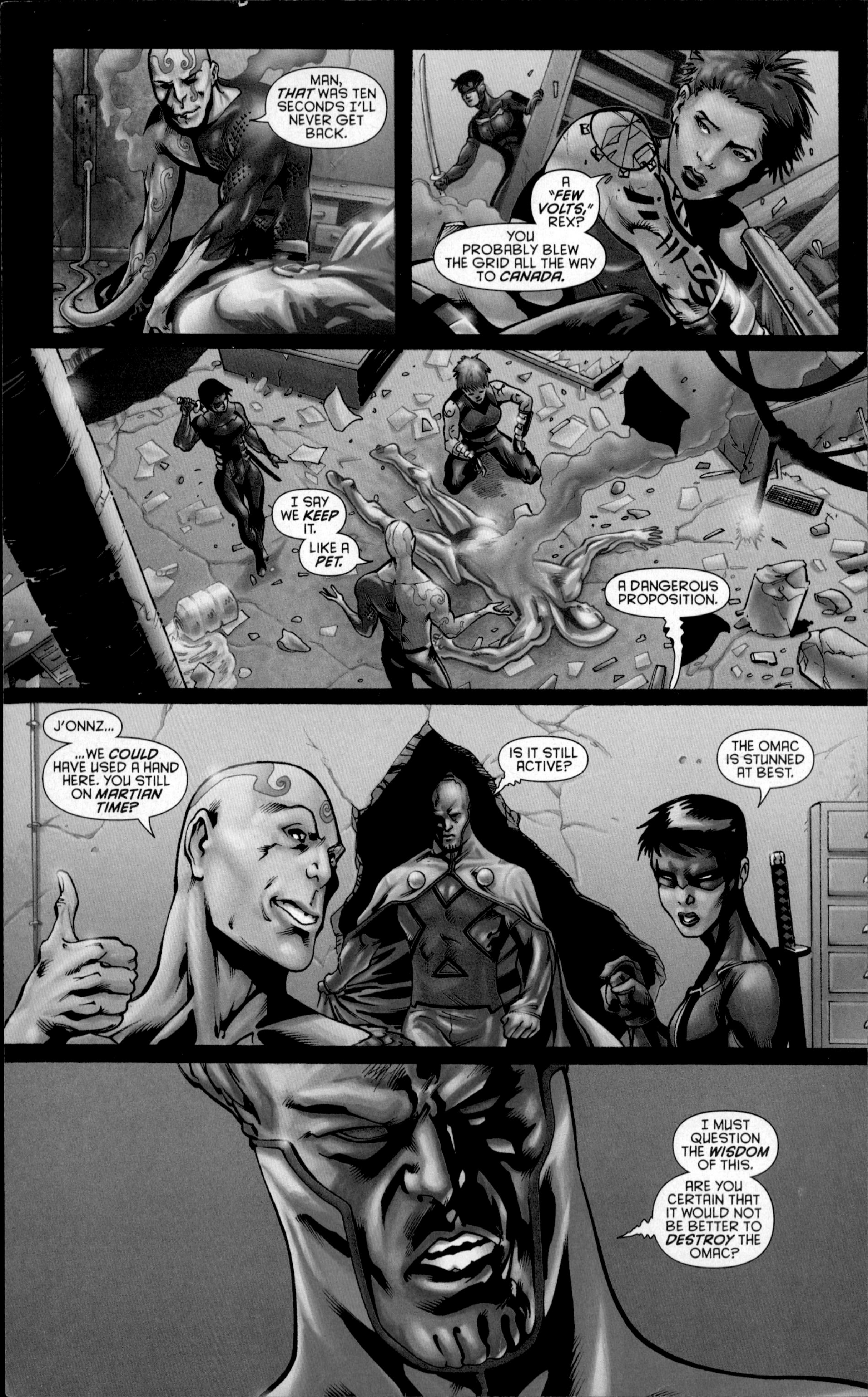
MAN, THAT WAS TEN SECONDS I'LL NEVER GET BACK.
A "FEW VOLTS," REX?
YOU PROBABLY BLEW THE GRID ALL THE WAY TO CANADA.
I SAY WE KEEP IT.
LIKE A PET.
A DANGEROUS PROPOSITION.
J'ONNZ...
...WE COULD HAVE USED A HAND HERE. YOU STILL ON MARTIAN TIME?
IS IT STILL ACTIVE?
THE OMAC IS STUNNED AT BEST.
I MUST QUESTION THE WISDOM OF THIS.
ARE YOU CERTAIN THAT IT WOULD NOT BE BETTER TO DESTROY THE OMAC?

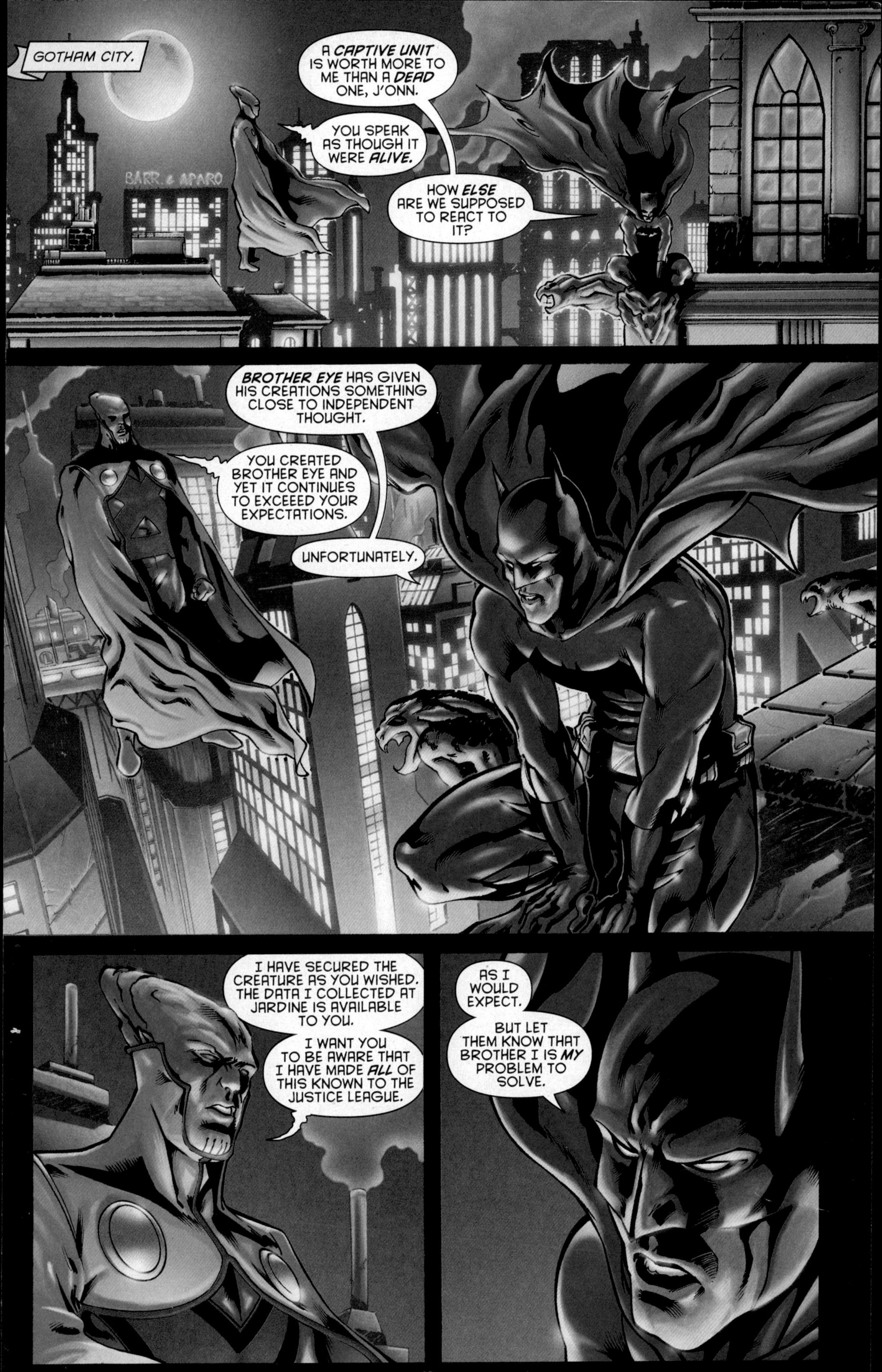
GOTHAM CITY.
A CAPTIVE UNIT IS WORTH MORE TO ME THAN A DEAD ONE, J'ONN.
YOU SPEAK AS THOUGH IT WERE ALIVE.
HOW ELSE ARE WE SUPPOSED TO REACT TO IT?
BARR. & APARO
BROTHER EYE HAS GIVEN HIS CREATIONS SOMETHING CLOSE TO INDEPENDENT THOUGHT.
YOU CREATED BROTHER EYE AND YET IT CONTINUES TO EXCEEED YOUR EXPECTATIONS.
UNFORTUNATELY.
I HAVE SECURED THE CREATURE AS YOU WISHED. THE DATA I COLLECTED AT JARDINE IS AVAILABLE TO YOU.
I WANT YOU TO BE AWARE THAT I HAVE MADE ALL OF THIS KNOWN TO THE JUSTICE LEAGUE.
AS I WOULD EXPECT.
BUT LET THEM KNOW THAT BROTHER I IS MY PROBLEM TO SOLVE.

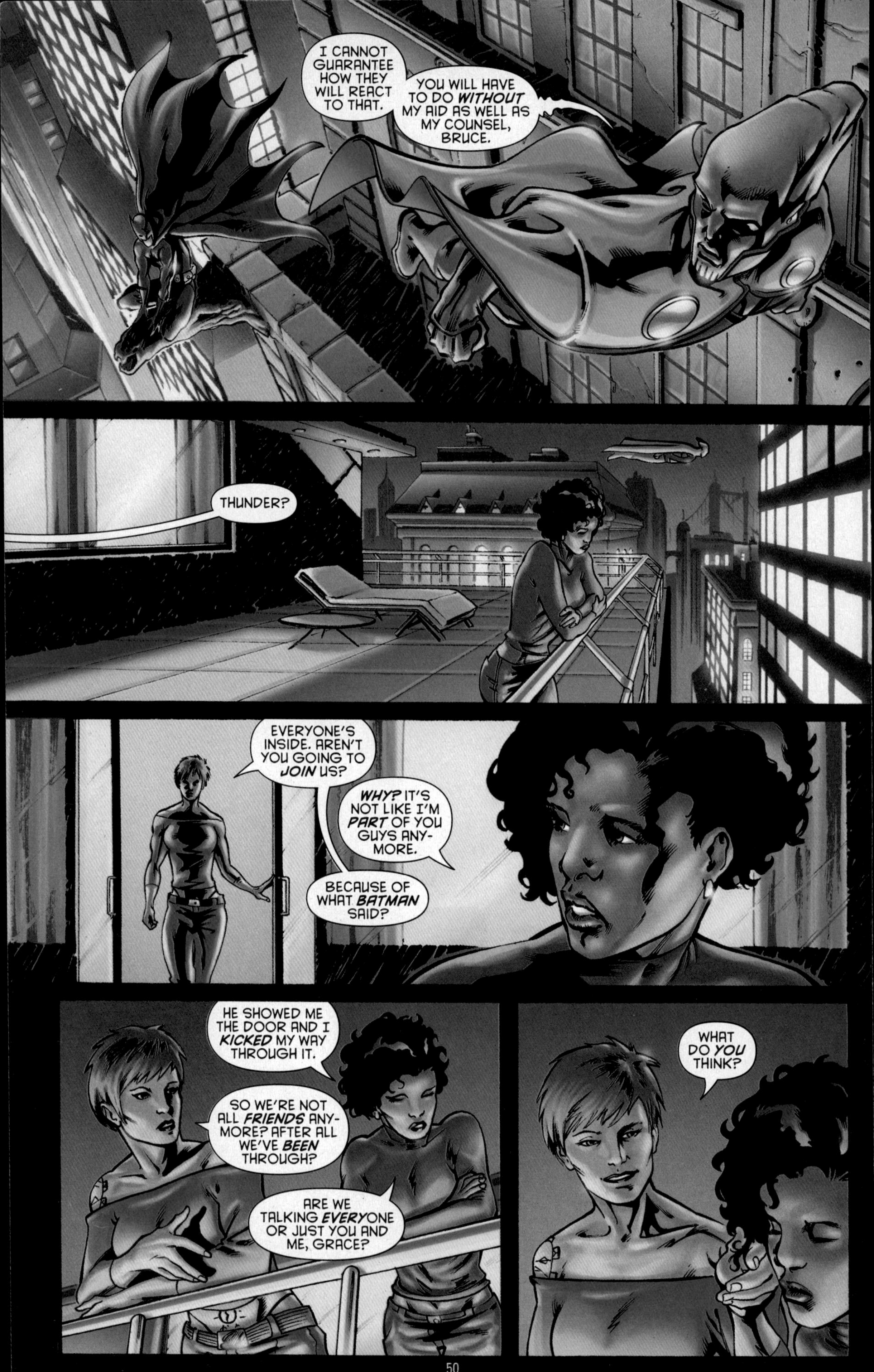
I CANNOT GUARANTEE HOW THEY WILL REACT TO THAT.
YOU WILL HAVE TO DO WITHOUT MY AID AS WELL AS MY COUNSEL, BRUCE.
THUNDER?
EVERYONE'S INSIDE. AREN'T YOU GOING TO JOIN US?
WHY? IT'S NOT LIKE I'M PART OF YOU GUYS ANY-MORE.
BECAUSE OF WHAT BATMAN SAID?
HE SHOWED ME THE DOOR AND I KICKED MY WAY THROUGH IT.
SO WE'RE NOT ALL FRIENDS ANY-MORE? AFTER ALL WE'VE BEEN THROUGH?
ARE WE TALKING EVERYONE OR JUST YOU AND ME, GRACE?
WHAT DO YOU THINK?

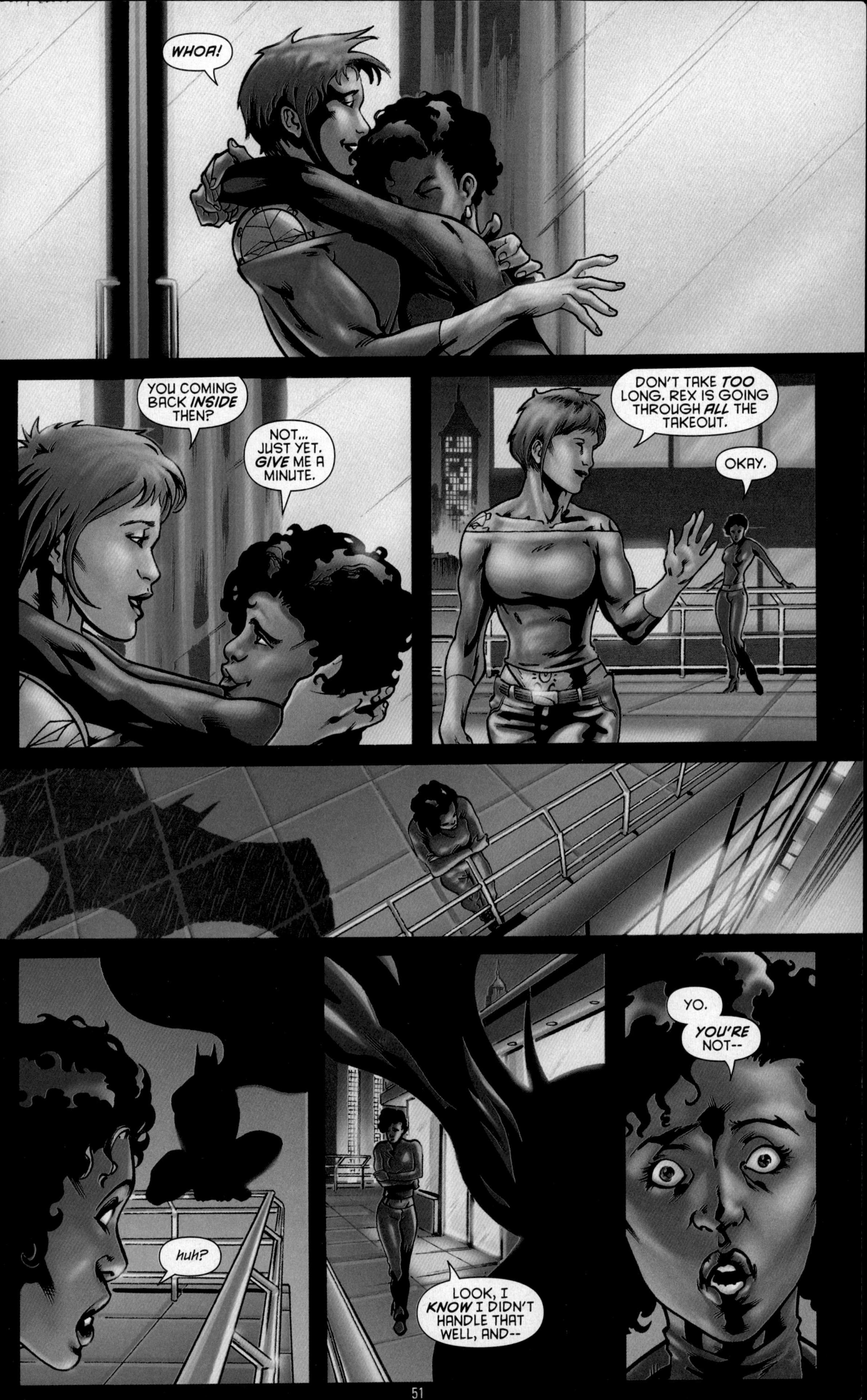

WHOA!
YOU COMING BACK INSIDE THEN?
NOT... JUST YET. GIVE ME A MINUTE.
DON'T TAKE TOO LONG. REX IS GOING THROUGH ALL THE TAKEOUT.
OKAY.
huh?
LOOK, I KNOW I DIDN'T HANDLE THAT WELL, AND--
YO.
YOU'RE NOT--

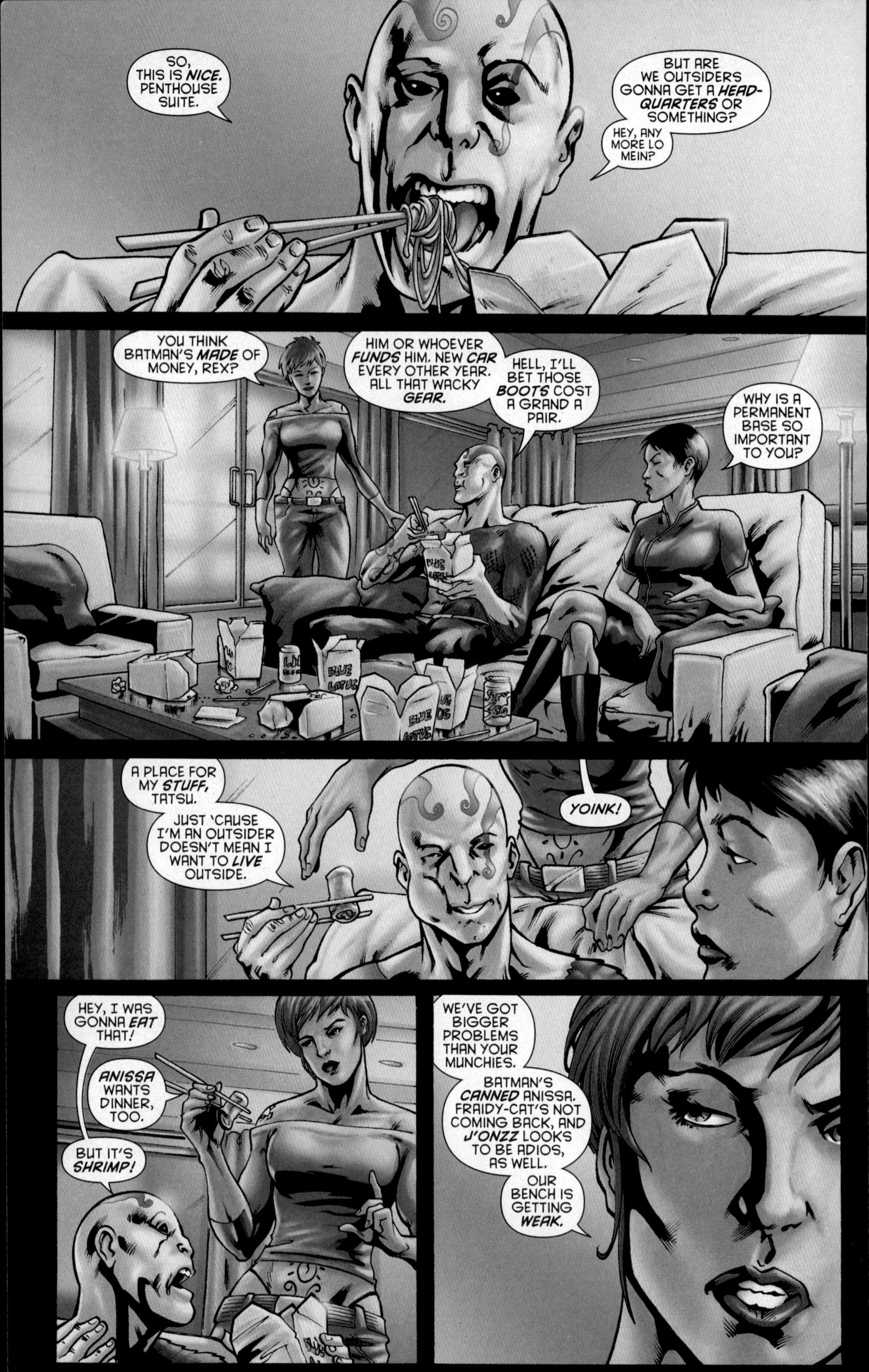

SO, THIS IS NICE. PENTHOUSE SUITE.
BUT ARE WE OUTSIDERS GONNA GET A HEAD-QUARTERS OR SOMETHING?
HEY, ANY MORE LO MEIN?
YOU THINK BATMAN'S MADE OF MONEY, REX?
HIM OR WHOEVER FUNDS HIM. NEW CAR EVERY OTHER YEAR. ALL THAT WACKY GEAR.
HELL, I'LL BET THOSE BOOTS COST A GRAND A PAIR.
WHY IS A PERMANENT BASE SO IMPORTANT TO YOU?
A PLACE FOR MY STUFF, TATSU.
JUST 'CAUSE I'M AN OUTSIDER DOESN'T MEAN I WANT TO LIVE OUTSIDE.
YOINK!
HEY, I WAS GONNA EAT THAT!
ANISSA WANTS DINNER, TOO.
BUT IT'S SHRIMP!
WE'VE GOT BIGGER PROBLEMS THAN YOUR MUNCHIES.
BATMAN'S CANNED ANISSA. FRAIDY-CAT'S NOT COMING BACK, AND J'ONZZ LOOKS TO BE ADIOS, AS WELL.
OUR BENCH IS GETTING WEAK.

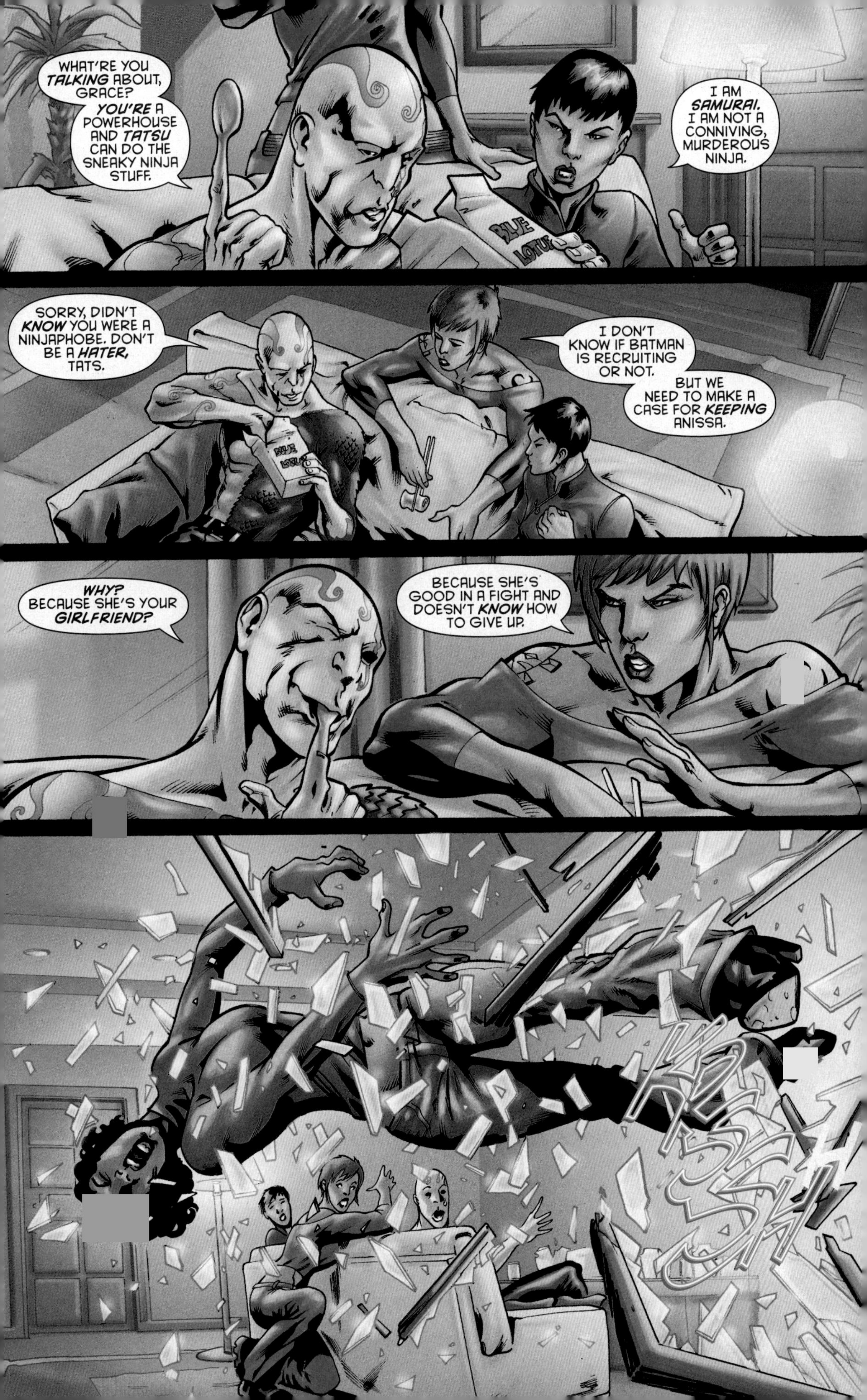
WHAT'RE YOU TALKING ABOUT, GRACE? YOU'RE A POWERHOUSE AND TATSU CAN DO THE SNEAKY NINJA STUFF.
I AM SAMURAI. I AM NOT A CONNIVING, MURDEROUS NINJA.
SORRY, DIDN'T KNOW YOU WERE A NINJAPHOBE. DON'T BE A HATER, TATS.
I DON'T KNOW IF BATMAN IS RECRUITING OR NOT.
BUT WE NEED TO MAKE A CASE FOR KEEPING ANISSA.
WHY? BECAUSE SHE'S YOUR GIRLFRIEND?
BECAUSE SHE'S GOOD IN A FIGHT AND DOESN'T KNOW HOW TO GIVE UP.

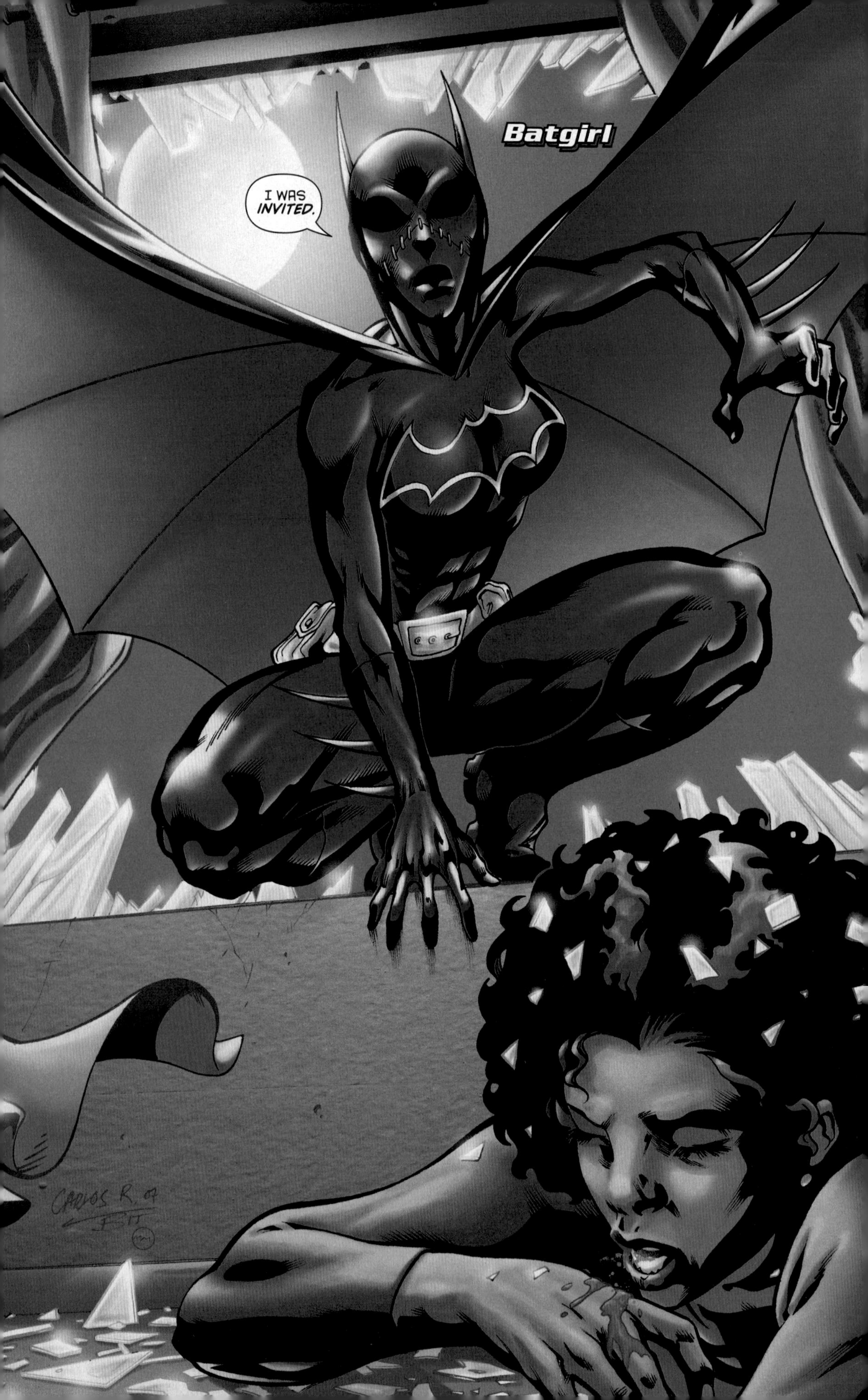
Batgirl
I WAS INVITED.
CARLOS R. 07

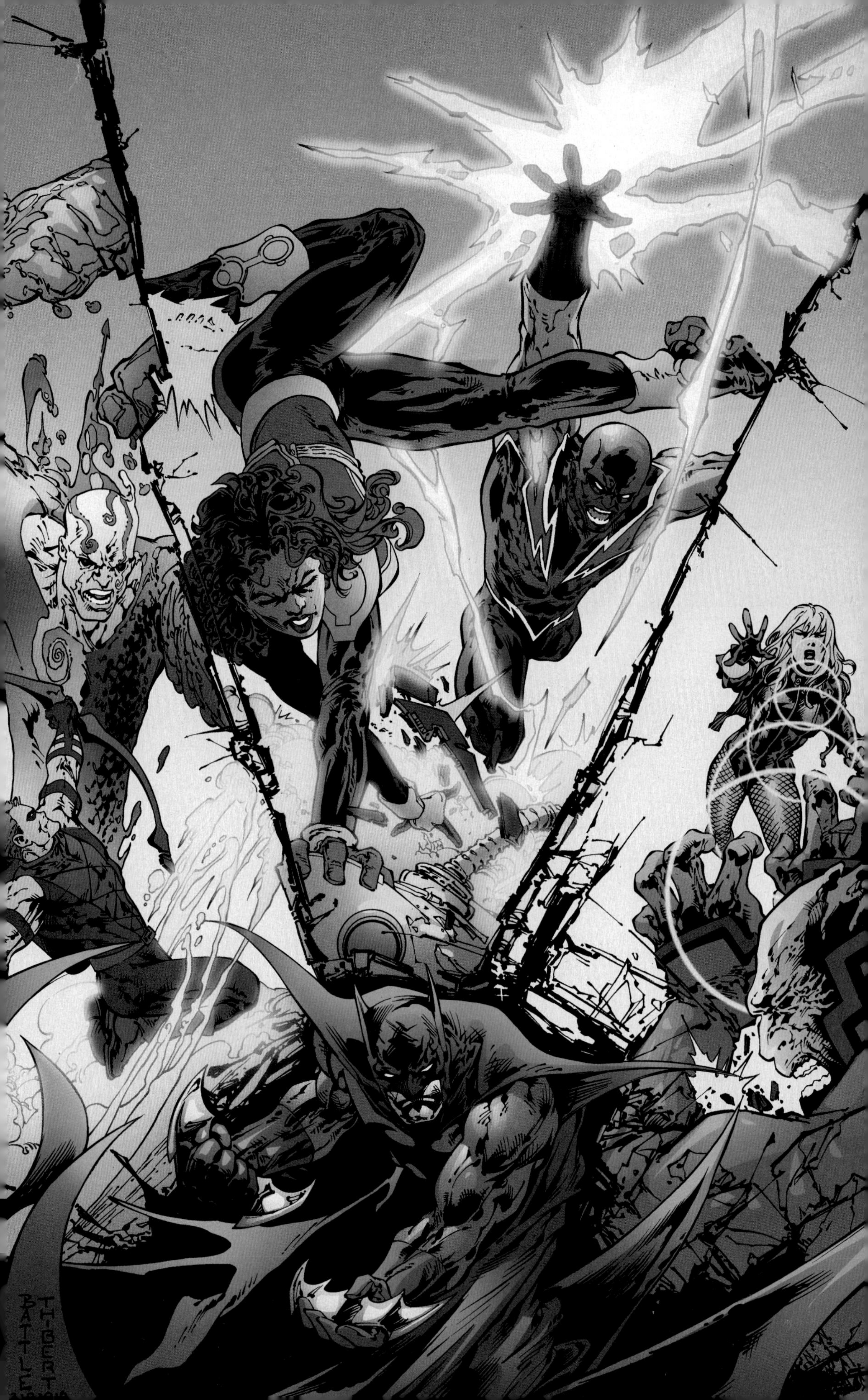

BATTLE
THIBERT

part THREE

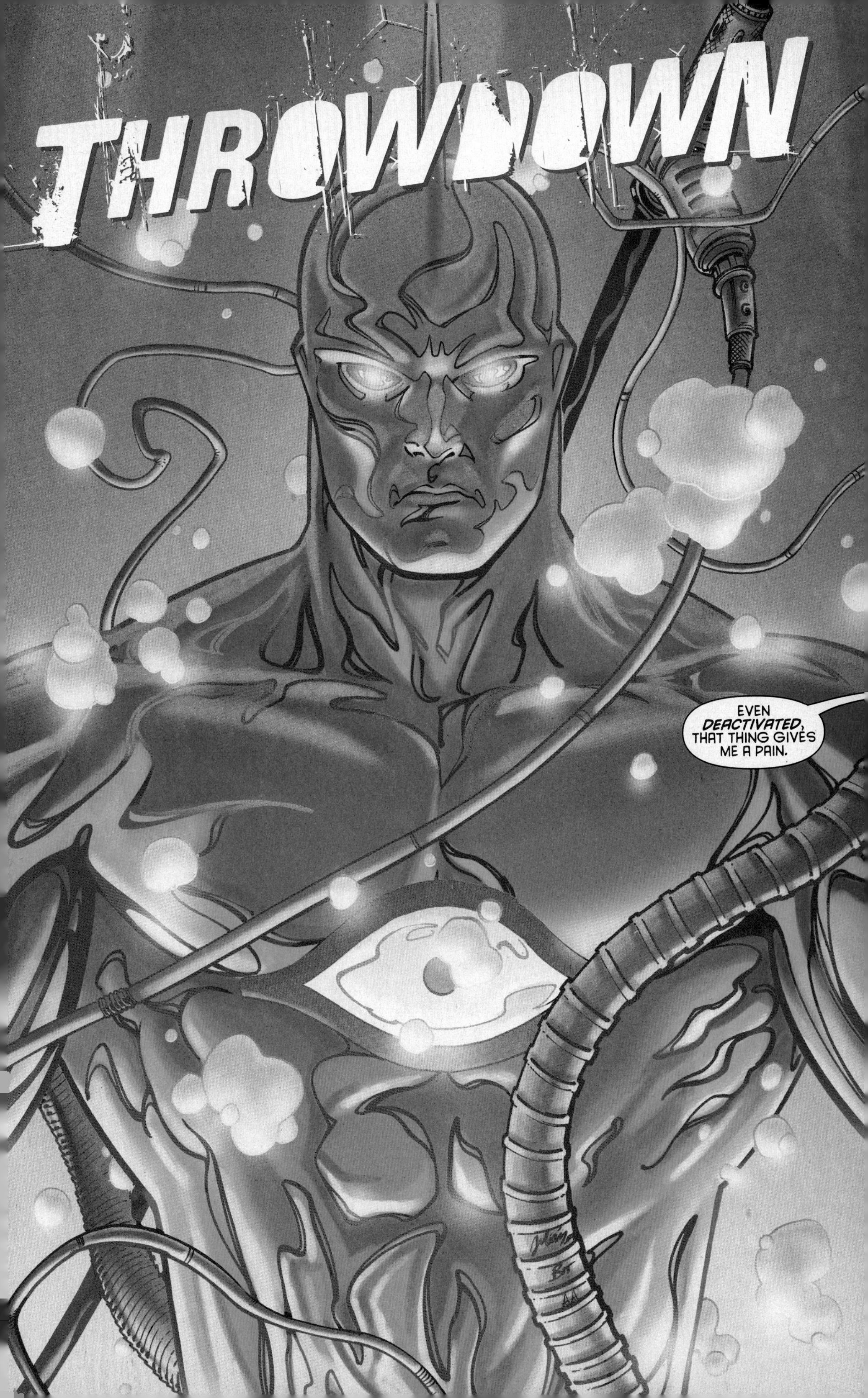
THROWDOWN
EVEN DEACTIVATED, THAT THING GIVES ME A PAIN.

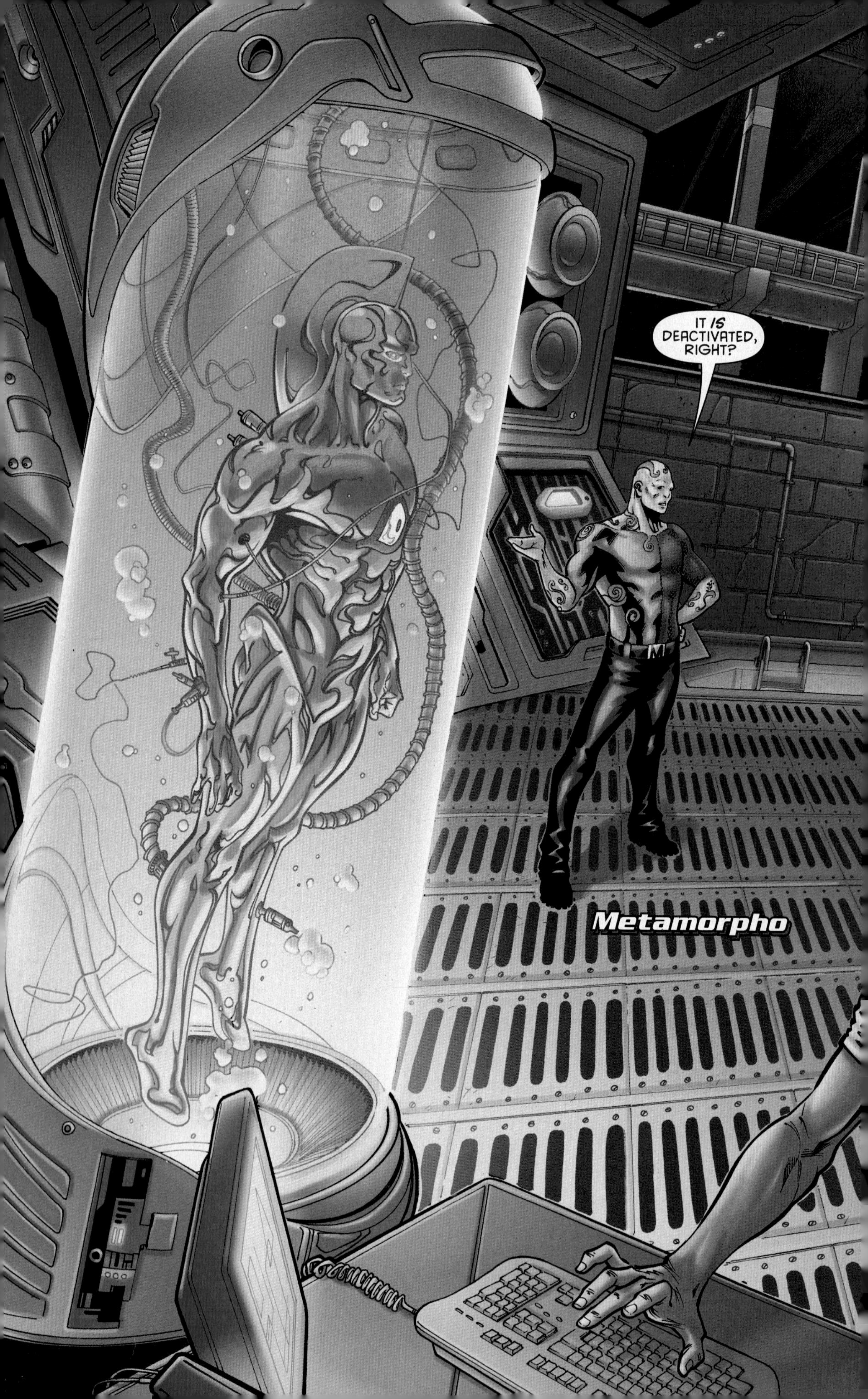
IT IS DEACTIVATED, RIGHT?
Metamorpho

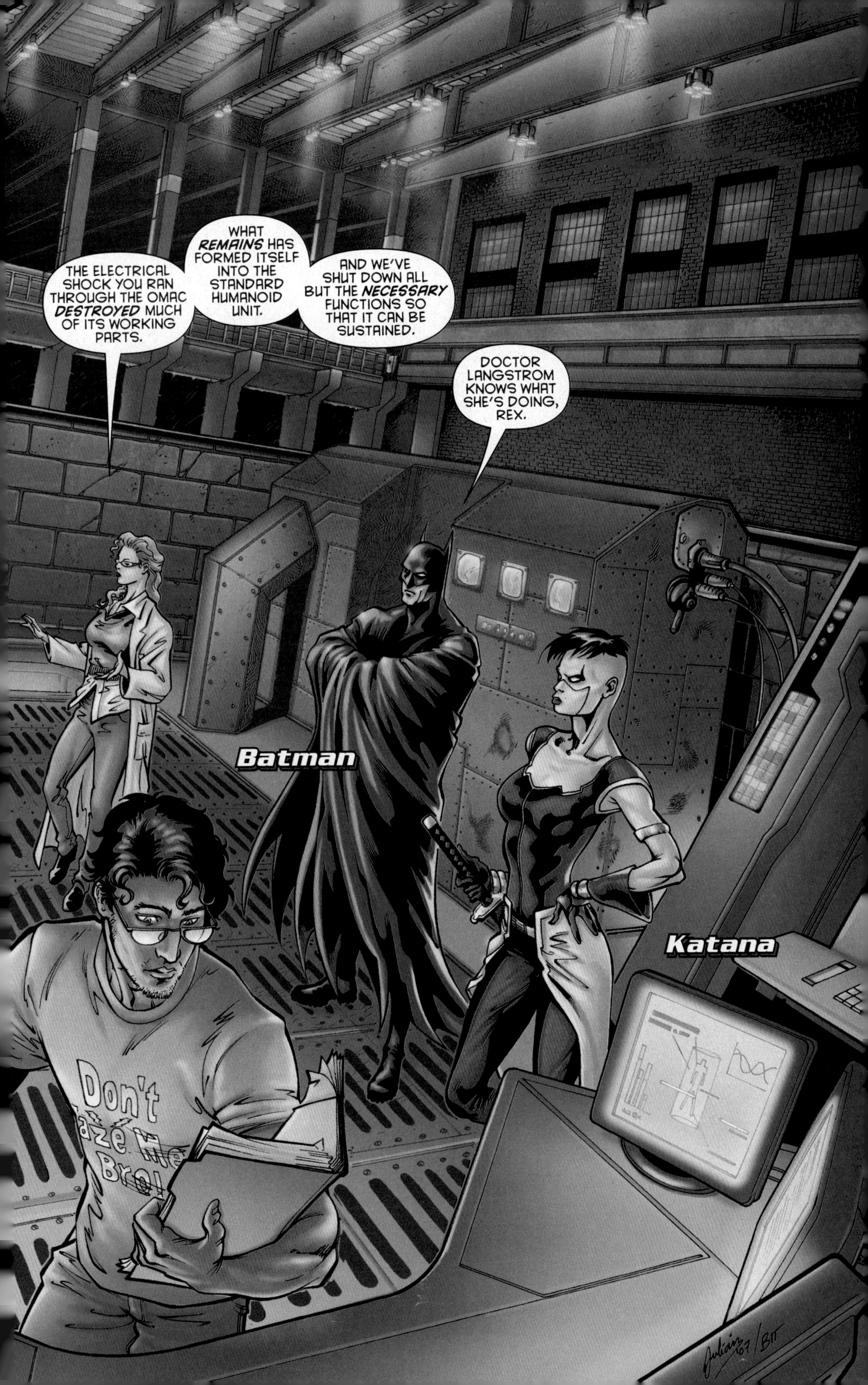
THE ELECTRICAL SHOCK YOU RAN THROUGH THE OMAC DESTROYED MUCH OF ITS WORKING PARTS.
WHAT REMAINS HAS FORMED ITSELF INTO THE STANDARD HUMANOID UNIT.
AND WE'VE SHUT DOWN ALL BUT THE NECESSARY FUNCTIONS SO THAT IT CAN BE SUSTAINED.
DOCTOR LANGSTROM KNOWS WHAT SHE'S DOING, REX.
Batman
Katana
Don't Taze Me Bro!

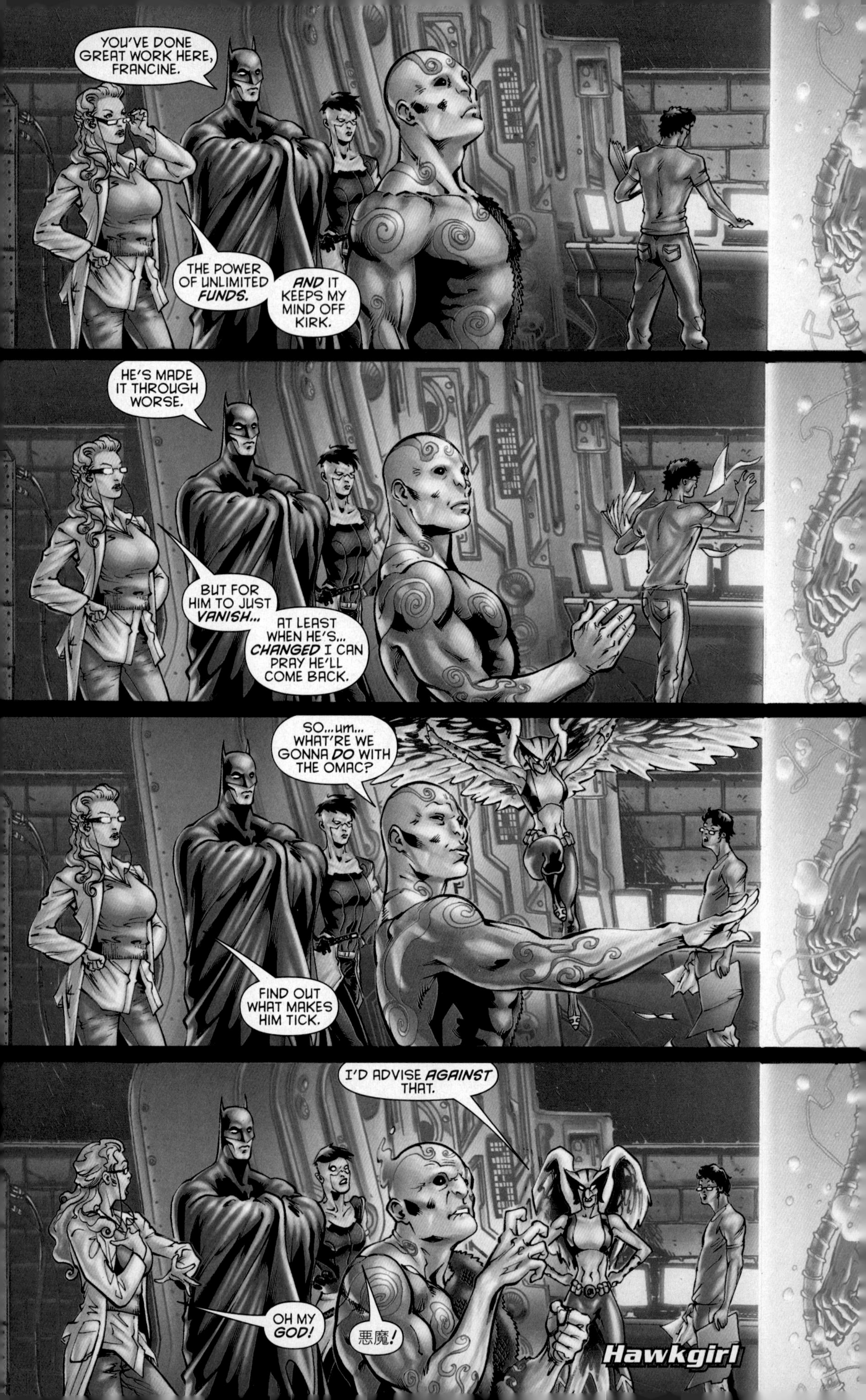
YOU'VE DONE GREAT WORK HERE, FRANCINE.
THE POWER OF UNLIMITED *FUNDS.*
AND IT KEEPS MY MIND OFF KIRK.
HE'S MADE IT THROUGH WORSE.
BUT FOR HIM TO JUST *VANISH...*
AT LEAST WHEN HE'S... *CHANGED* I CAN PRAY HE'LL COME BACK.
SO...um... WHAT'RE WE GONNA *DO* WITH THE OMAC?
FIND OUT WHAT MAKES HIM TICK.
I'D ADVISE *AGAINST* THAT.
OH MY *GOD!*
悪魔*!*
Hawkgirl

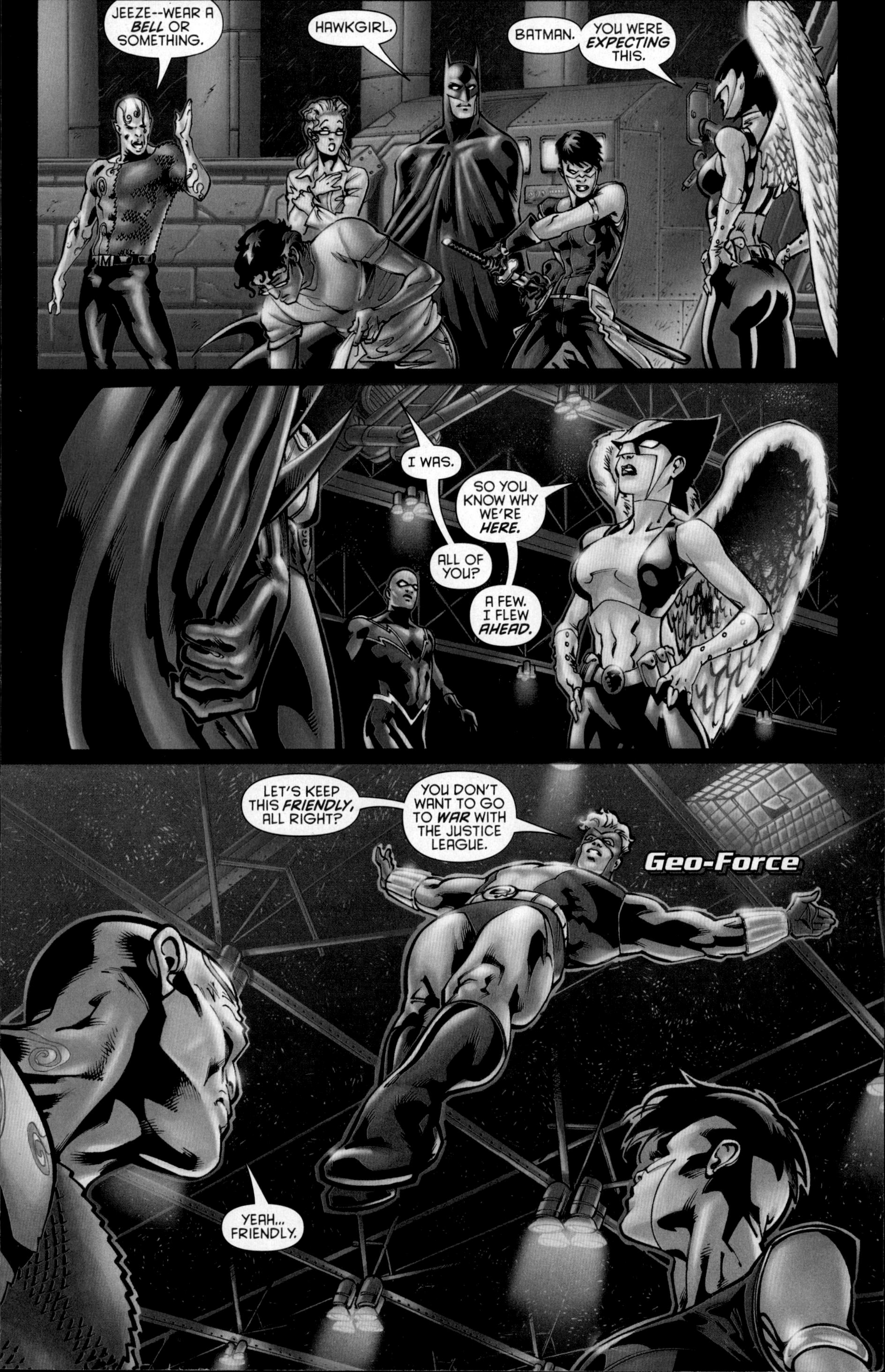
JEEZE--WEAR A *BELL* OR SOMETHING.
HAWKGIRL.
BATMAN.
YOU WERE *EXPECTING* THIS.
I WAS.
SO YOU KNOW WHY WE'RE *HERE*.
ALL OF YOU?
A FEW. I FLEW *AHEAD*.
LET'S KEEP THIS *FRIENDLY*, ALL RIGHT?
YOU DON'T WANT TO GO TO *WAR* WITH THE JUSTICE LEAGUE.
Geo-Force
YEAH... FRIENDLY.

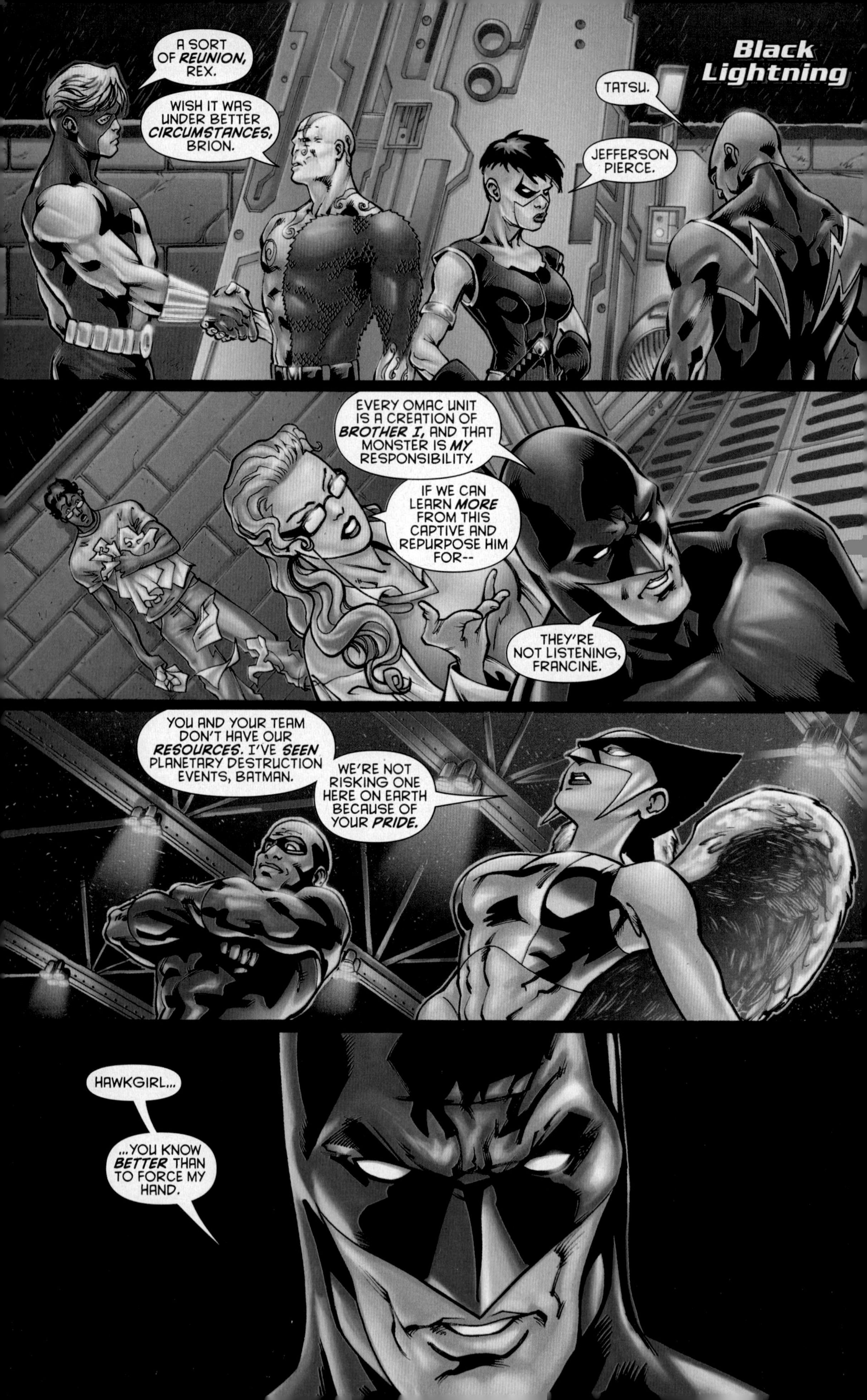
A SORT OF REUNION, REX.
WISH IT WAS UNDER BETTER CIRCUMSTANCES, BRION.
Black Lightning
TATSU.
JEFFERSON PIERCE.
EVERY OMAC UNIT IS A CREATION OF BROTHER I, AND THAT MONSTER IS MY RESPONSIBILITY.
IF WE CAN LEARN MORE FROM THIS CAPTIVE AND REPURPOSE HIM FOR--
THEY'RE NOT LISTENING, FRANCINE.
YOU AND YOUR TEAM DON'T HAVE OUR RESOURCES. I'VE SEEN PLANETARY DESTRUCTION EVENTS, BATMAN.
WE'RE NOT RISKING ONE HERE ON EARTH BECAUSE OF YOUR PRIDE.
HAWKGIRL...
...YOU KNOW BETTER THAN TO FORCE MY HAND.

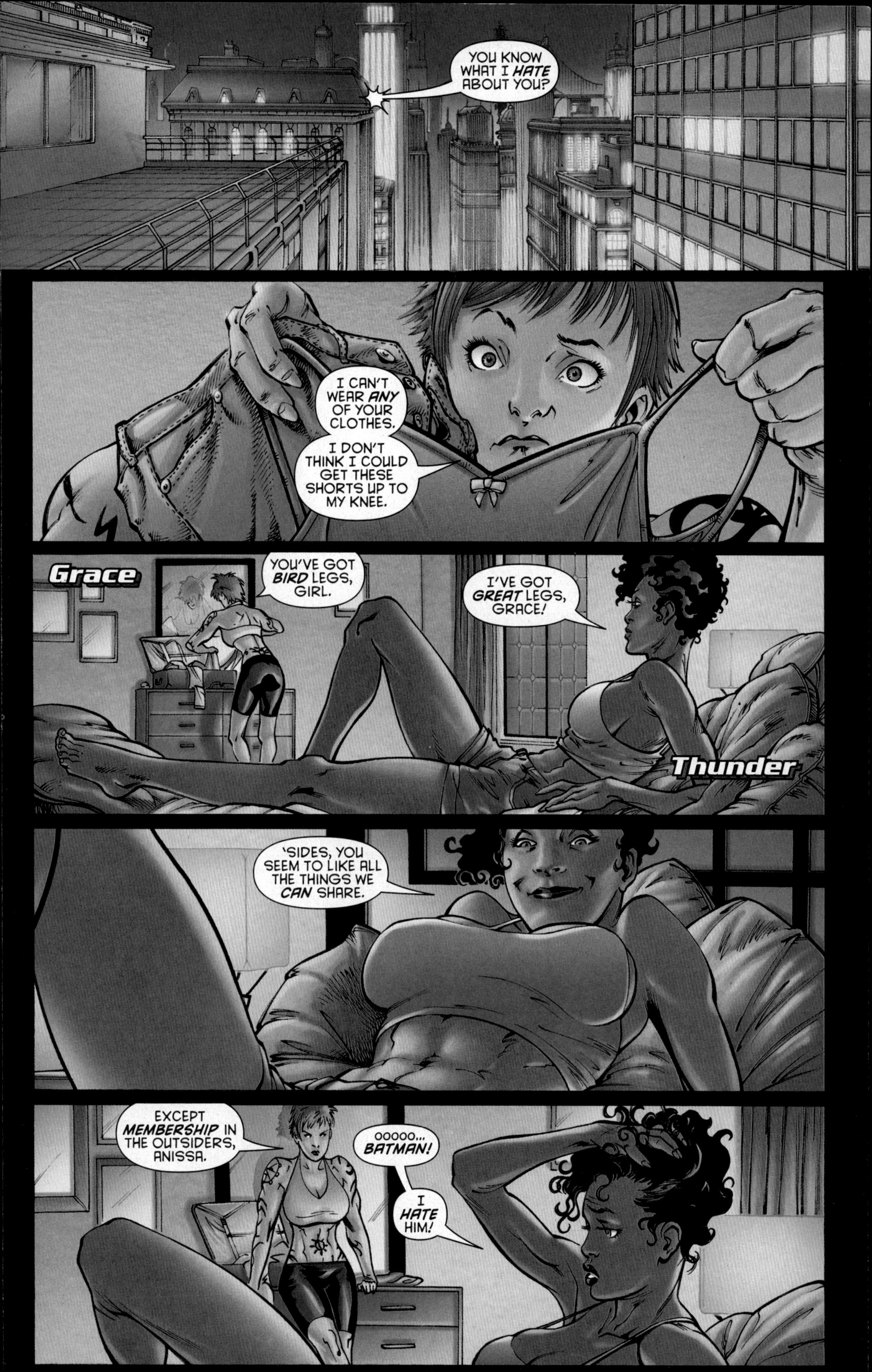

YOU KNOW WHAT I HATE ABOUT YOU?
I CAN'T WEAR ANY OF YOUR CLOTHES.
I DON'T THINK I COULD GET THESE SHORTS UP TO MY KNEE.
Grace
YOU'VE GOT BIRD LEGS, GIRL.
I'VE GOT GREAT LEGS, GRACE!
Thunder
'SIDES, YOU SEEM TO LIKE ALL THE THINGS WE CAN SHARE.
EXCEPT MEMBERSHIP IN THE OUTSIDERS, ANISSA.
OOOOO... BATMAN!
I HATE HIM!

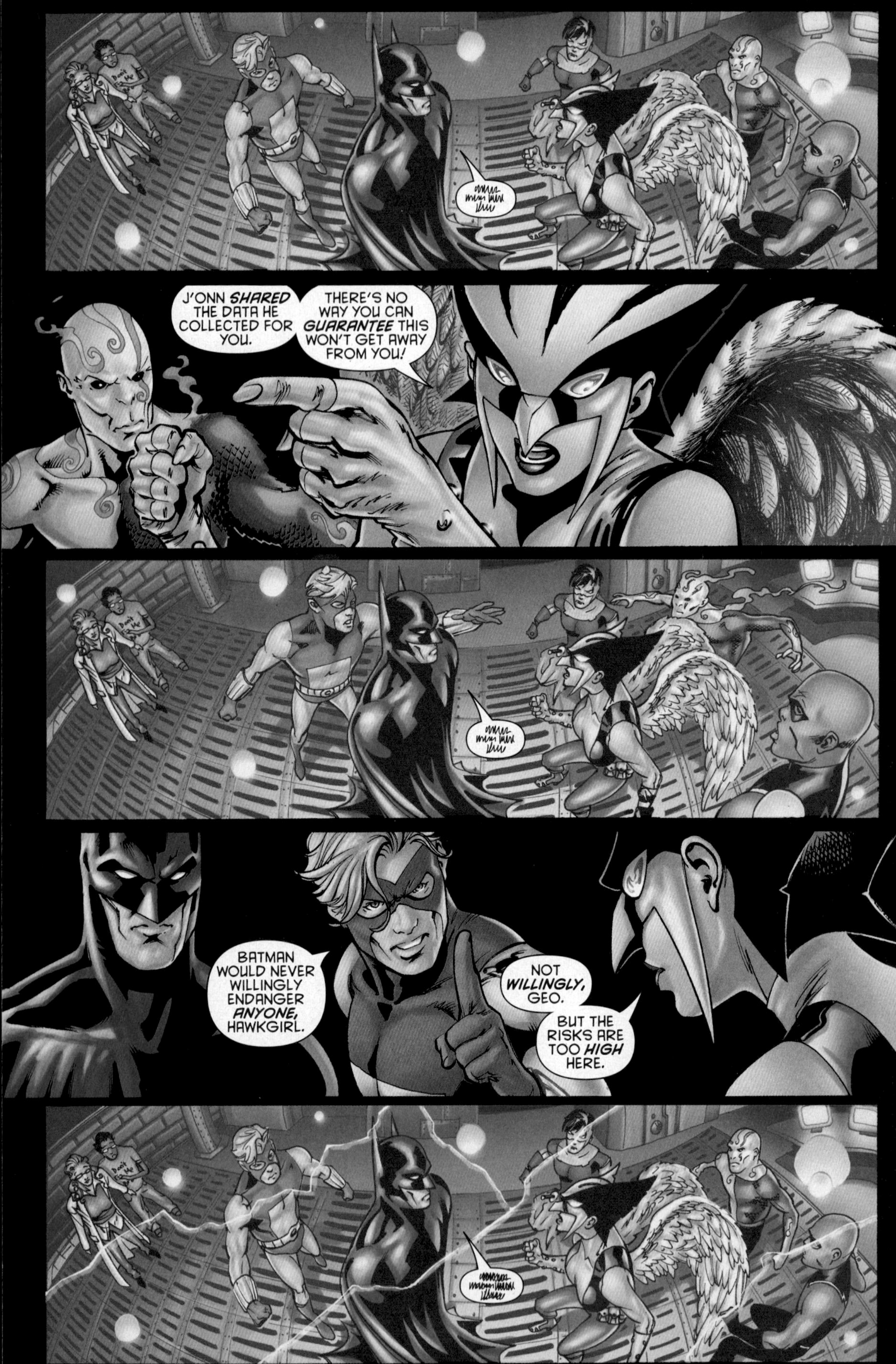
J'ONN SHARED THE DATA HE COLLECTED FOR YOU.
THERE'S NO WAY YOU CAN GUARANTEE THIS WON'T GET AWAY FROM YOU!
BATMAN WOULD NEVER WILLINGLY ENDANGER ANYONE, HAWKGIRL.
NOT WILLINGLY, GEO.
BUT THE RISKS ARE TOO HIGH HERE.

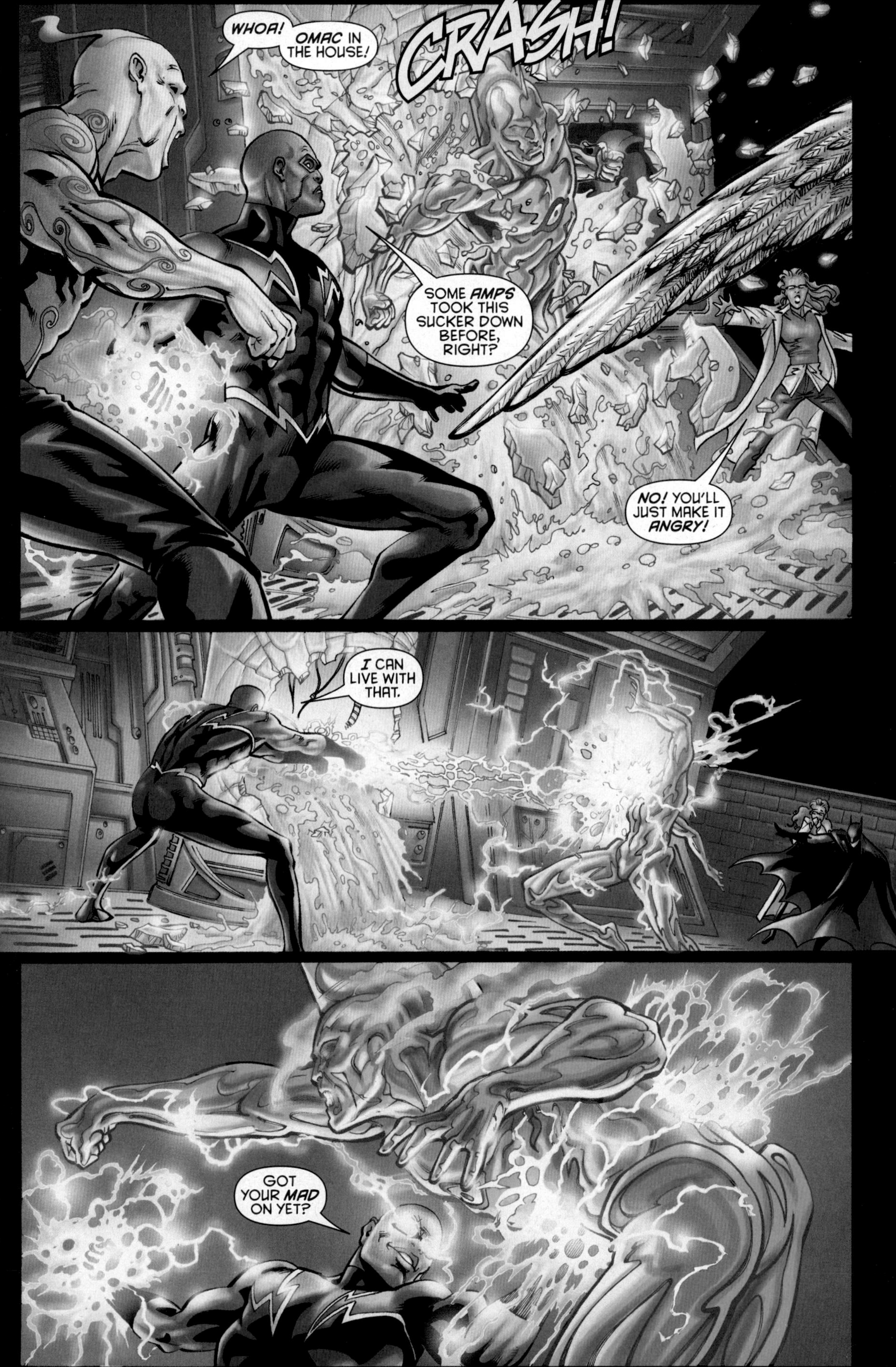
CRASH!
WHOA! OMAC IN THE HOUSE!
SOME AMPS TOOK THIS SUCKER DOWN BEFORE, RIGHT?
NO! YOU'LL JUST MAKE IT ANGRY!
I CAN LIVE WITH THAT.
GOT YOUR MAD ON YET?

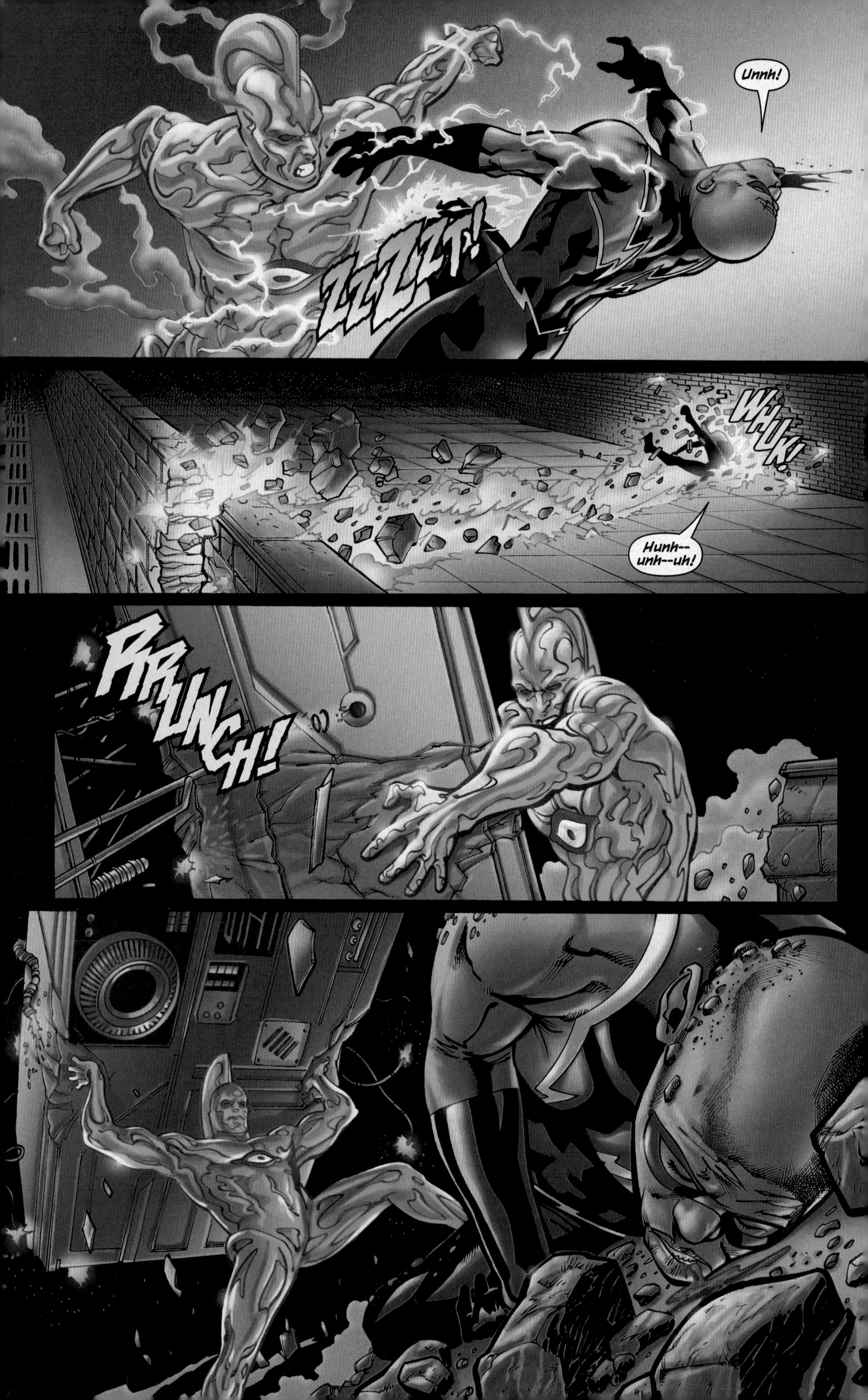
ZZZZZT!
Unnh!
WHUK!
Hunh-- unh--uh!
RRRUNCH!

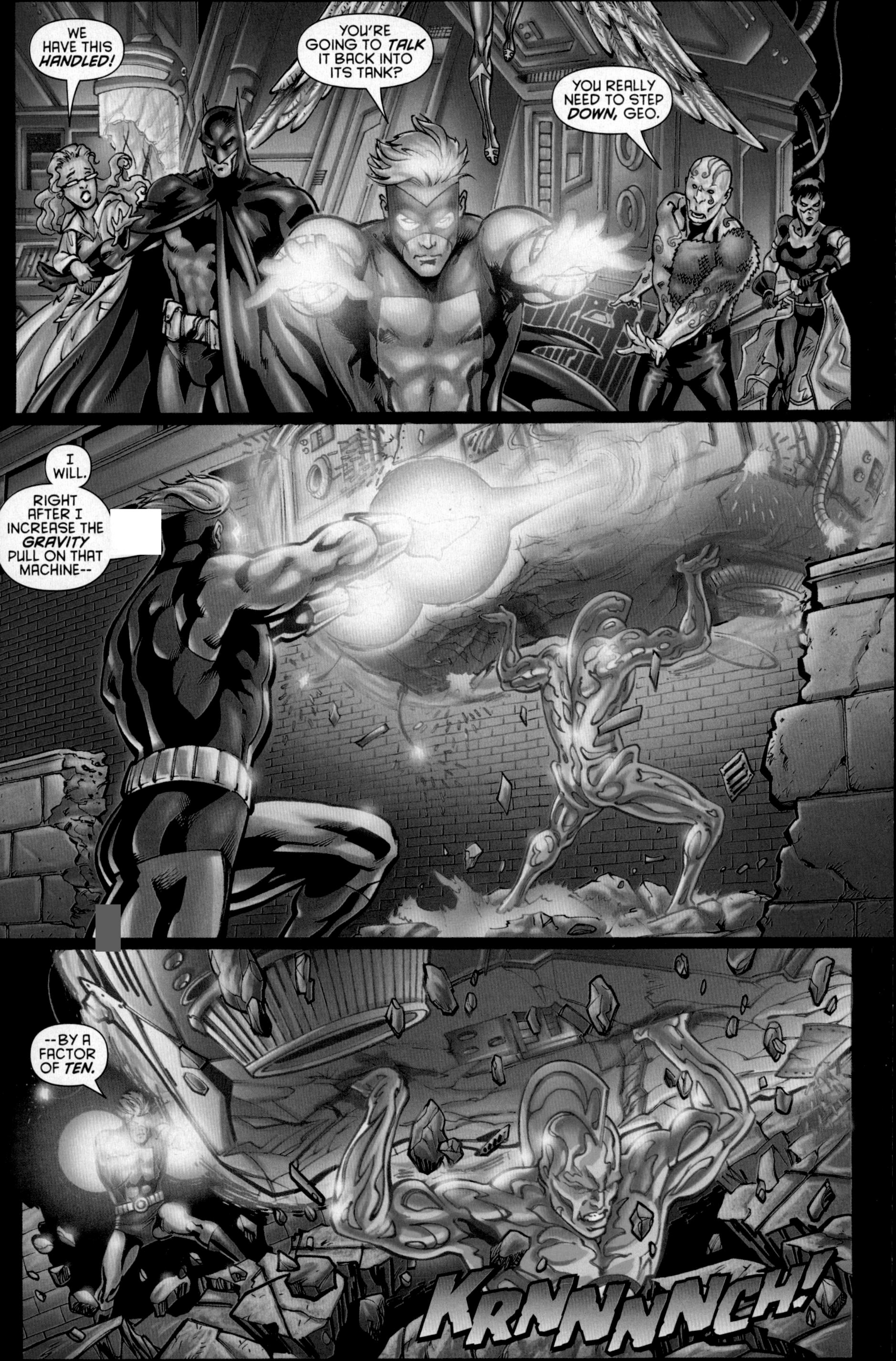
WE HAVE THIS HANDLED!
YOU'RE GOING TO TALK IT BACK INTO ITS TANK?
YOU REALLY NEED TO STEP DOWN, GEO.
I WILL.
RIGHT AFTER I INCREASE THE GRAVITY PULL ON THAT MACHINE--
--BY A FACTOR OF TEN.
KRNNNNCH!

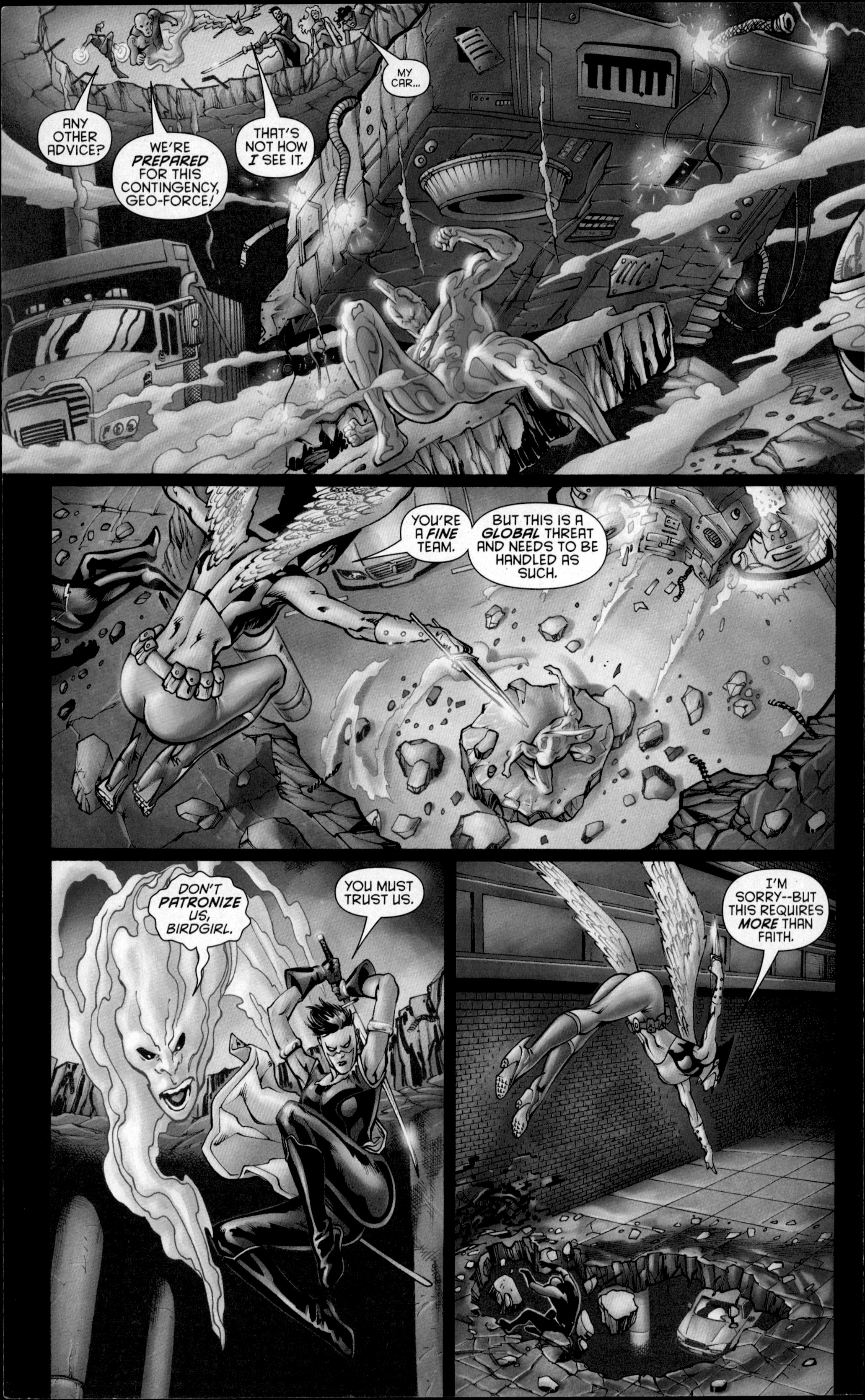
ANY OTHER ADVICE?
WE'RE PREPARED FOR THIS CONTINGENCY, GEO-FORCE!
THAT'S NOT HOW I SEE IT.
MY CAR...
YOU'RE A FINE TEAM.
BUT THIS IS A GLOBAL THREAT AND NEEDS TO BE HANDLED AS SUCH.
DON'T PATRONIZE US, BIRDGIRL.
YOU MUST TRUST US.
I'M SORRY--BUT THIS REQUIRES MORE THAN FAITH.

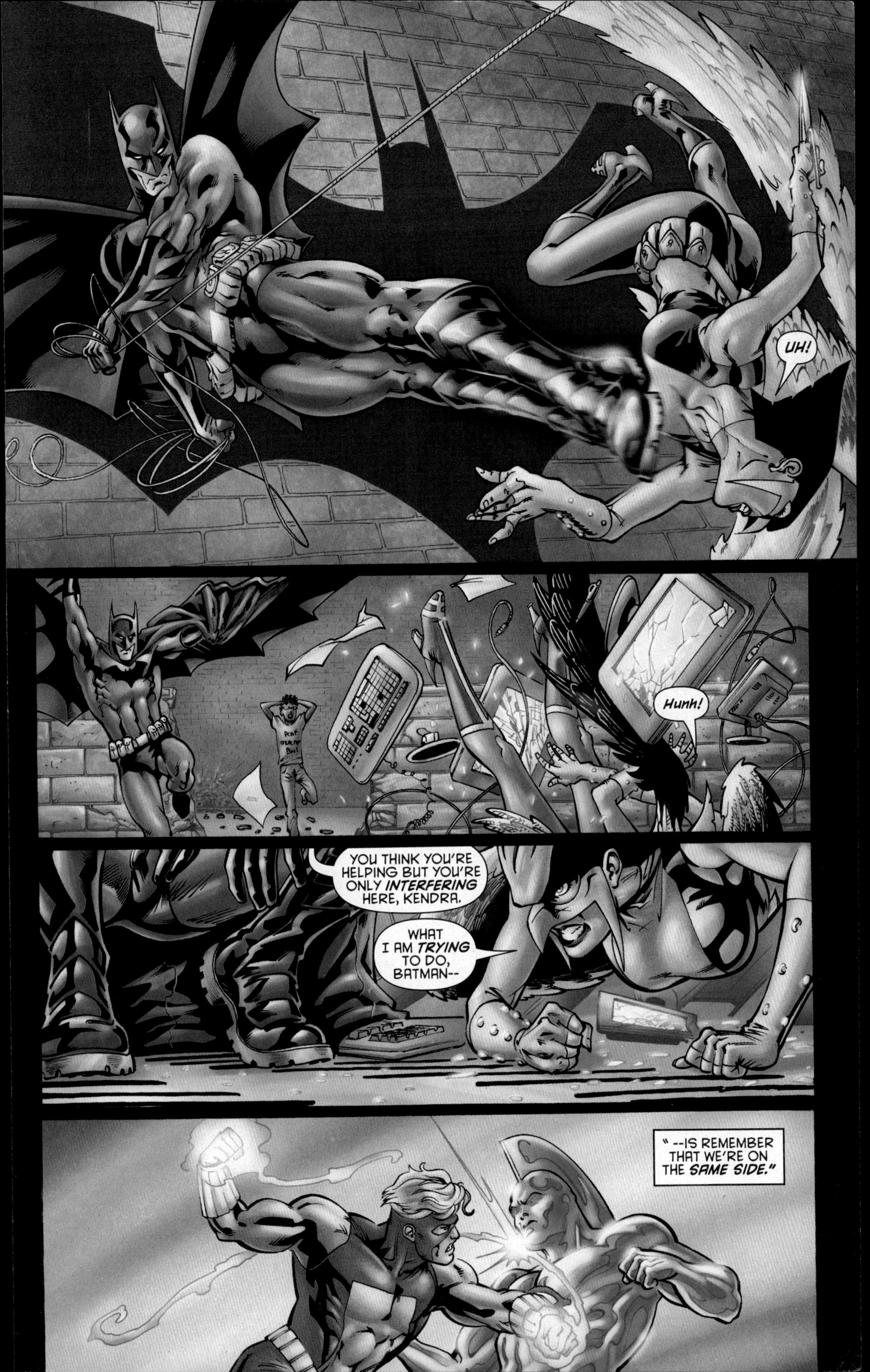
UH!
Hunh!
YOU THINK YOU'RE HELPING BUT YOU'RE ONLY INTERFERING HERE, KENDRA.
WHAT I AM TRYING TO DO, BATMAN--
"--IS REMEMBER THAT WE'RE ON THE SAME SIDE."

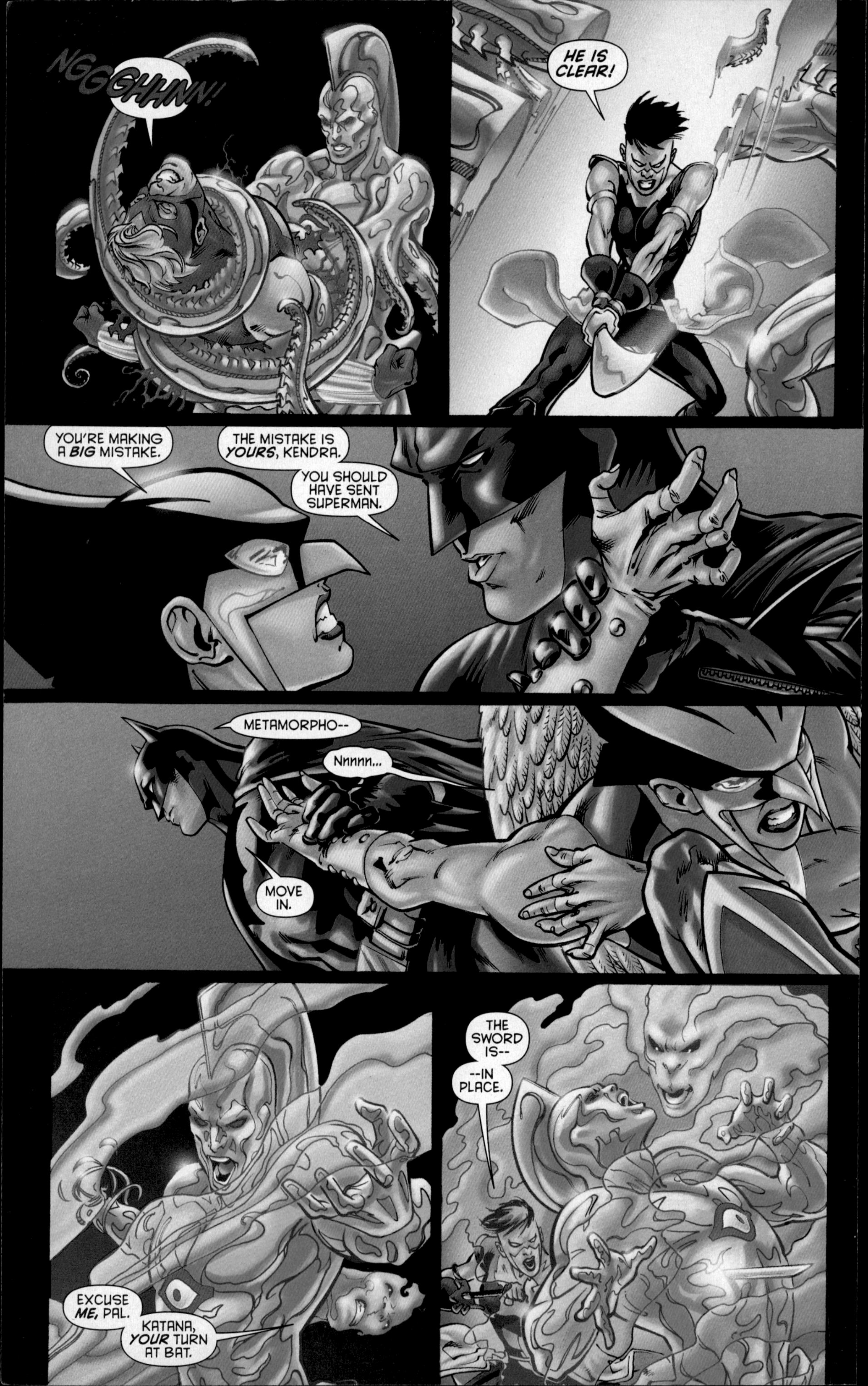
NGGGHHNN!
HE IS CLEAR!
YOU'RE MAKING A *BIG* MISTAKE.
THE MISTAKE IS *YOURS*, KENDRA.
YOU SHOULD HAVE SENT SUPERMAN.
METAMORPHO--
Nnnnn...
MOVE IN.
EXCUSE *ME*, PAL.
KATANA, *YOUR* TURN AT BAT.
THE SWORD IS--
--IN PLACE.

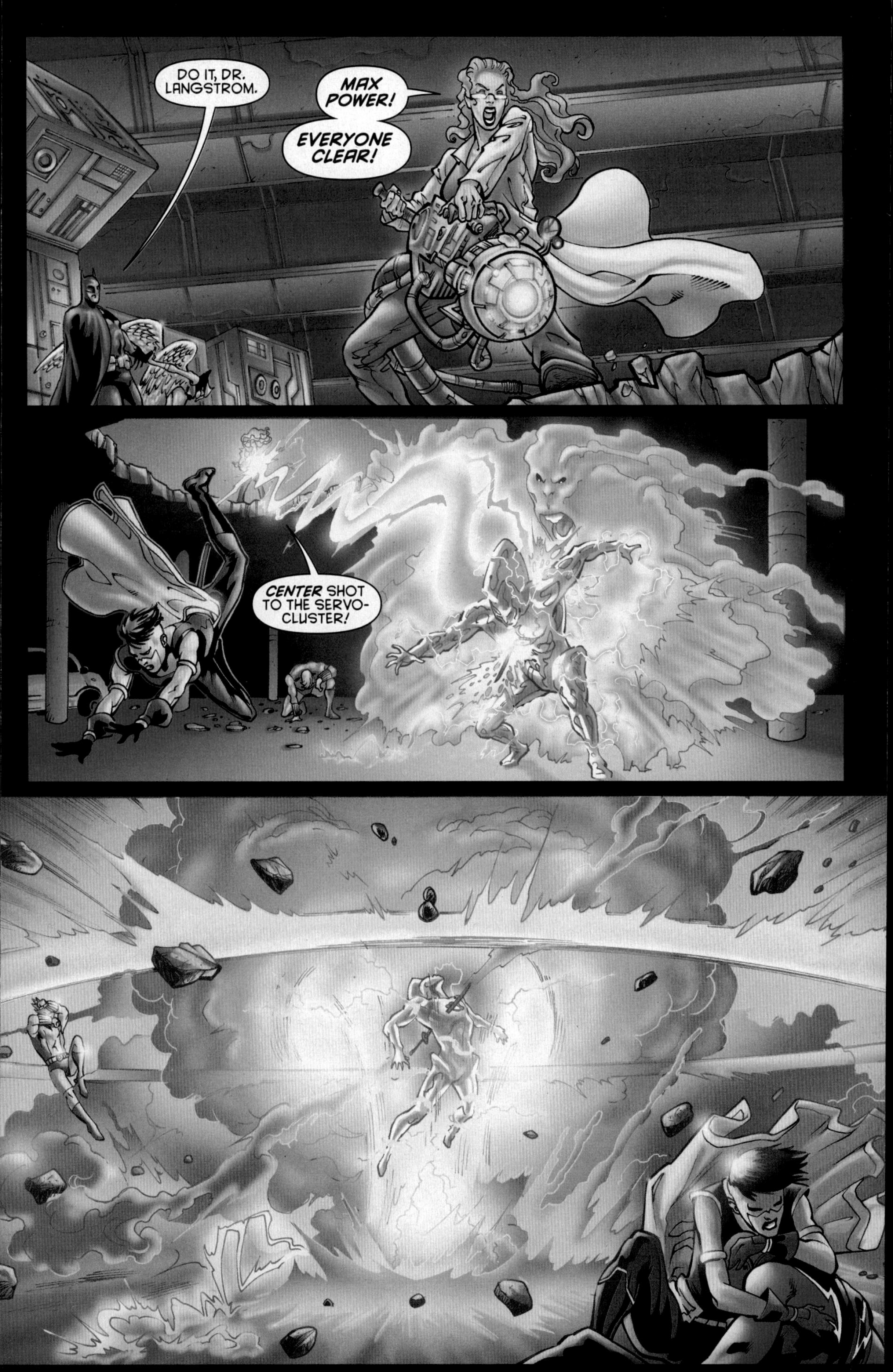
DO IT, DR. LANGSTROM.
MAX POWER!
EVERYONE CLEAR!
CENTER SHOT TO THE SERVO-CLUSTER!

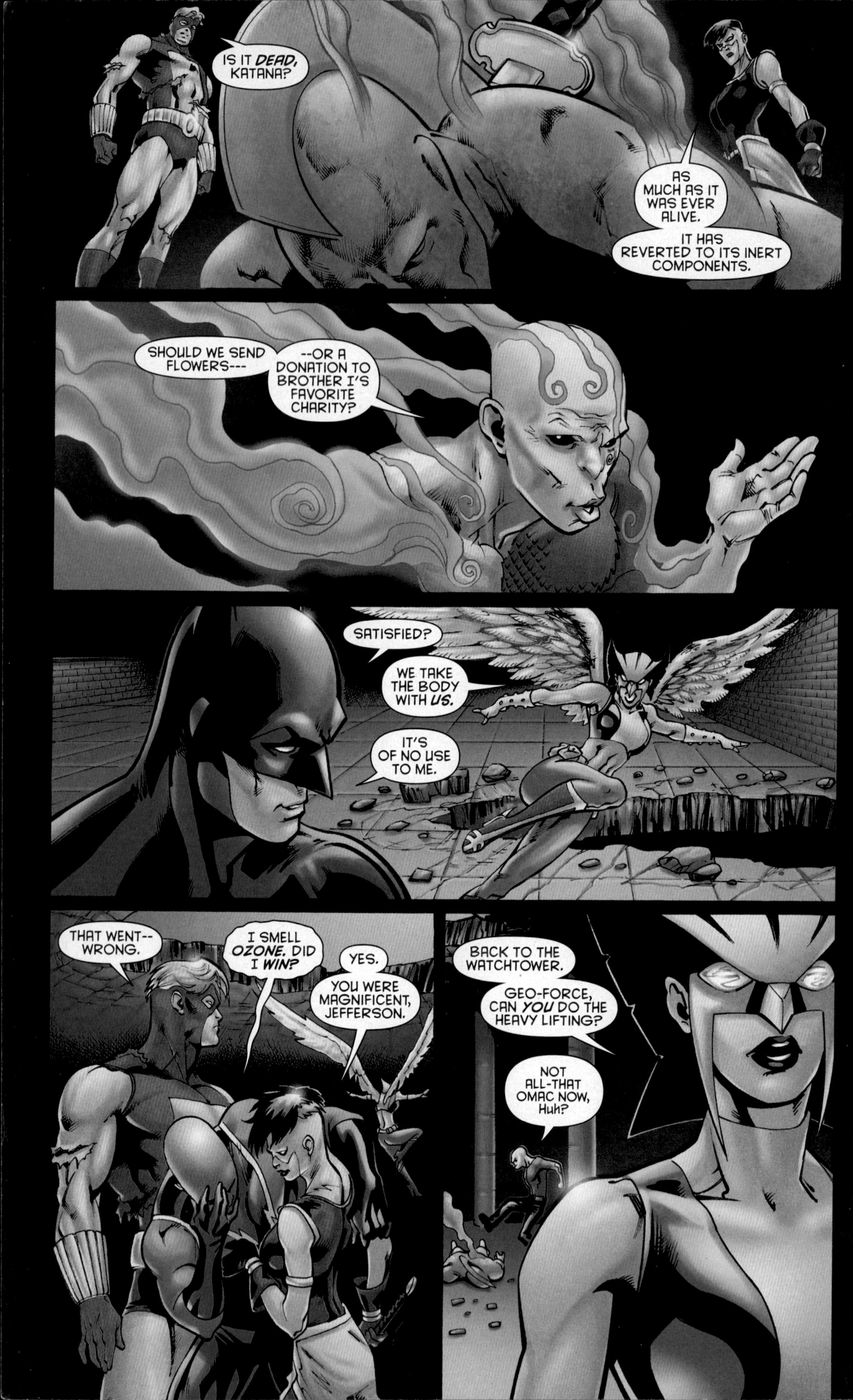
IS IT DEAD, KATANA?
AS MUCH AS IT WAS EVER ALIVE.
IT HAS REVERTED TO ITS INERT COMPONENTS.
SHOULD WE SEND FLOWERS---
--OR A DONATION TO BROTHER I'S FAVORITE CHARITY?
SATISFIED?
WE TAKE THE BODY WITH US.
IT'S OF NO USE TO ME.
THAT WENT--WRONG.
I SMELL OZONE. DID I WIN?
YES.
YOU WERE MAGNIFICENT, JEFFERSON.
BACK TO THE WATCHTOWER.
GEO-FORCE, CAN YOU DO THE HEAVY LIFTING?
NOT ALL-THAT OMAC NOW, Huh?

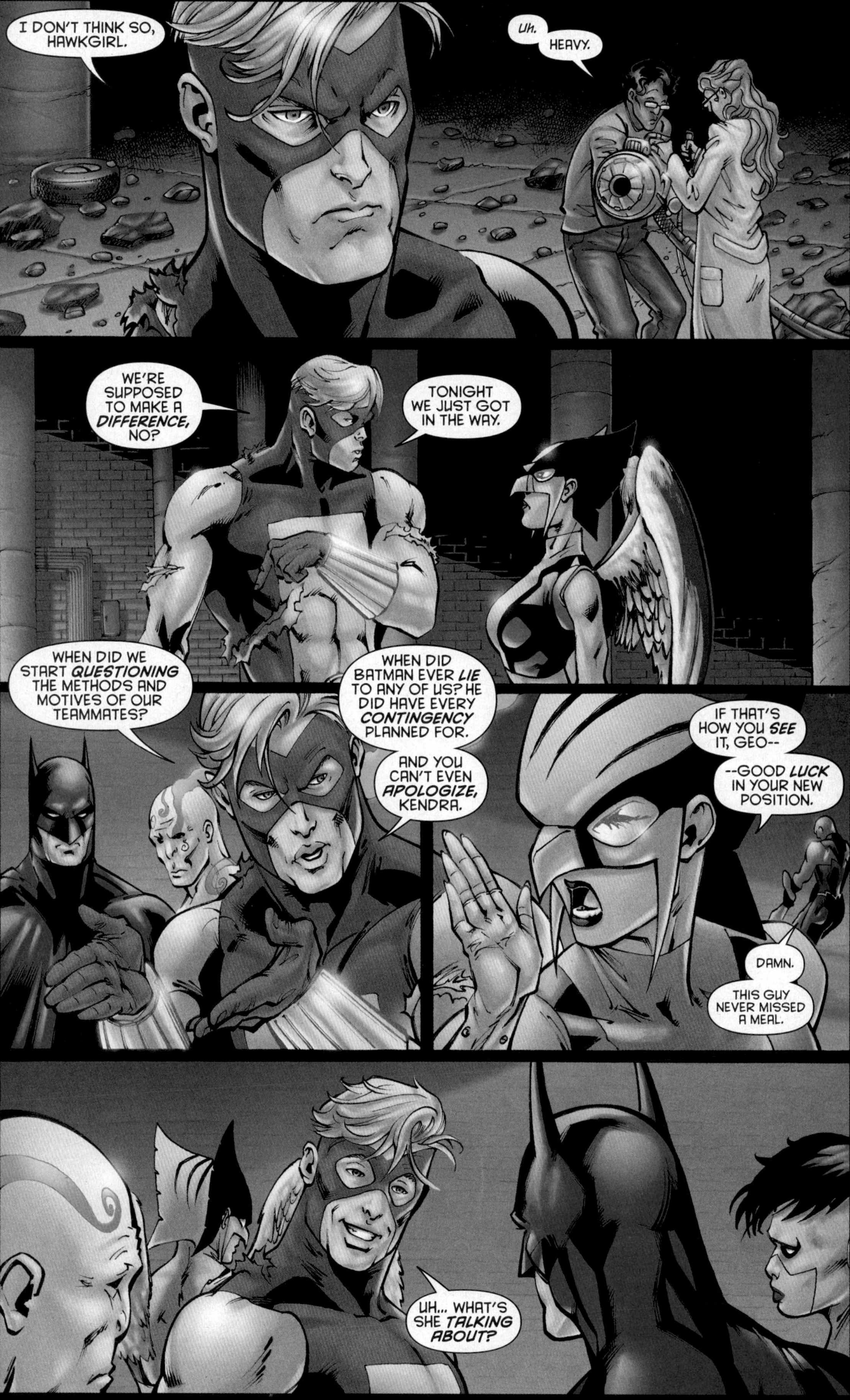
I DON'T THINK SO, HAWKGIRL.
UH. HEAVY.
WE'RE SUPPOSED TO MAKE A *DIFFERENCE,* NO?
TONIGHT WE JUST GOT IN THE WAY.
WHEN DID WE START *QUESTIONING* THE METHODS AND MOTIVES OF OUR TEAMMATES?
WHEN DID BATMAN EVER *LIE* TO ANY OF US? HE DID HAVE EVERY *CONTINGENCY* PLANNED FOR.
AND YOU CAN'T EVEN *APOLOGIZE,* KENDRA.
IF THAT'S HOW YOU *SEE* IT, GEO--
--GOOD *LUCK* IN YOUR NEW POSITION.
DAMN.
THIS GUY NEVER MISSED A MEAL.
UH... WHAT'S SHE *TALKING ABOUT?*

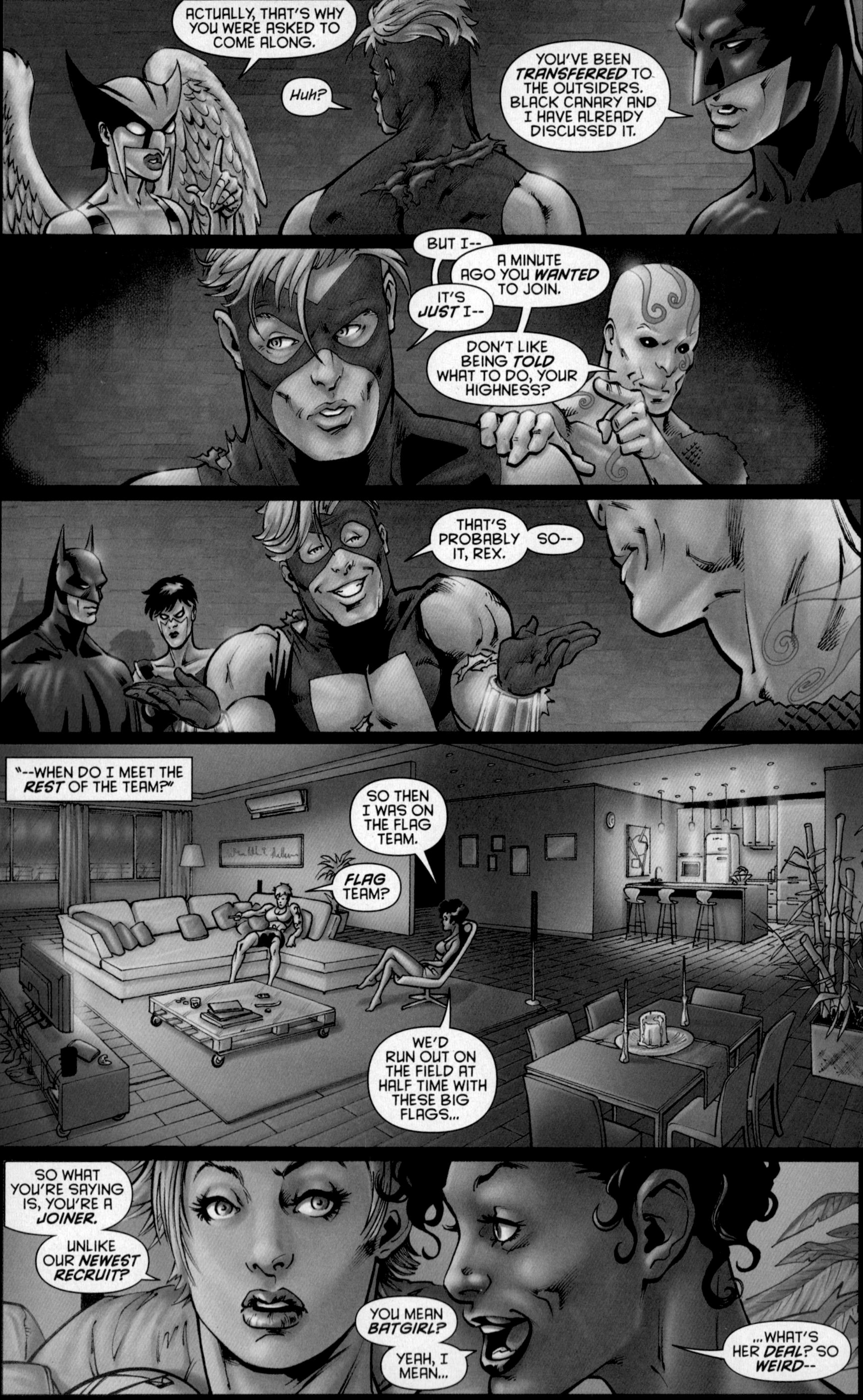
ACTUALLY, THAT'S WHY YOU WERE ASKED TO COME ALONG.
Huh?
YOU'VE BEEN *TRANSFERRED* TO THE OUTSIDERS. BLACK CANARY AND I HAVE ALREADY DISCUSSED IT.
BUT I--
A MINUTE AGO YOU *WANTED* TO JOIN.
IT'S *JUST* I--
DON'T LIKE BEING *TOLD* WHAT TO DO, YOUR HIGHNESS?
THAT'S PROBABLY IT, REX.
SO--
"--WHEN DO I MEET THE *REST* OF THE TEAM?"
SO THEN I WAS ON THE FLAG TEAM.
FLAG TEAM?
WE'D RUN OUT ON THE FIELD AT HALF TIME WITH THESE BIG FLAGS...
SO WHAT YOU'RE SAYING IS, YOU'RE A *JOINER.*
UNLIKE OUR *NEWEST RECRUIT?*
YOU MEAN *BATGIRL?*
YEAH, I MEAN...
...WHAT'S HER *DEAL*? SO *WEIRD*--

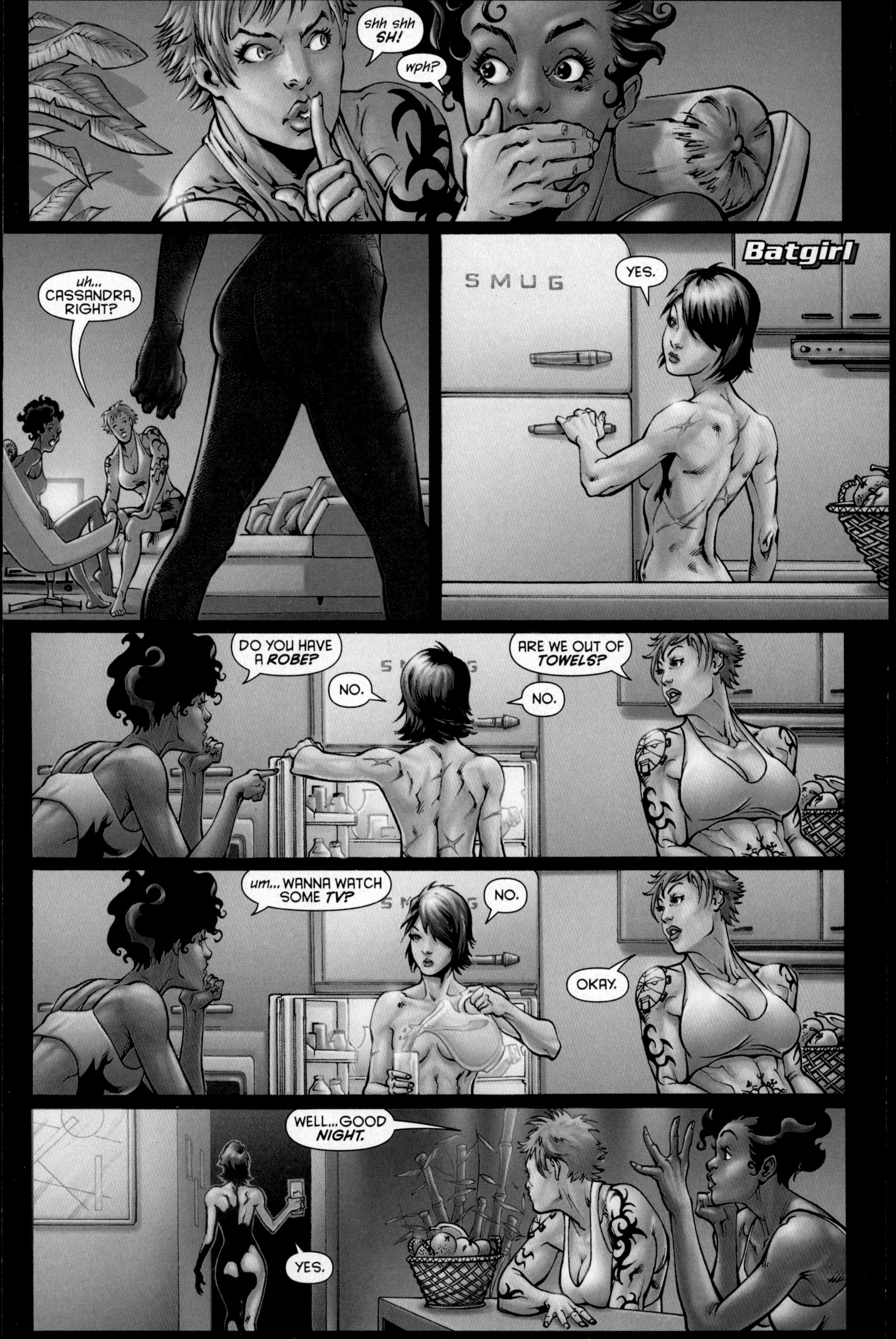

shh shh SH!
wph?
uh... CASSANDRA, RIGHT?
Batgirl
SMUG
YES.
DO YOU HAVE A ROBE?
NO.
ARE WE OUT OF TOWELS?
NO.
um... WANNA WATCH SOME TV?
NO.
OKAY.
WELL... GOOD NIGHT.
YES.

DIDN'T *KNOW* THE BAT CROWD WAS CLOTHING OPTIONAL.

SHE HAS SO MANY *SCARS.*

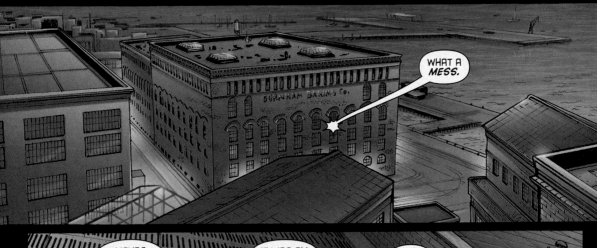

WHAT A *MESS.*

MAYBE ONE OF YOUR *METAHUMAN* PALS CAN HELP WITH THE CLEANUP?

IT WAS ALL NECESSARY, FRANCINE.

A HECK OF A *SHOW.*

THE SUBJECT PERFORMED PERFECTLY.

YOU AND SALAH DID MIRACULOUS WORK UNDER A CRUSHING DEADLINE.

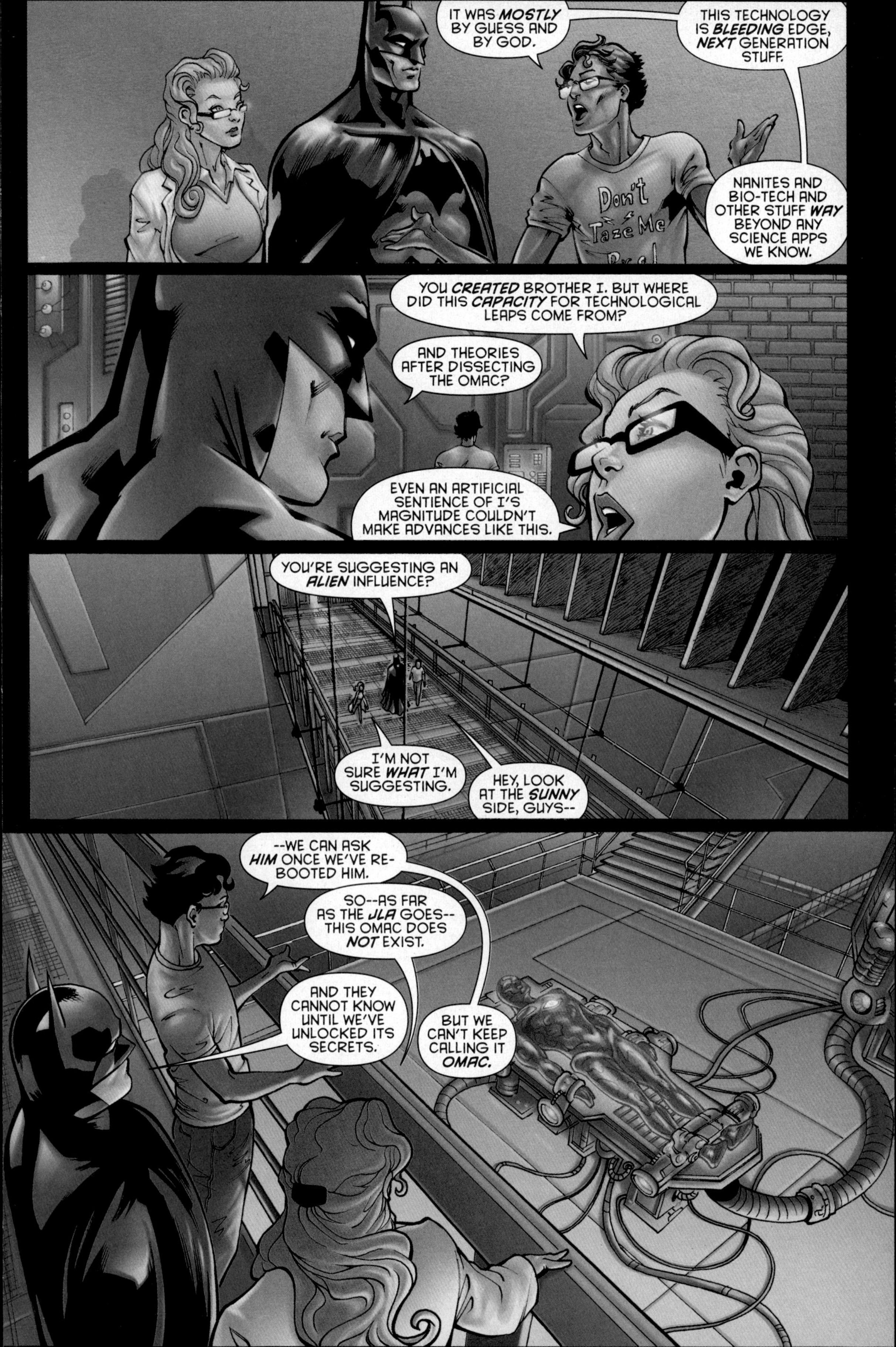
IT WAS MOSTLY BY GUESS AND BY GOD.
THIS TECHNOLOGY IS BLEEDING EDGE, NEXT GENERATION STUFF.
NANITES AND BIO-TECH AND OTHER STUFF WAY BEYOND ANY SCIENCE APPS WE KNOW.
Don't Taze Me
YOU CREATED BROTHER I. BUT WHERE DID THIS CAPACITY FOR TECHNOLOGICAL LEAPS COME FROM?
AND THEORIES AFTER DISSECTING THE OMAC?
EVEN AN ARTIFICIAL SENTIENCE OF I'S MAGNITUDE COULDN'T MAKE ADVANCES LIKE THIS.
YOU'RE SUGGESTING AN ALIEN INFLUENCE?
I'M NOT SURE WHAT I'M SUGGESTING.
HEY, LOOK AT THE SUNNY SIDE, GUYS--
--WE CAN ASK HIM ONCE WE'VE RE-BOOTED HIM.
SO--AS FAR AS THE JLA GOES--THIS OMAC DOES NOT EXIST.
AND THEY CANNOT KNOW UNTIL WE'VE UNLOCKED ITS SECRETS.
BUT WE CAN'T KEEP CALLING IT OMAC.

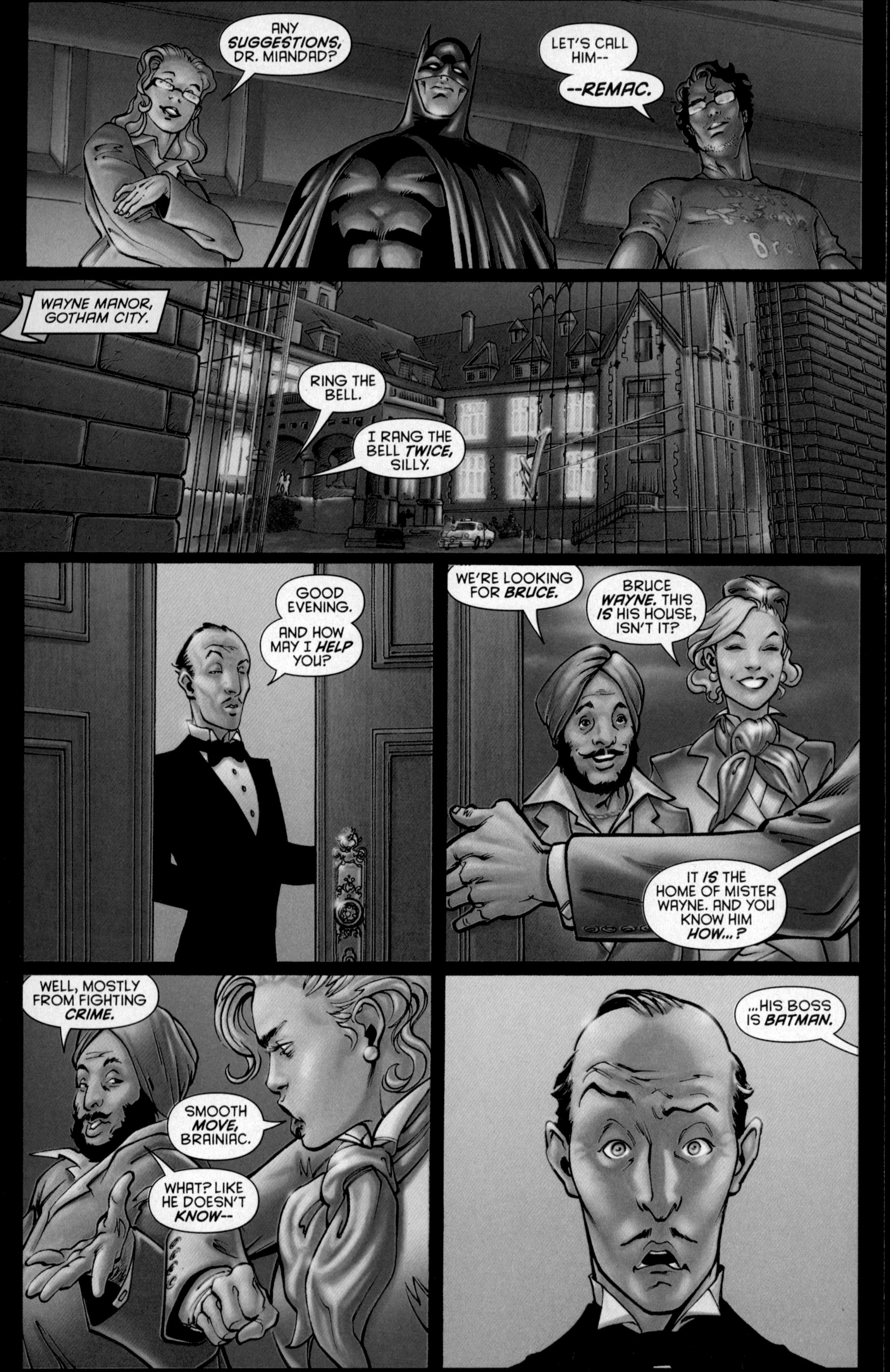
ANY SUGGESTIONS, DR. MIANDAD?
LET'S CALL HIM--
--REMAC.
WAYNE MANOR, GOTHAM CITY.
RING THE BELL.
I RANG THE BELL TWICE, SILLY.
GOOD EVENING.
AND HOW MAY I HELP YOU?
WE'RE LOOKING FOR BRUCE.
BRUCE WAYNE. THIS IS HIS HOUSE, ISN'T IT?
IT IS THE HOME OF MISTER WAYNE. AND YOU KNOW HIM HOW...?
WELL, MOSTLY FROM FIGHTING CRIME.
SMOOTH MOVE, BRAINIAC.
WHAT? LIKE HE DOESN'T KNOW--
...HIS BOSS IS BATMAN.

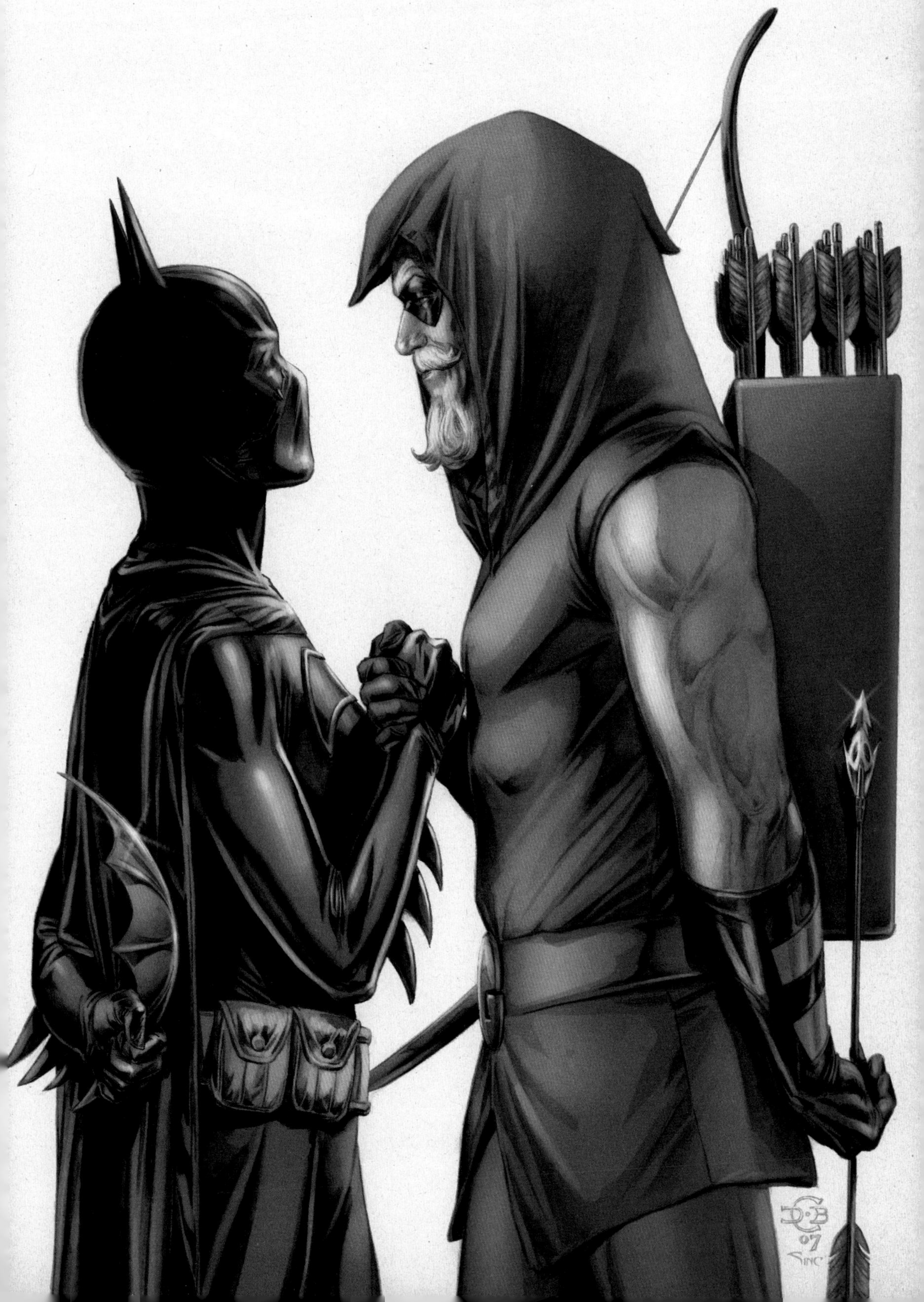

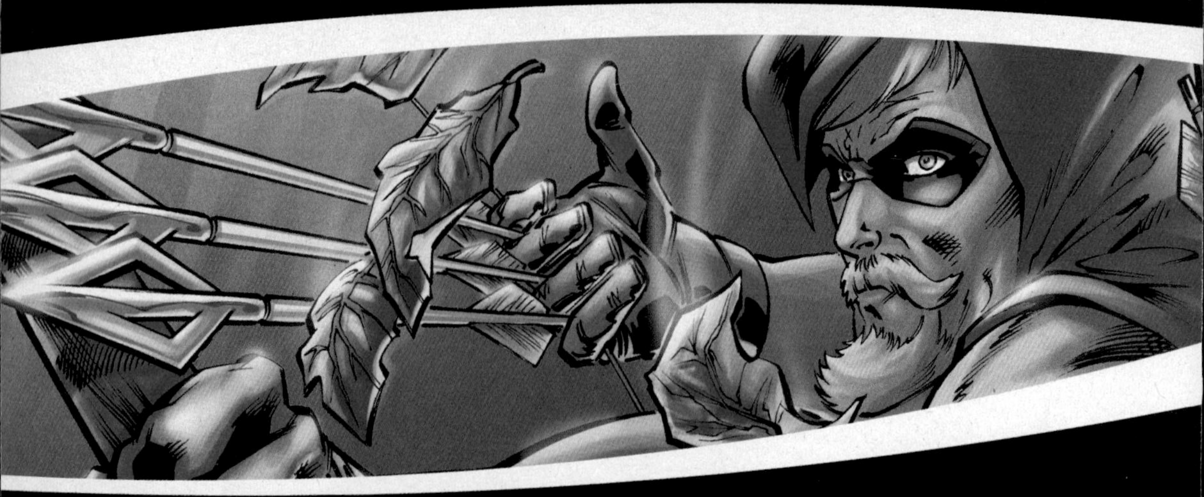

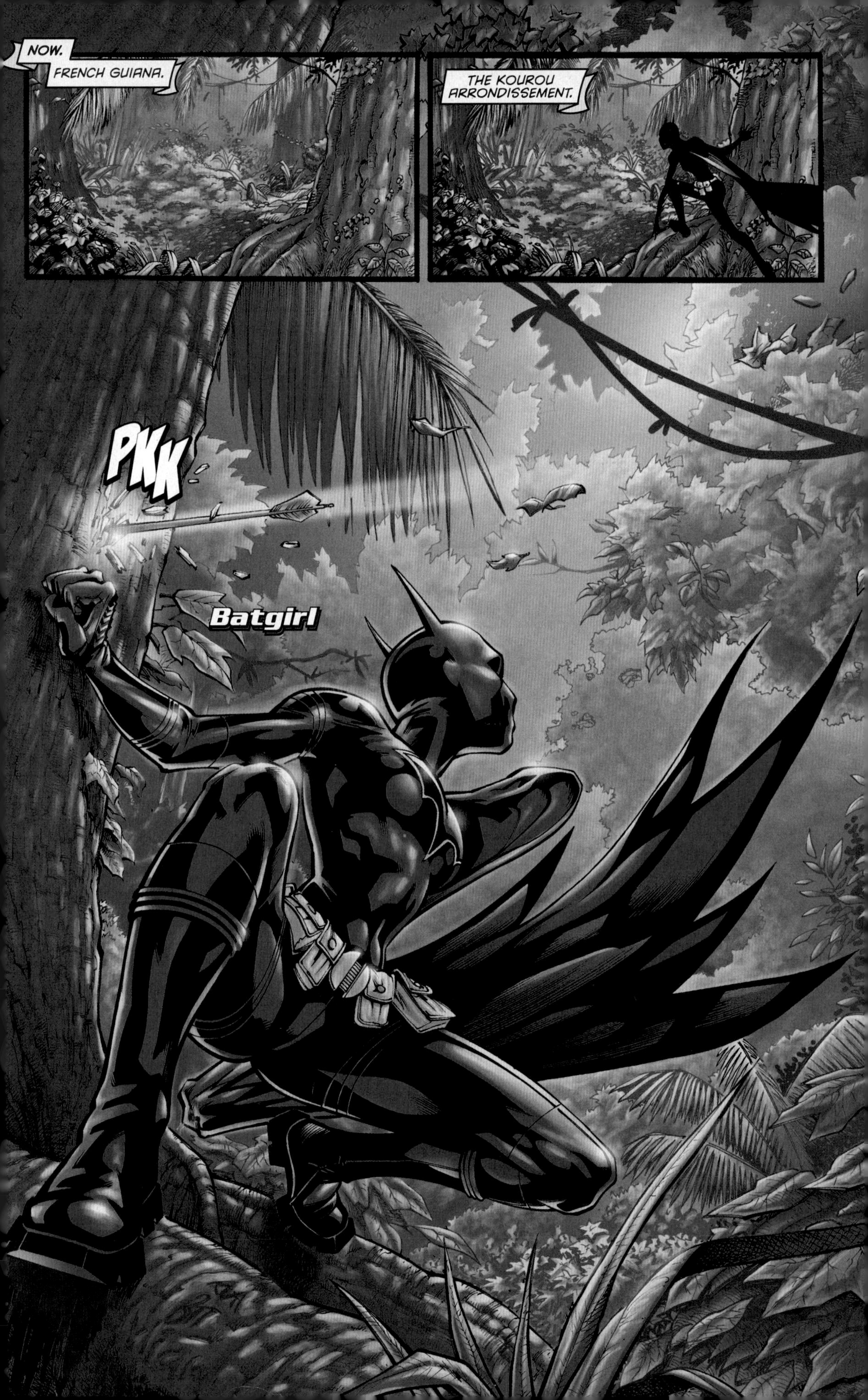
NOW.
FRENCH GUIANA.
THE KOUROU ARRONDISSEMENT.
PKK
Batgirl

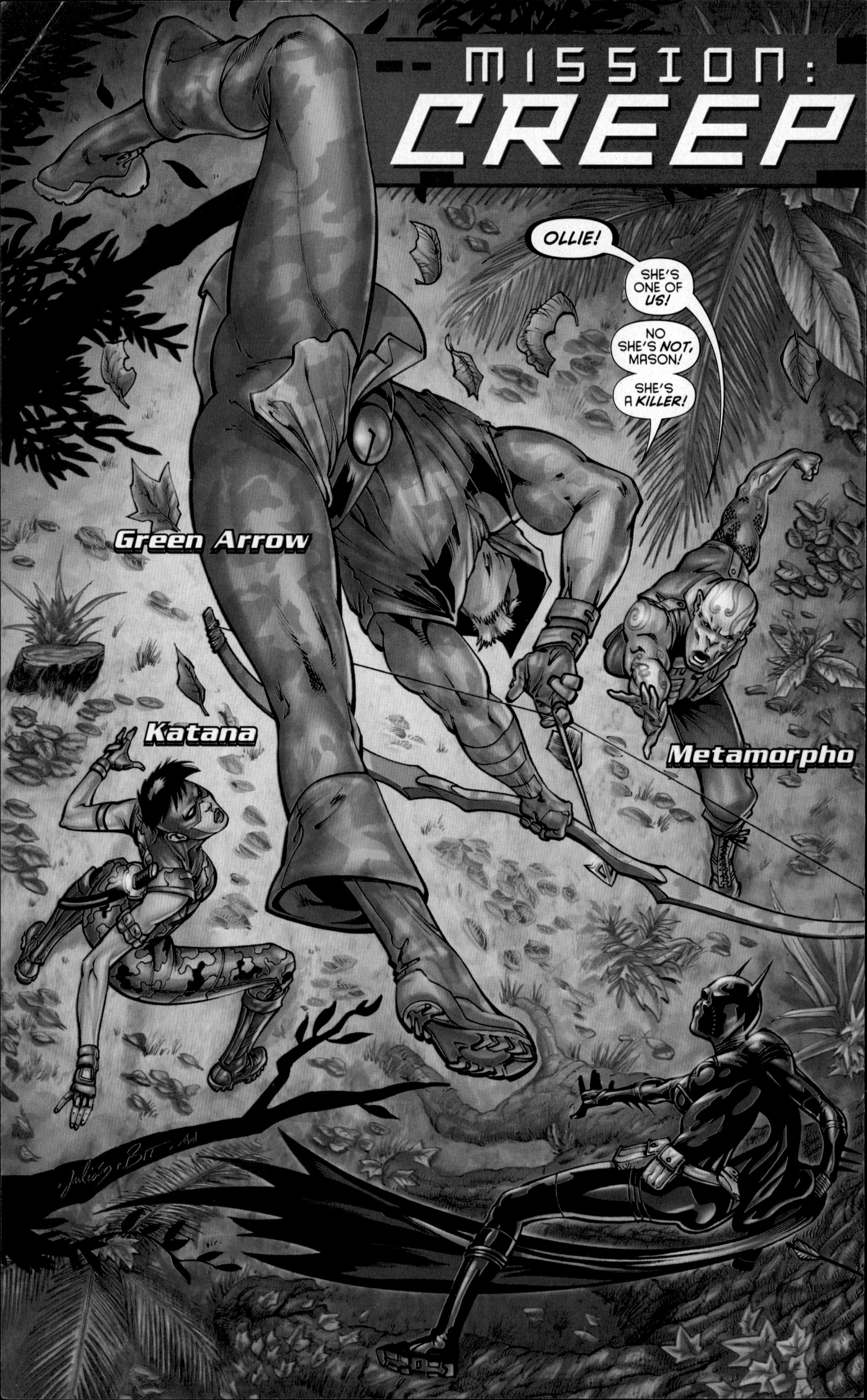
MISSION: CREEP
OLLIE!
SHE'S ONE OF US!
NO SHE'S NOT, MASON!
SHE'S A KILLER!
Green Arrow
Katana
Metamorpho

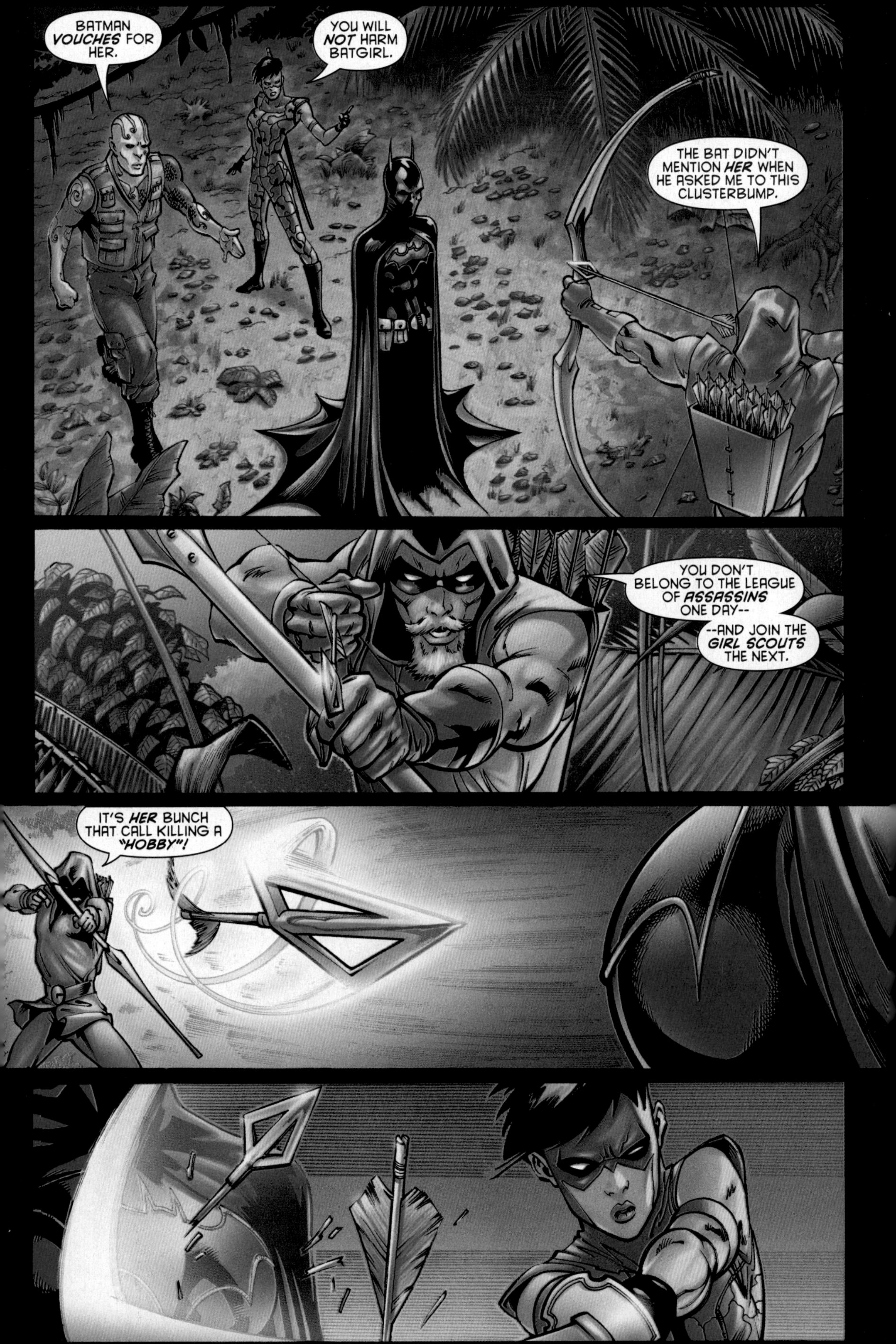
BATMAN VOUCHES FOR HER.
YOU WILL NOT HARM BATGIRL.
THE BAT DIDN'T MENTION HER WHEN HE ASKED ME TO THIS CLUSTERBUMP.
YOU DON'T BELONG TO THE LEAGUE OF ASSASSINS ONE DAY--
--AND JOIN THE GIRL SCOUTS THE NEXT.
IT'S HER BUNCH THAT CALL KILLING A "HOBBY"!

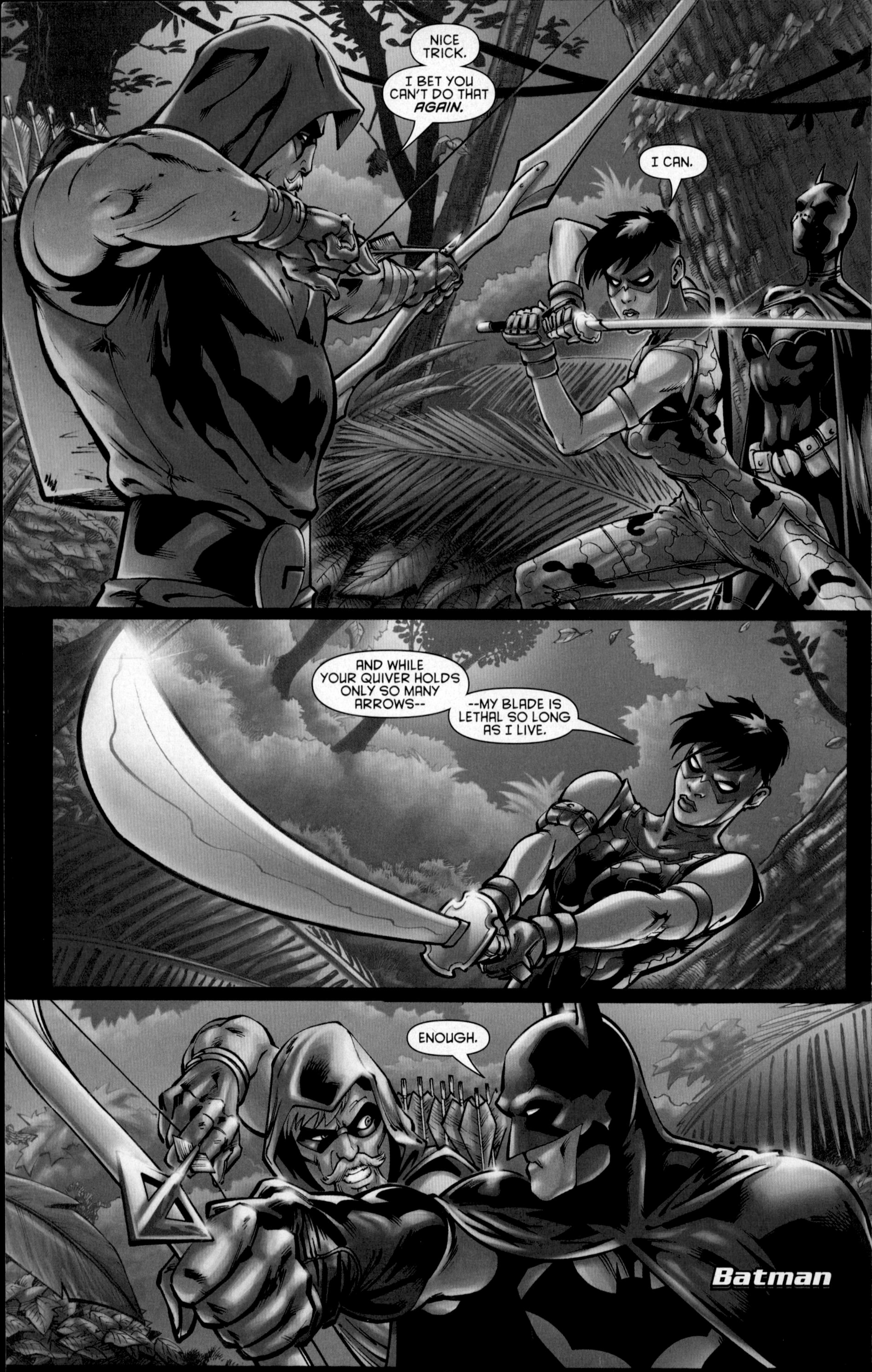
NICE TRICK.
I BET YOU CAN'T DO THAT *AGAIN.*
I CAN.
AND WHILE YOUR QUIVER HOLDS ONLY SO MANY ARROWS--
--MY BLADE IS LETHAL SO LONG AS I LIVE.
ENOUGH.
Batman

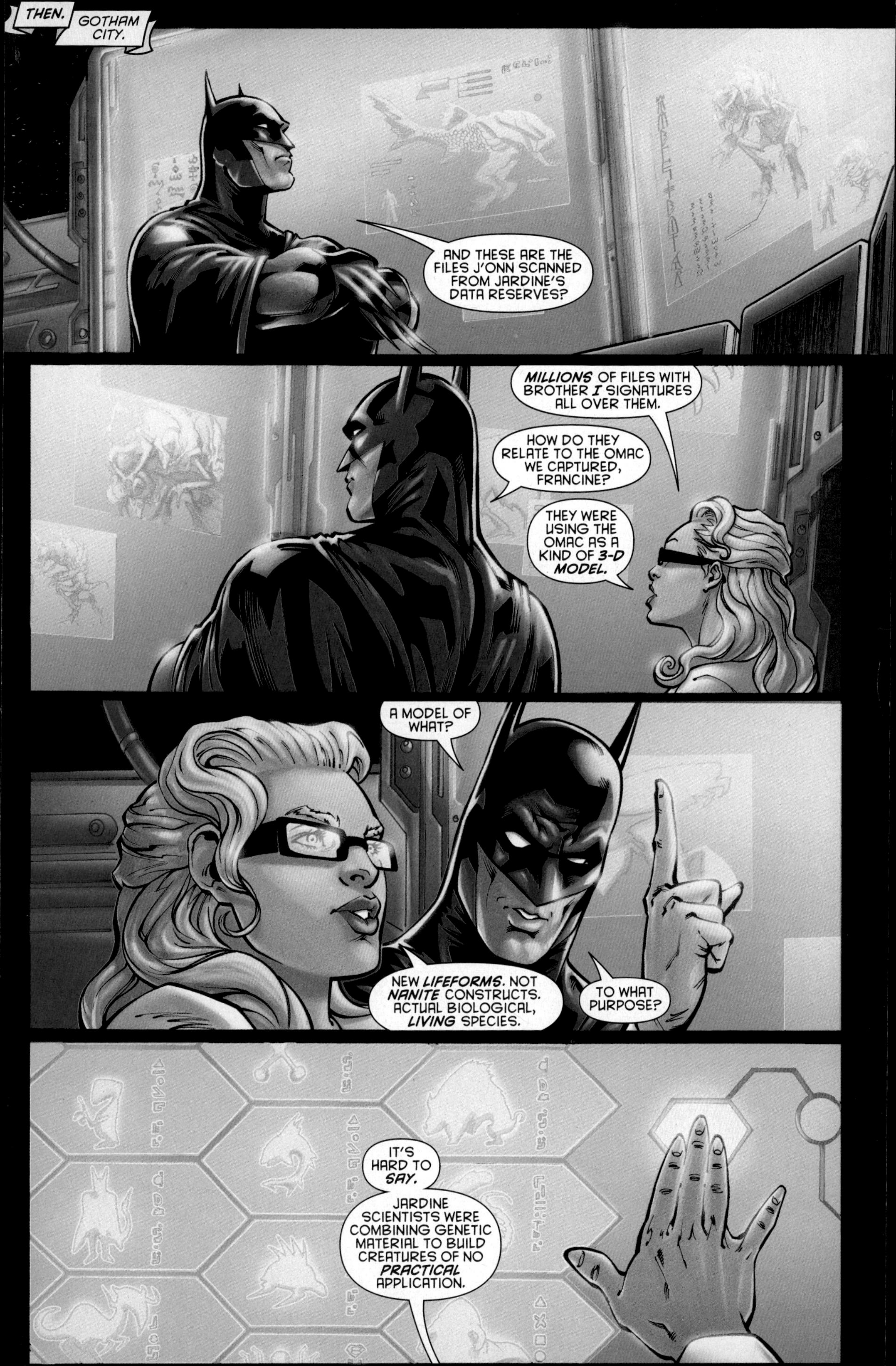
THEN.
GOTHAM CITY.
AND THESE ARE THE FILES J'ONN SCANNED FROM JARDINE'S DATA RESERVES?
MILLIONS OF FILES WITH BROTHER I SIGNATURES ALL OVER THEM.
HOW DO THEY RELATE TO THE OMAC WE CAPTURED, FRANCINE?
THEY WERE USING THE OMAC AS A KIND OF 3-D MODEL.
A MODEL OF WHAT?
NEW LIFEFORMS. NOT NANITE CONSTRUCTS. ACTUAL BIOLOGICAL, LIVING SPECIES.
TO WHAT PURPOSE?
IT'S HARD TO SAY.
JARDINE SCIENTISTS WERE COMBINING GENETIC MATERIAL TO BUILD CREATURES OF NO PRACTICAL APPLICATION.

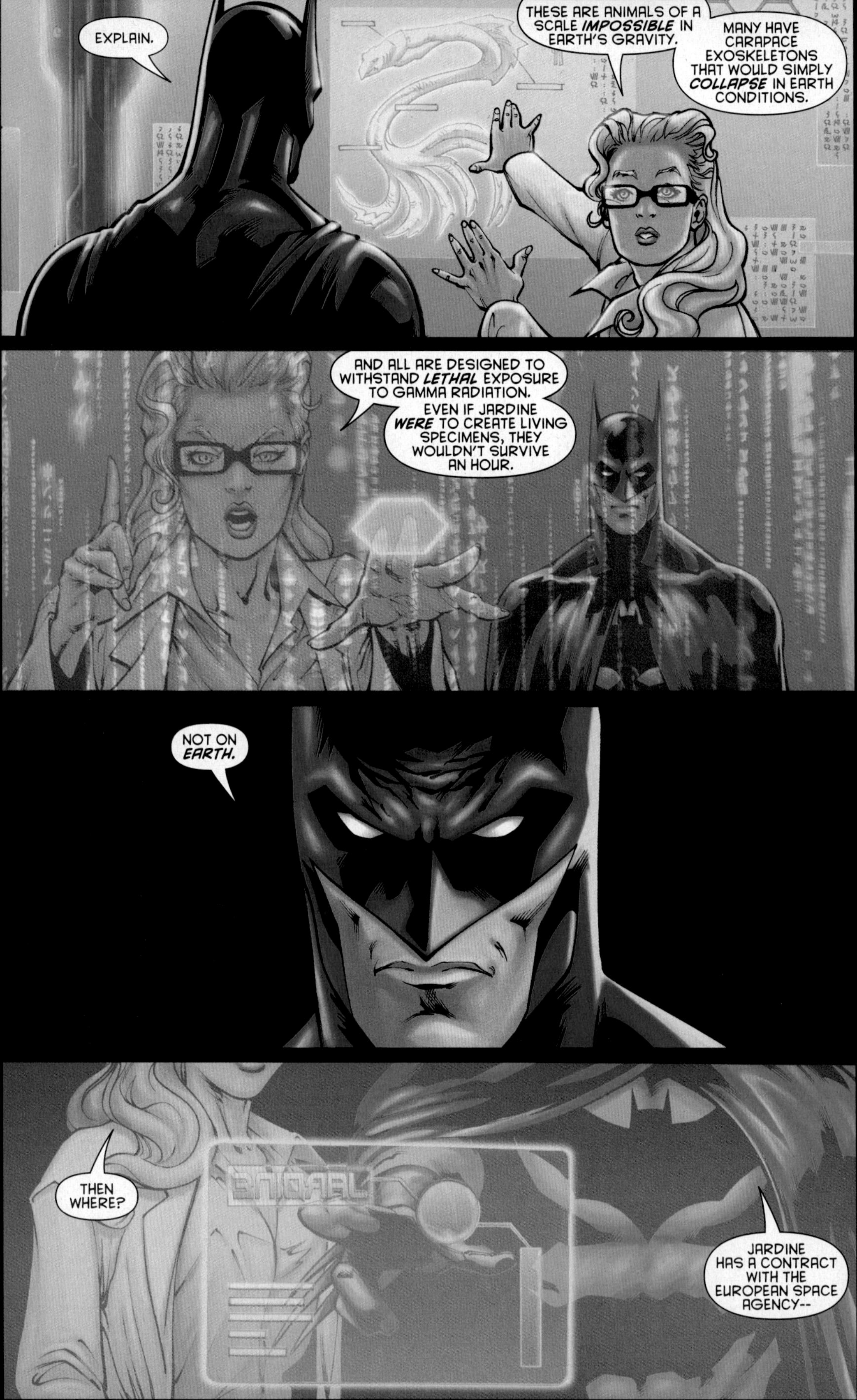
EXPLAIN.
THESE ARE ANIMALS OF A SCALE IMPOSSIBLE IN EARTH'S GRAVITY.
MANY HAVE CARAPACE EXOSKELETONS THAT WOULD SIMPLY COLLAPSE IN EARTH CONDITIONS.
AND ALL ARE DESIGNED TO WITHSTAND LETHAL EXPOSURE TO GAMMA RADIATION.
EVEN IF JARDINE WERE TO CREATE LIVING SPECIMENS, THEY WOULDN'T SURVIVE AN HOUR.
NOT ON EARTH.
THEN WHERE?
JARDINE HAS A CONTRACT WITH THE EUROPEAN SPACE AGENCY--

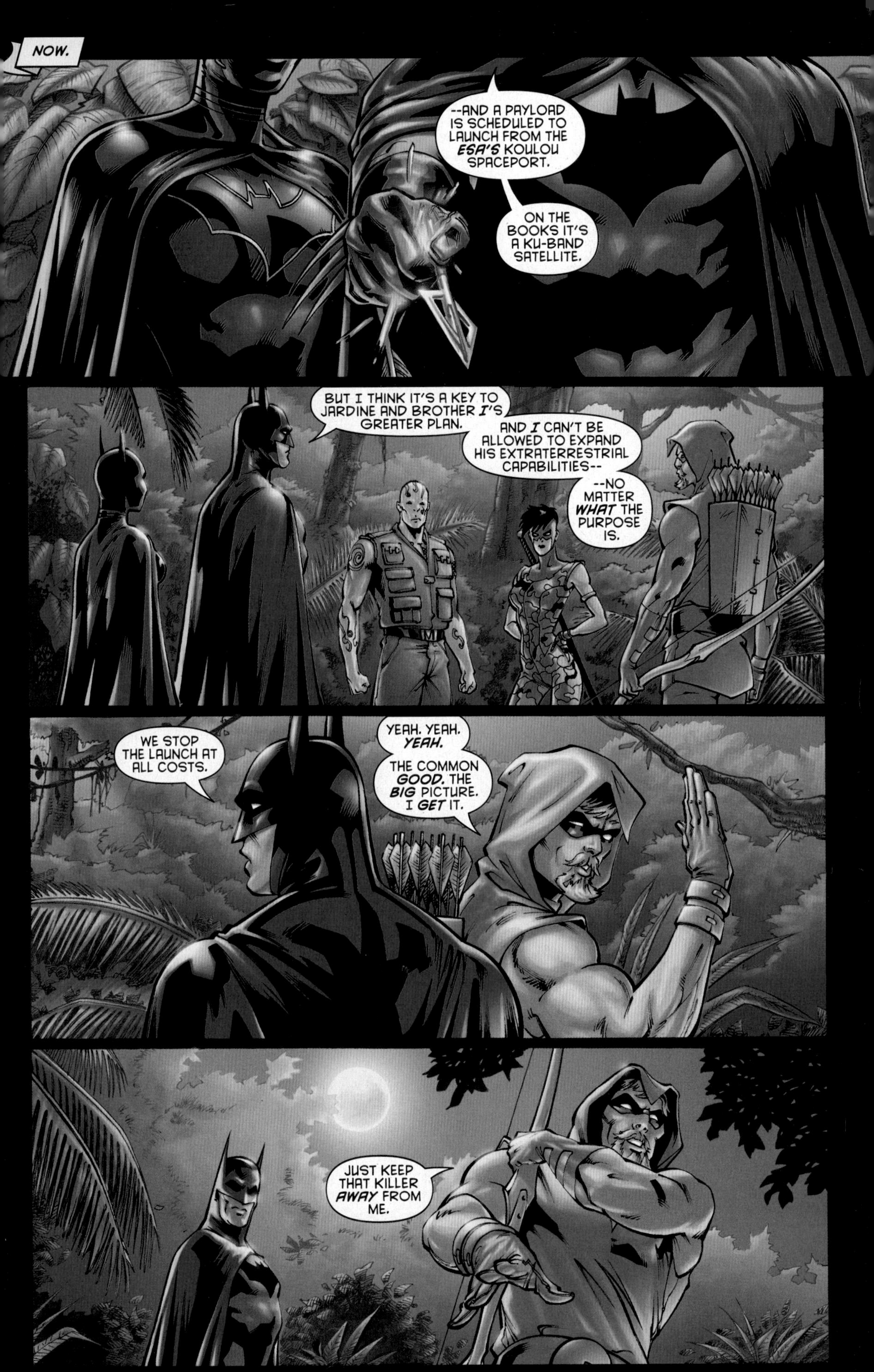
NOW.
--AND A PAYLOAD IS SCHEDULED TO LAUNCH FROM THE ESA'S KOULOU SPACEPORT.
ON THE BOOKS IT'S A KU-BAND SATELLITE.
BUT I THINK IT'S A KEY TO JARDINE AND BROTHER I'S GREATER PLAN.
AND I CAN'T BE ALLOWED TO EXPAND HIS EXTRATERRESTRIAL CAPABILITIES--
--NO MATTER WHAT THE PURPOSE IS.
WE STOP THE LAUNCH AT ALL COSTS.
YEAH. YEAH. YEAH.
THE COMMON GOOD. THE BIG PICTURE. I GET IT.
JUST KEEP THAT KILLER AWAY FROM ME.

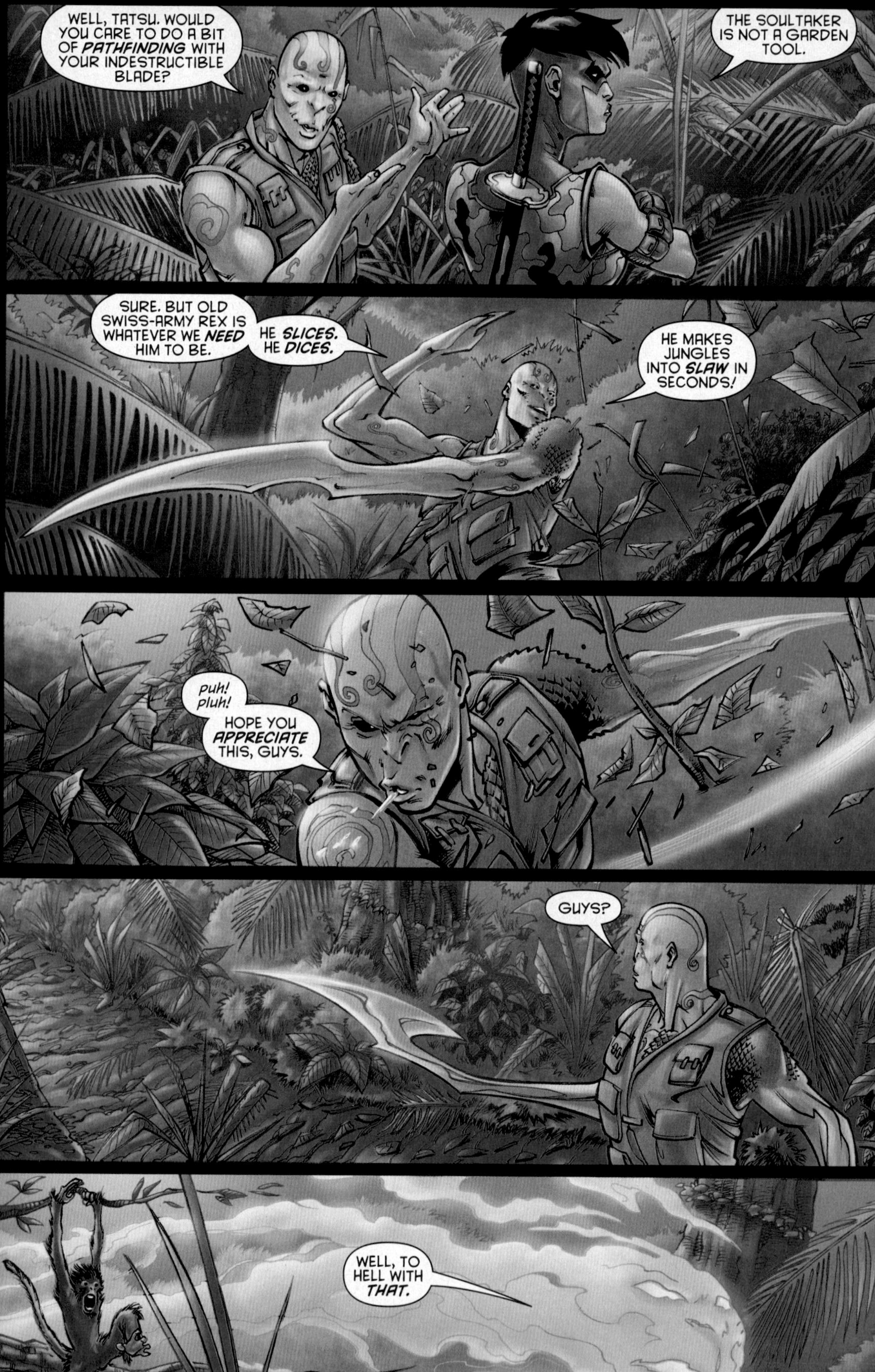
WELL, TATSU. WOULD YOU CARE TO DO A BIT OF PATHFINDING WITH YOUR INDESTRUCTIBLE BLADE?
THE SOULTAKER IS NOT A GARDEN TOOL.
SURE. BUT OLD SWISS-ARMY REX IS WHATEVER WE NEED HIM TO BE.
HE SLICES. HE DICES.
HE MAKES JUNGLES INTO SLAW IN SECONDS!
puh! pluh!
HOPE YOU APPRECIATE THIS, GUYS.
GUYS?
WELL, TO HELL WITH THAT.

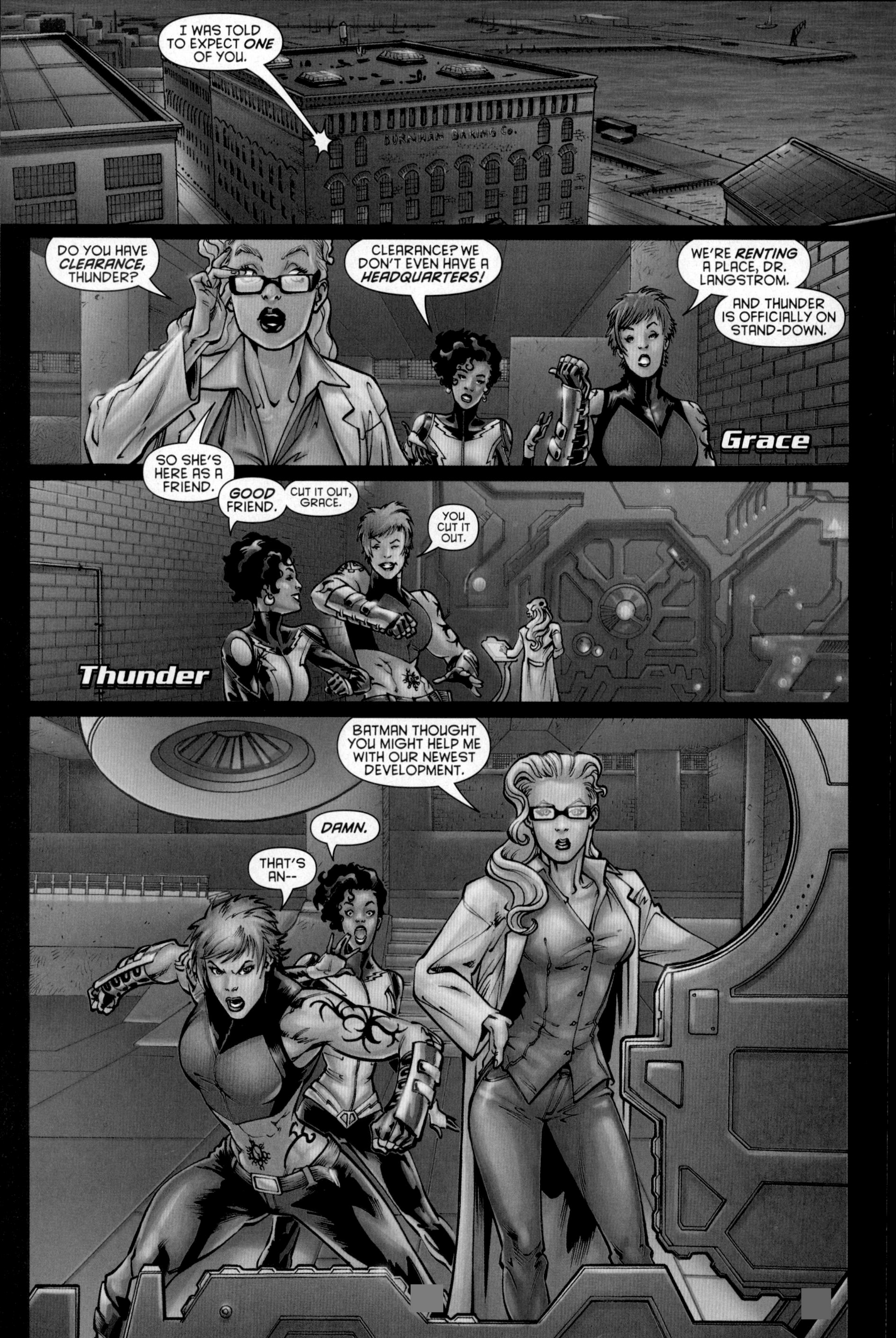
I WAS TOLD TO EXPECT *ONE* OF YOU.
BURNHAM BAKING Co.
DO YOU HAVE *CLEARANCE,* THUNDER?
CLEARANCE? WE DON'T EVEN HAVE A *HEADQUARTERS!*
WE'RE *RENTING* A PLACE, DR. LANGSTROM.
AND THUNDER IS OFFICIALLY ON STAND-DOWN.
Grace
SO SHE'S HERE AS A FRIEND.
GOOD FRIEND.
CUT IT OUT, GRACE.
YOU CUT IT OUT.
Thunder
BATMAN THOUGHT YOU MIGHT HELP ME WITH OUR NEWEST DEVELOPMENT.
DAMN.
THAT'S AN--

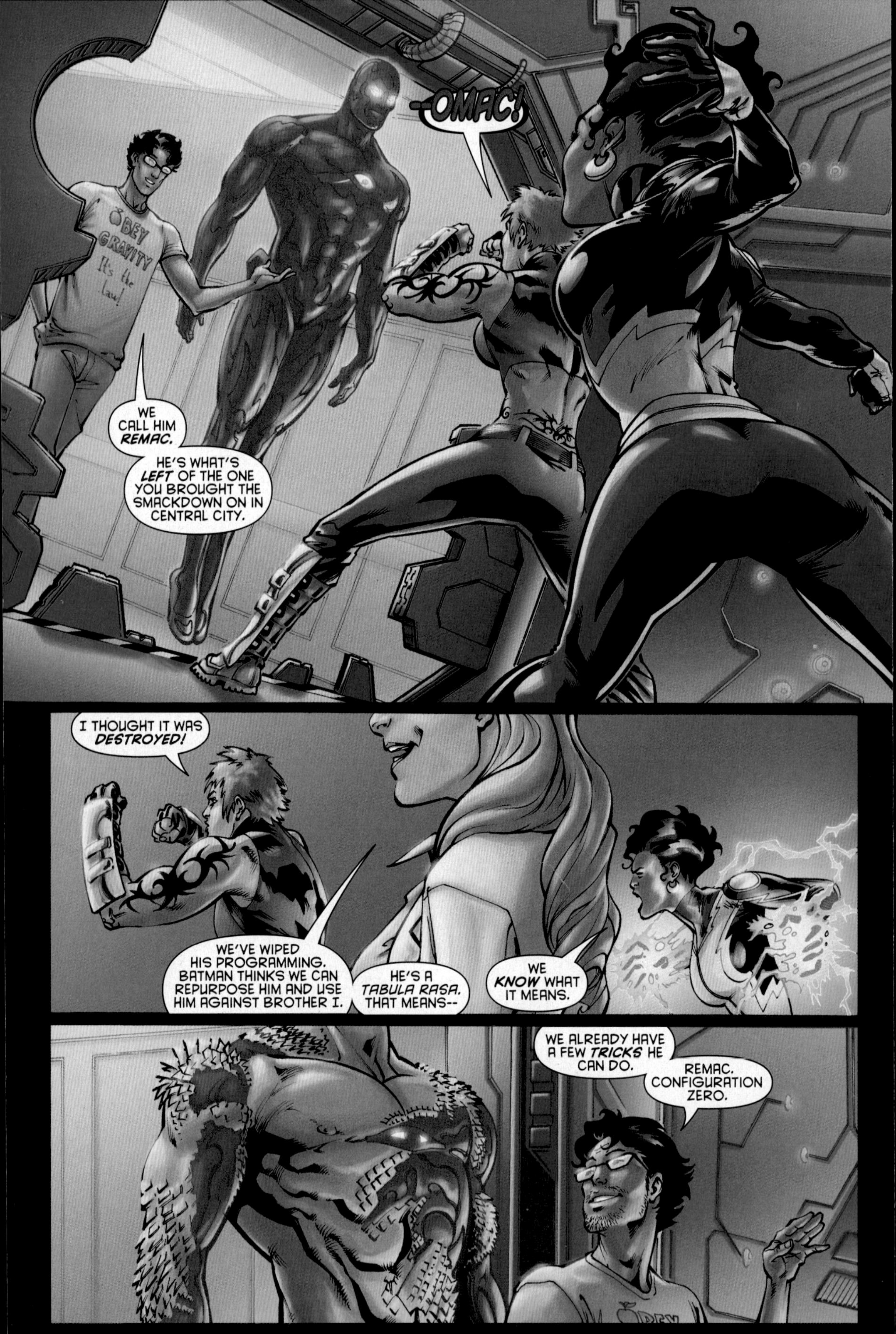
--OMAC!
WE CALL HIM *REMAC.*
HE'S WHAT'S *LEFT* OF THE ONE YOU BROUGHT THE SMACKDOWN ON IN CENTRAL CITY.
OBEY GRAVITY It's the law!
I THOUGHT IT WAS *DESTROYED!*
WE'VE WIPED HIS PROGRAMMING. BATMAN THINKS WE CAN REPURPOSE HIM AND USE HIM AGAINST BROTHER I.
HE'S A *TABULA RASA.* THAT MEANS--
WE *KNOW* WHAT IT MEANS.
WE ALREADY HAVE A FEW *TRICKS* HE CAN DO.
REMAC. CONFIGURATION ZERO.

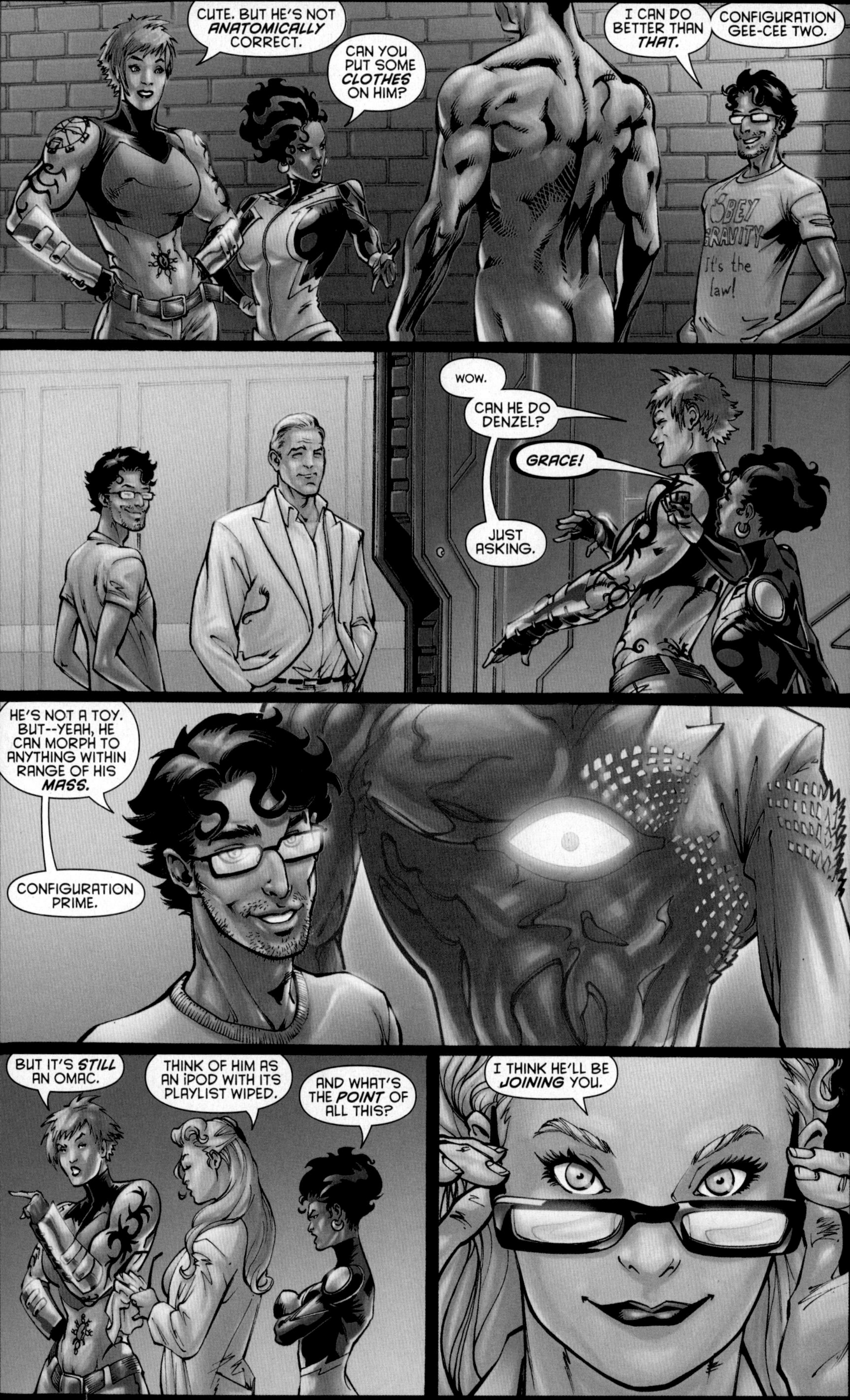
CUTE. BUT HE'S NOT ANATOMICALLY CORRECT.
CAN YOU PUT SOME CLOTHES ON HIM?
I CAN DO BETTER THAN THAT.
CONFIGURATION GEE-CEE TWO.
OBEY GRAVITY It's the law!
WOW.
CAN HE DO DENZEL?
GRACE!
JUST ASKING.
HE'S NOT A TOY. BUT--YEAH, HE CAN MORPH TO ANYTHING WITHIN RANGE OF HIS MASS.
CONFIGURATION PRIME.
BUT IT'S STILL AN OMAC.
THINK OF HIM AS AN iPOD WITH ITS PLAYLIST WIPED.
AND WHAT'S THE POINT OF ALL THIS?
I THINK HE'LL BE JOINING YOU.

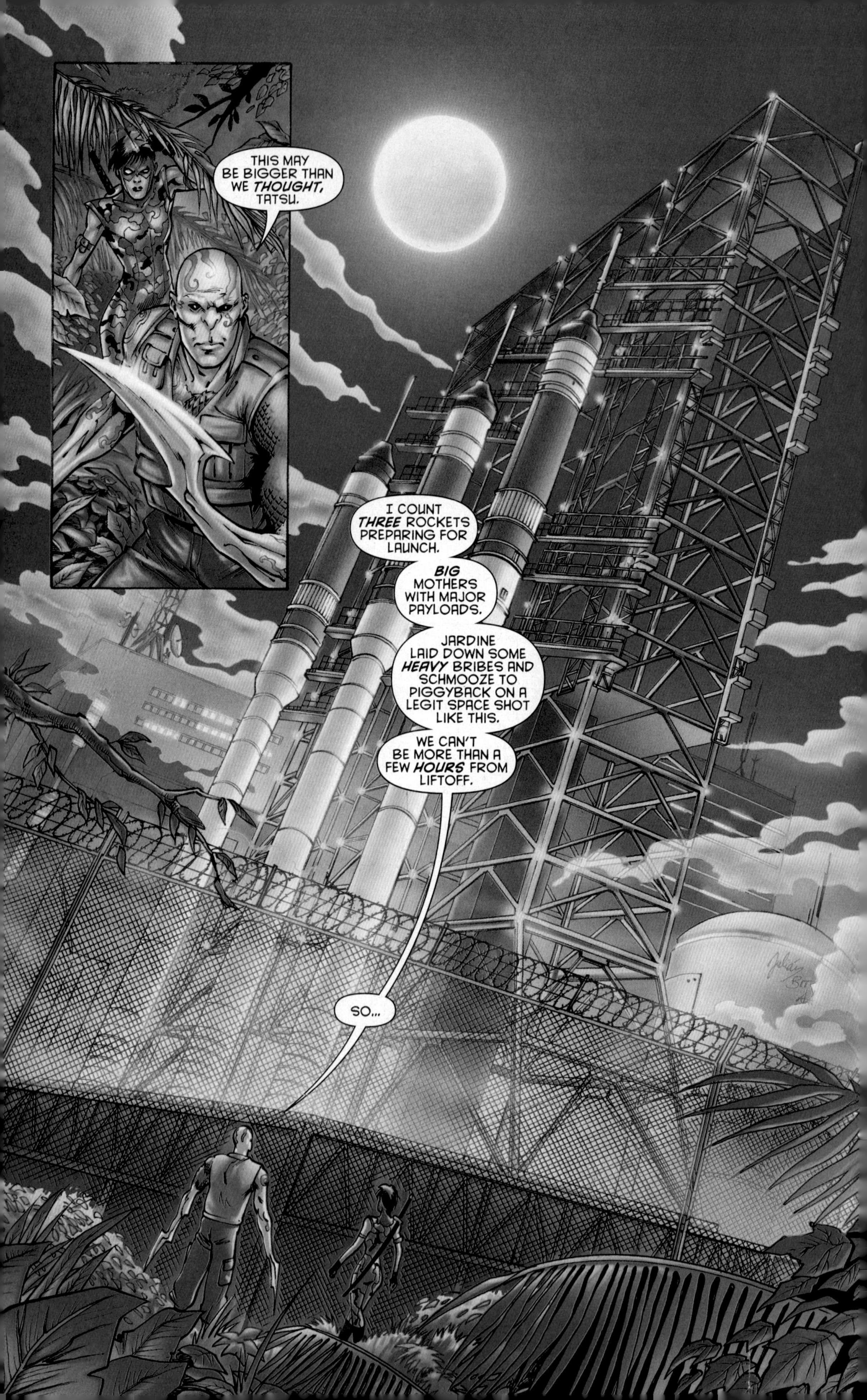
THIS MAY BE BIGGER THAN WE *THOUGHT,* TATSU.
I COUNT *THREE* ROCKETS PREPARING FOR LAUNCH.
BIG MOTHERS WITH MAJOR PAYLOADS.
JARDINE LAID DOWN SOME *HEAVY* BRIBES AND SCHMOOZE TO PIGGYBACK ON A LEGIT SPACE SHOT LIKE THIS.
WE CAN'T BE MORE THAN A FEW *HOURS* FROM LIFTOFF.
SO...

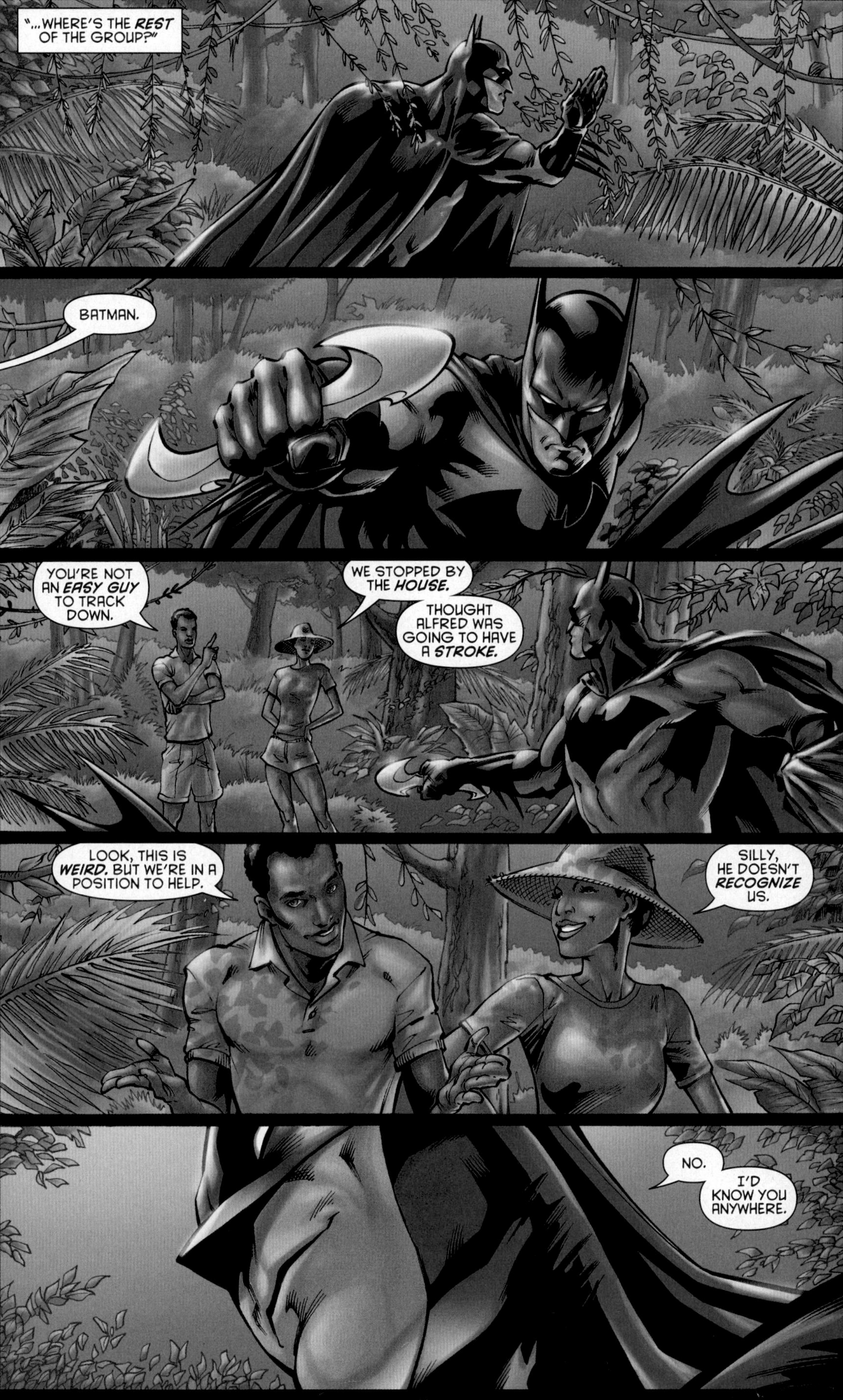

"...WHERE'S THE REST OF THE GROUP?"
BATMAN.
YOU'RE NOT AN EASY GUY TO TRACK DOWN.
WE STOPPED BY THE HOUSE.
THOUGHT ALFRED WAS GOING TO HAVE A STROKE.
LOOK, THIS IS WEIRD. BUT WE'RE IN A POSITION TO HELP.
SILLY, HE DOESN'T RECOGNIZE US.
NO.
I'D KNOW YOU ANYWHERE.

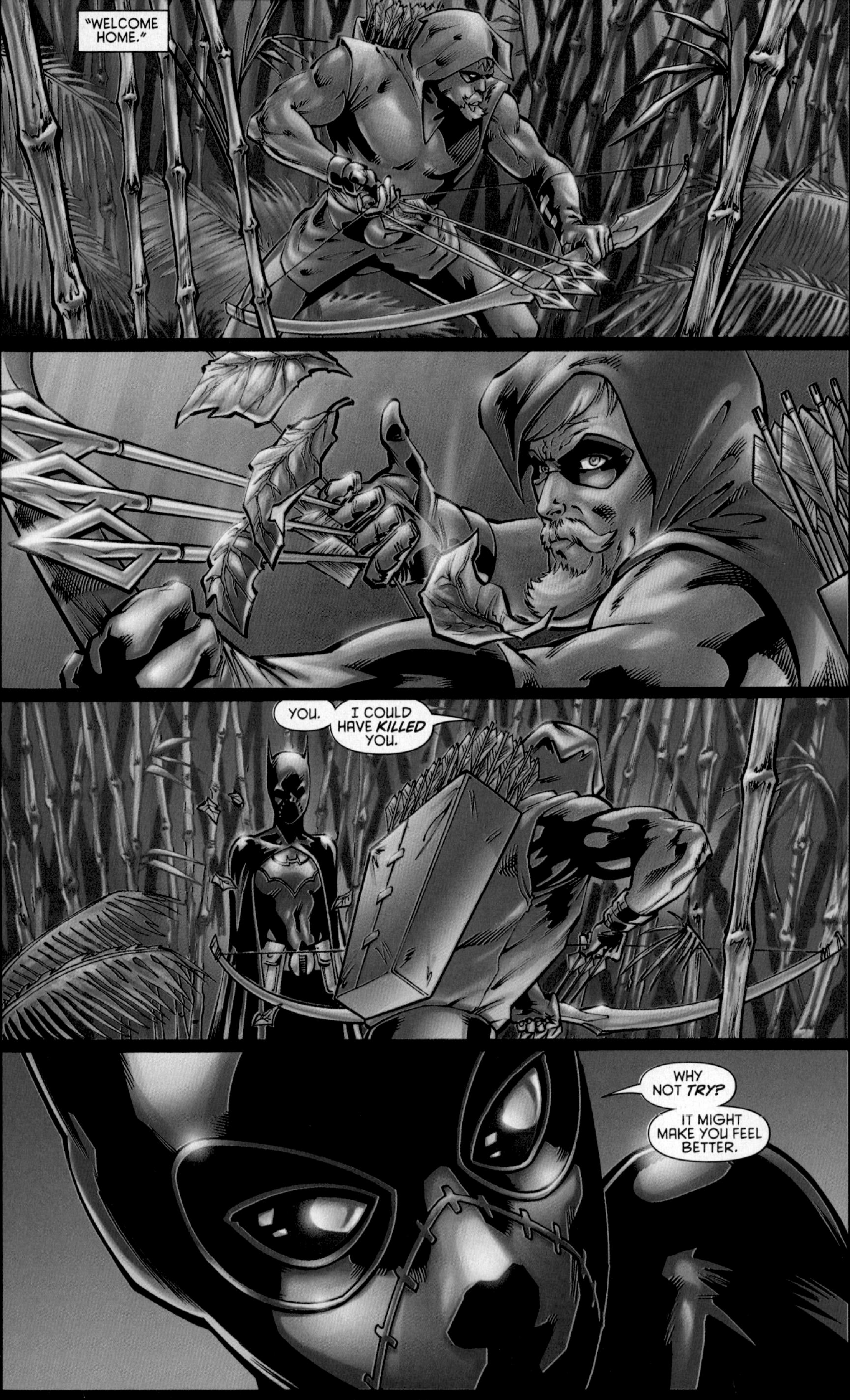
"WELCOME HOME."
YOU.
I COULD HAVE KILLED YOU.
WHY NOT TRY?
IT MIGHT MAKE YOU FEEL BETTER.

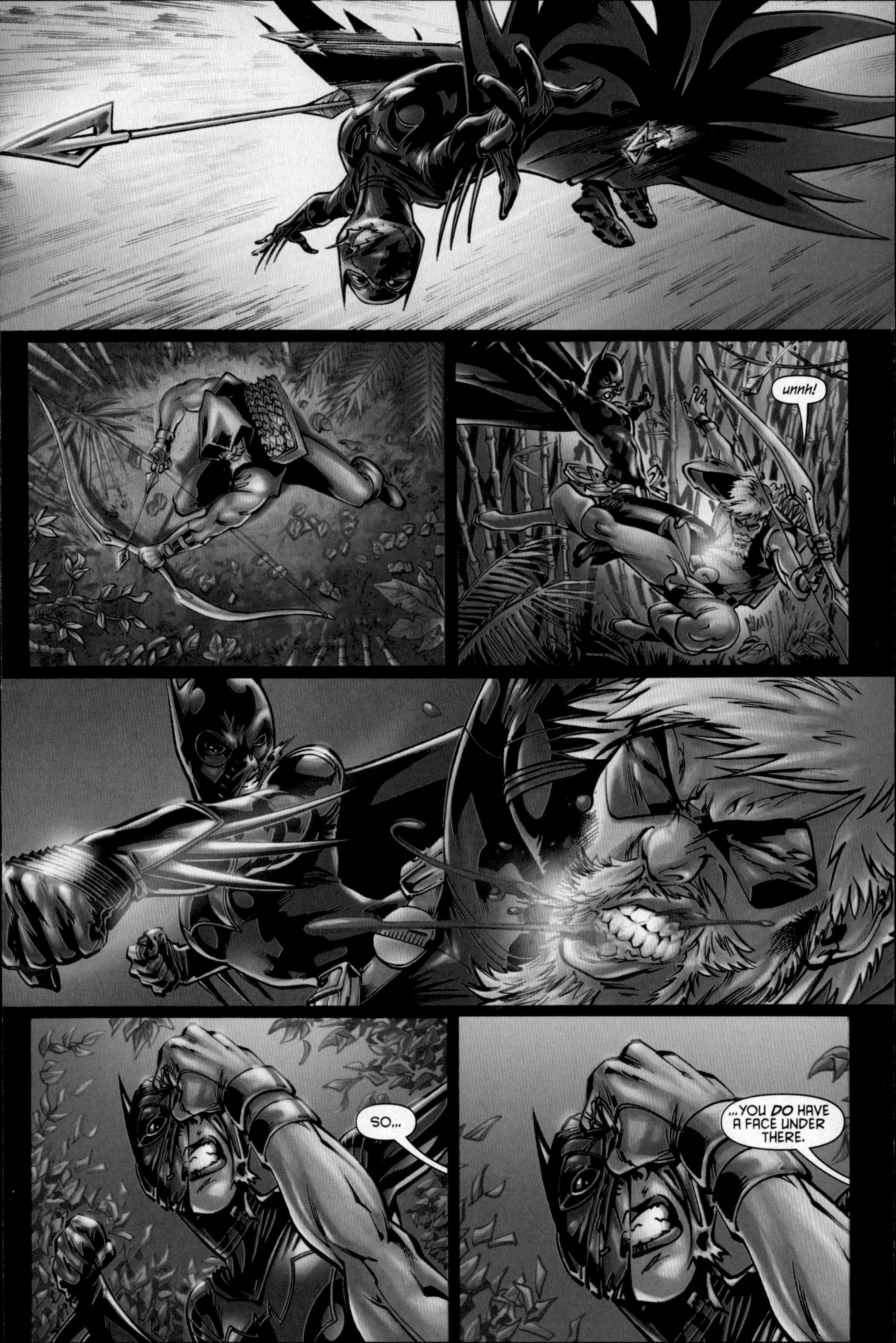
unnh!
SO...
...YOU DO HAVE A FACE UNDER THERE.

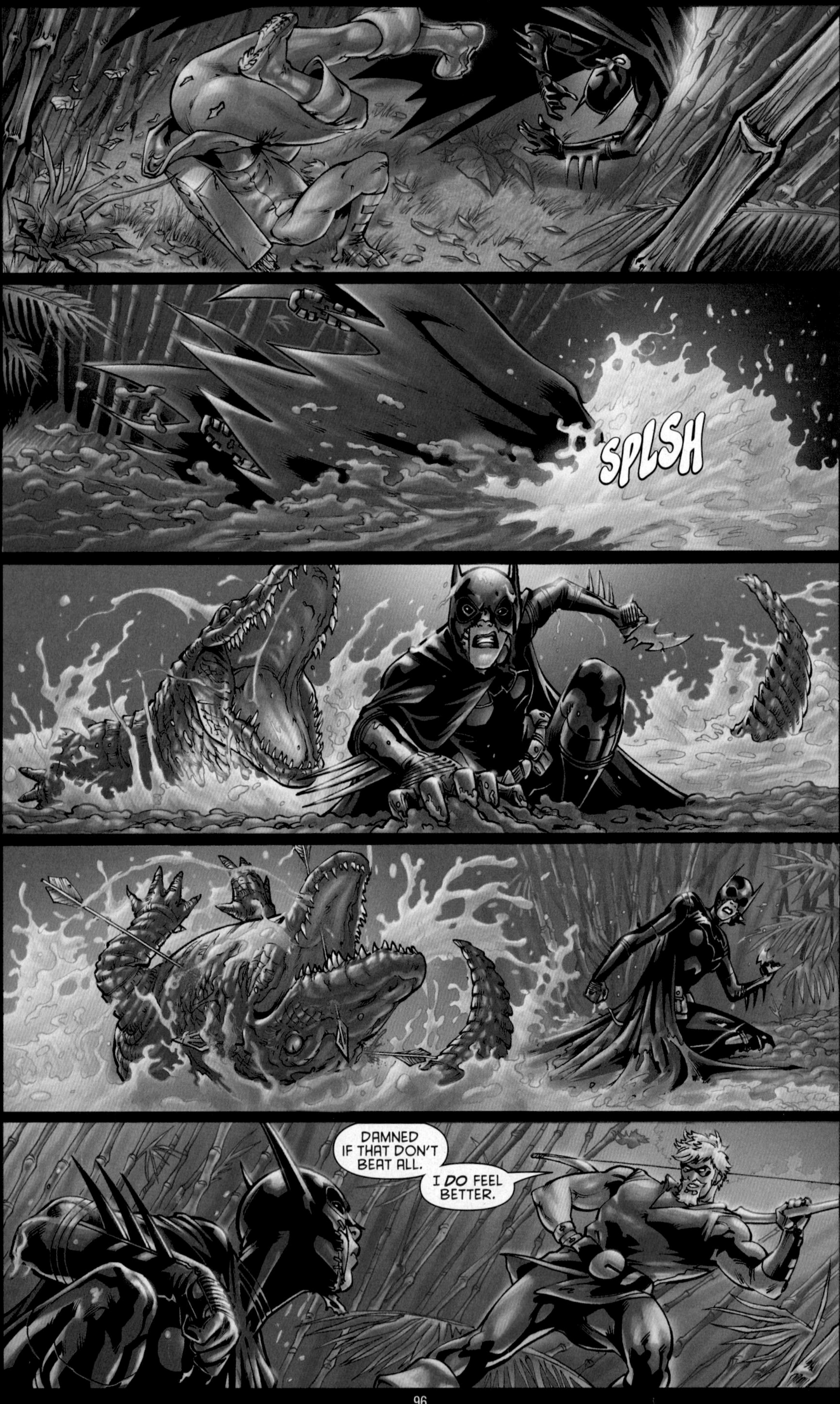
SPLSH
DAMNED IF THAT DON'T BEAT ALL.
I *DO* FEEL BETTER.

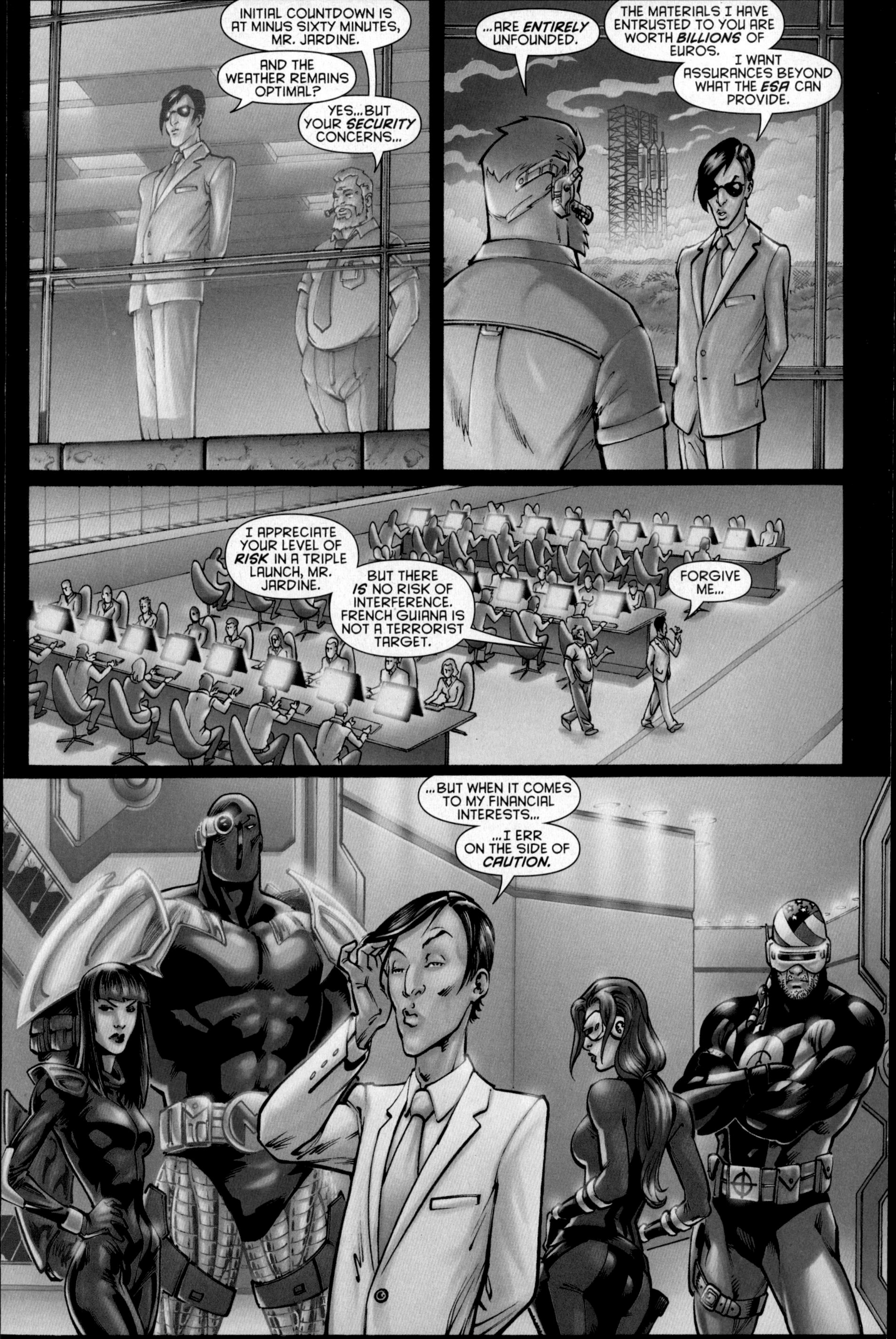
INITIAL COUNTDOWN IS AT MINUS SIXTY MINUTES, MR. JARDINE.
AND THE WEATHER REMAINS OPTIMAL?
YES...BUT YOUR SECURITY CONCERNS...
...ARE ENTIRELY UNFOUNDED.
THE MATERIALS I HAVE ENTRUSTED TO YOU ARE WORTH BILLIONS OF EUROS.
I WANT ASSURANCES BEYOND WHAT THE ESA CAN PROVIDE.
I APPRECIATE YOUR LEVEL OF RISK IN A TRIPLE LAUNCH, MR. JARDINE.
BUT THERE IS NO RISK OF INTERFERENCE. FRENCH GUIANA IS NOT A TERRORIST TARGET.
FORGIVE ME...
...BUT WHEN IT COMES TO MY FINANCIAL INTERESTS...
...I ERR ON THE SIDE OF CAUTION.

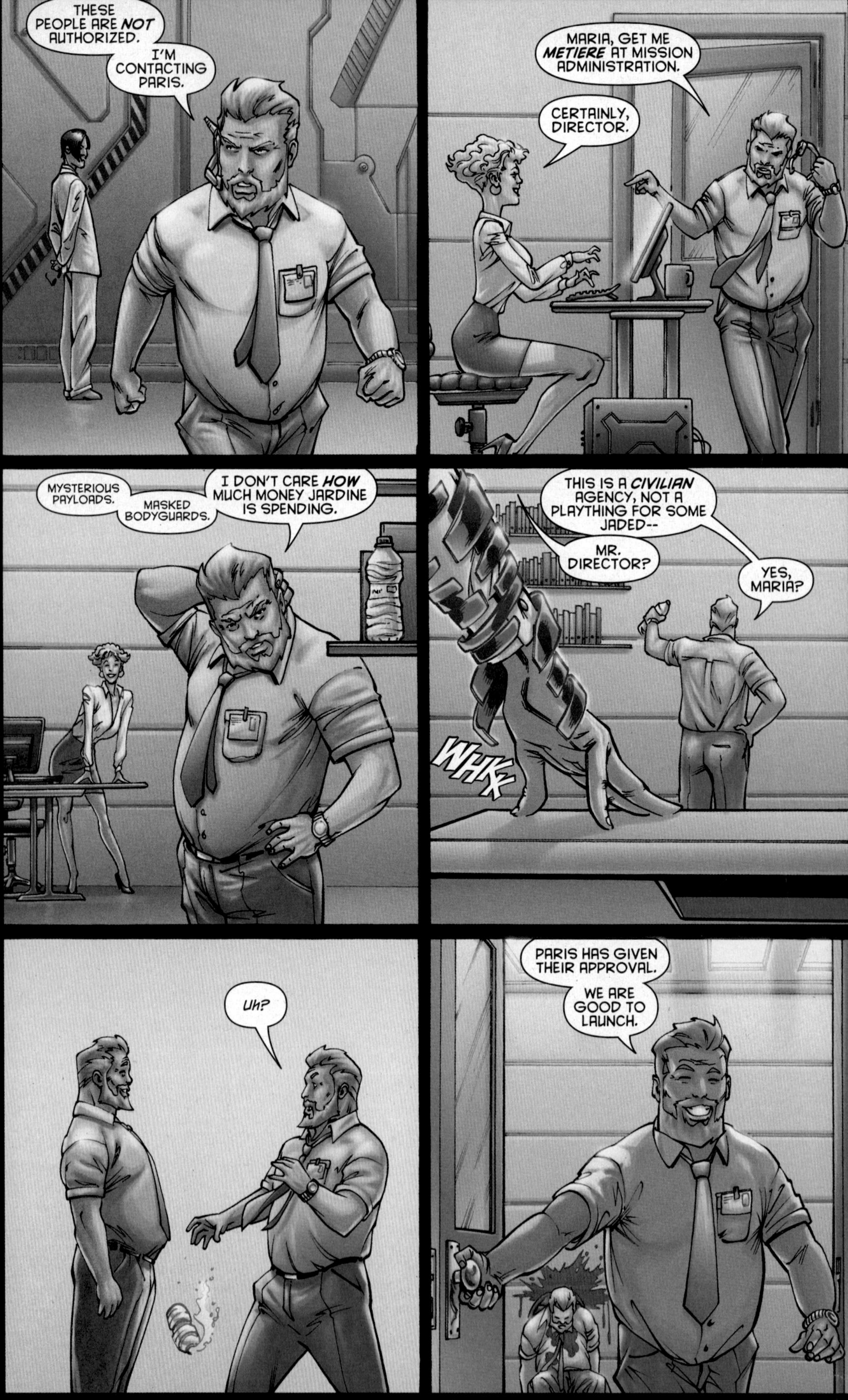
THESE PEOPLE ARE NOT AUTHORIZED.
I'M CONTACTING PARIS.
MARIA, GET ME METIERE AT MISSION ADMINISTRATION.
CERTAINLY, DIRECTOR.
MYSTERIOUS PAYLOADS.
MASKED BODYGUARDS.
I DON'T CARE HOW MUCH MONEY JARDINE IS SPENDING.
THIS IS A CIVILIAN AGENCY, NOT A PLAYTHING FOR SOME JADED--
MR. DIRECTOR?
YES, MARIA?
WHKK
Uh?
PARIS HAS GIVEN THEIR APPROVAL.
WE ARE GOOD TO LAUNCH.

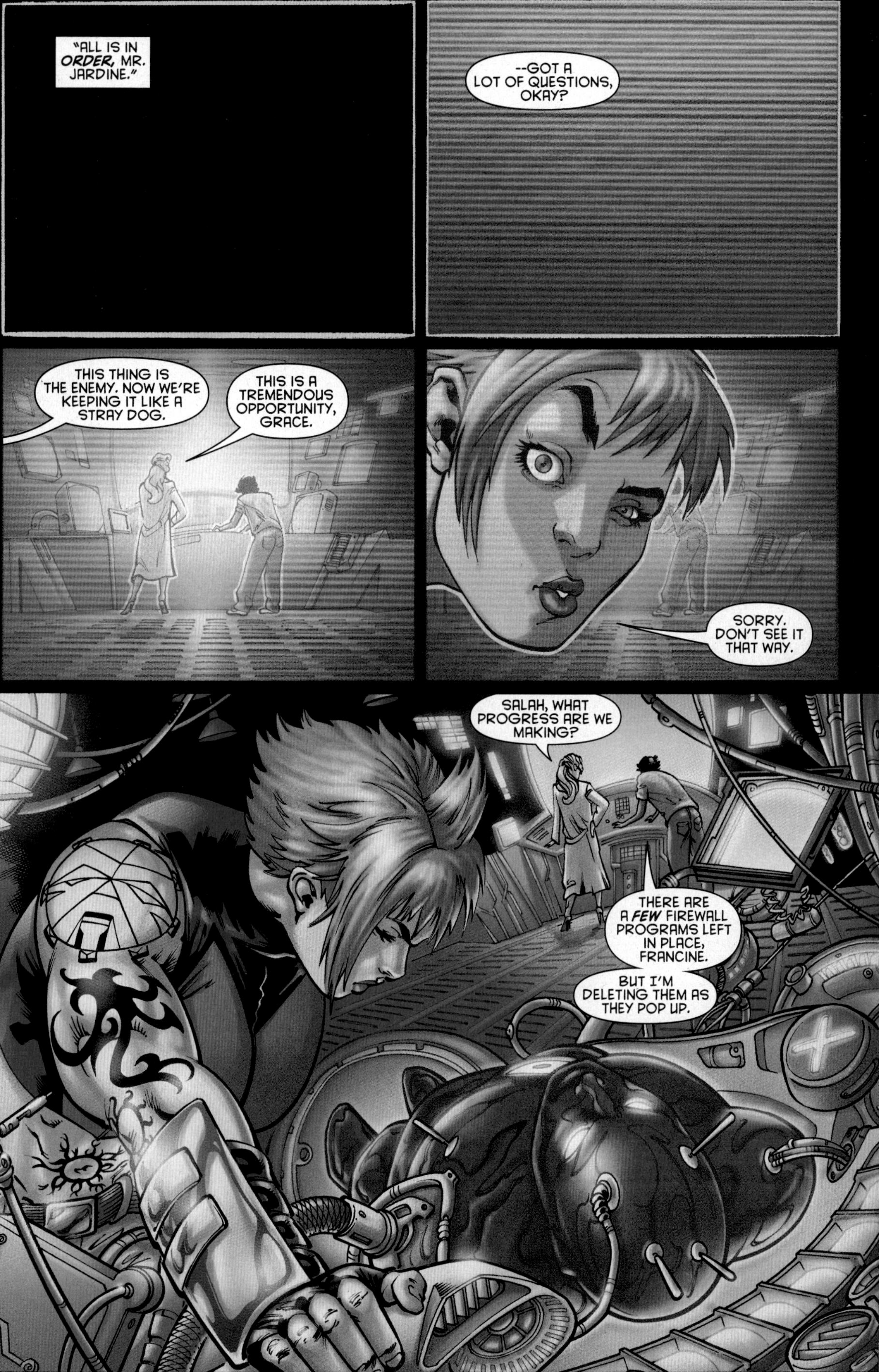
"ALL IS IN ORDER, MR. JARDINE."
--GOT A LOT OF QUESTIONS, OKAY?
THIS THING IS THE ENEMY. NOW WE'RE KEEPING IT LIKE A STRAY DOG.
THIS IS A TREMENDOUS OPPORTUNITY, GRACE.
SORRY. DON'T SEE IT THAT WAY.
SALAH, WHAT PROGRESS ARE WE MAKING?
THERE ARE A FEW FIREWALL PROGRAMS LEFT IN PLACE, FRANCINE.
BUT I'M DELETING THEM AS THEY POP UP.

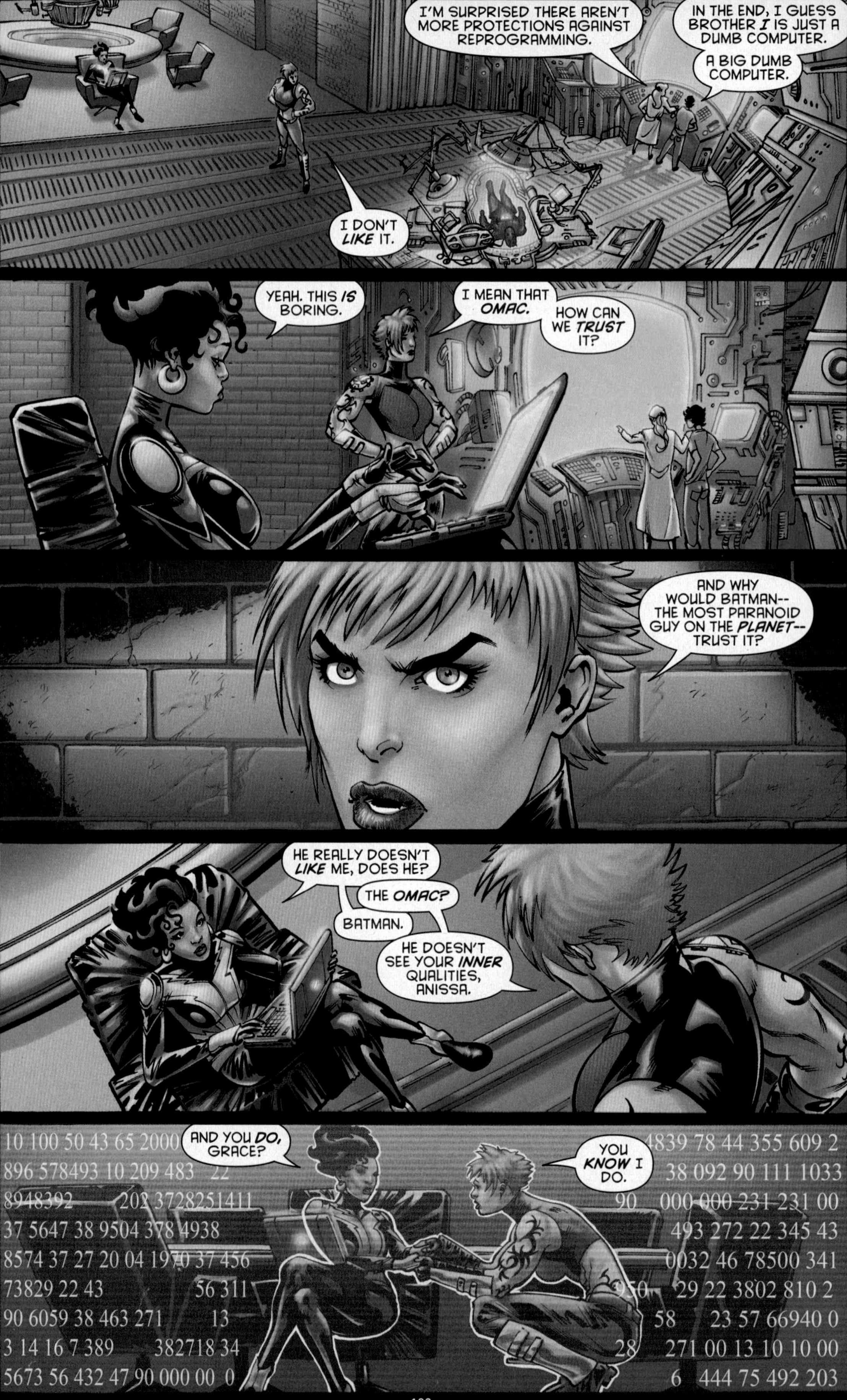
I'M SURPRISED THERE AREN'T MORE PROTECTIONS AGAINST REPROGRAMMING.
IN THE END, I GUESS BROTHER *I* IS JUST A DUMB COMPUTER.
A BIG DUMB COMPUTER.
I DON'T *LIKE* IT.
YEAH. THIS *IS* BORING.
I MEAN THAT *OMAC.*
HOW CAN WE *TRUST* IT?
AND WHY WOULD BATMAN-- THE MOST PARANOID GUY ON THE *PLANET*-- TRUST IT?
HE REALLY DOESN'T *LIKE* ME, DOES HE?
THE *OMAC?*
BATMAN.
HE DOESN'T SEE YOUR *INNER* QUALITIES, ANISSA.
AND YOU *DO,* GRACE?
YOU *KNOW* I DO.

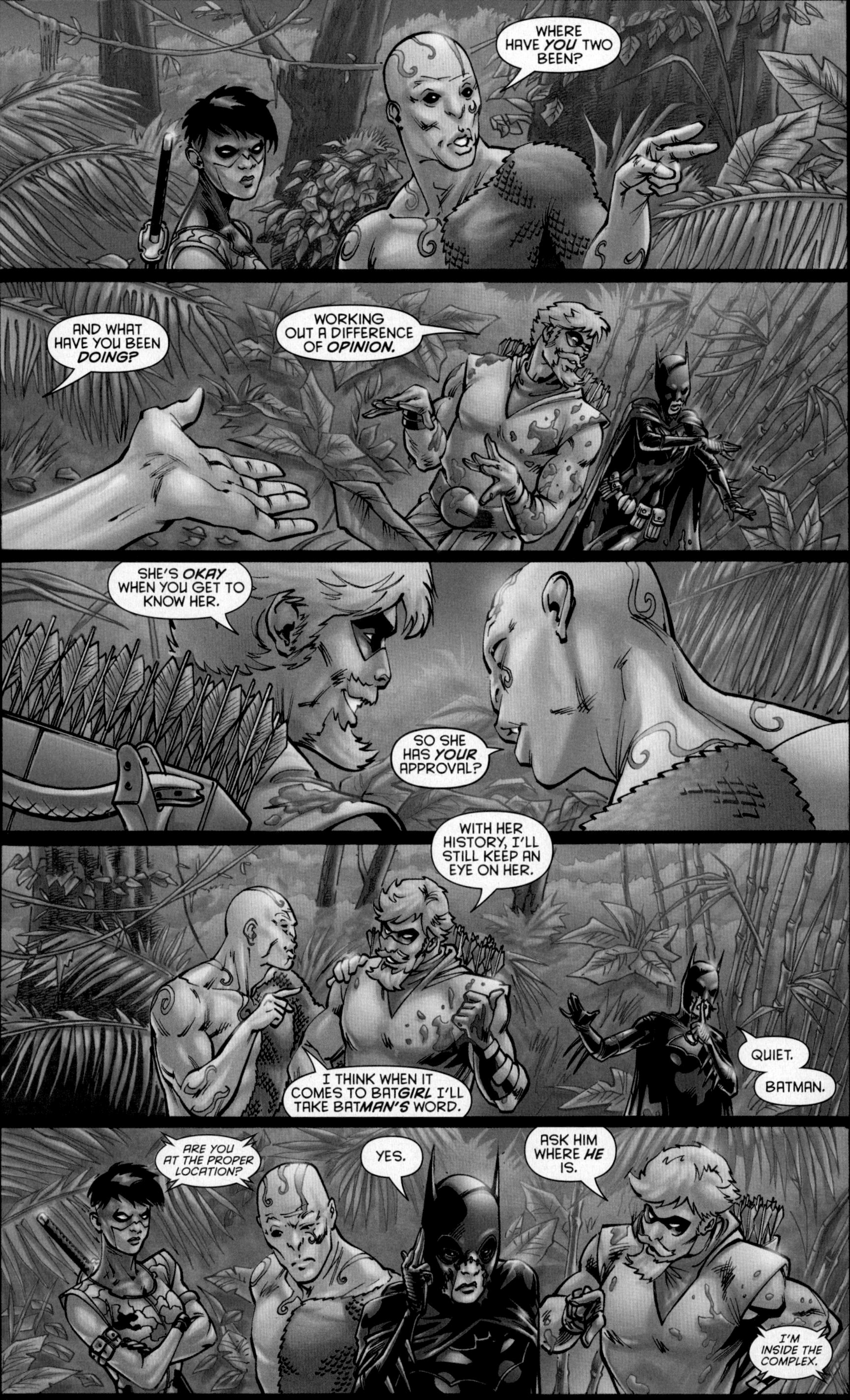
WHERE HAVE *YOU* TWO BEEN?
AND WHAT HAVE YOU BEEN *DOING?*
WORKING OUT A DIFFERENCE OF *OPINION.*
SHE'S *OKAY* WHEN YOU GET TO KNOW HER.
SO SHE HAS *YOUR* APPROVAL?
WITH HER HISTORY, I'LL STILL KEEP AN EYE ON HER.
I THINK WHEN IT COMES TO BAT*GIRL* I'LL TAKE BAT*MAN'S* WORD.
QUIET.
BATMAN.
ARE YOU AT THE PROPER LOCATION?
YES.
ASK HIM WHERE *HE* IS.
I'M INSIDE THE COMPLEX.

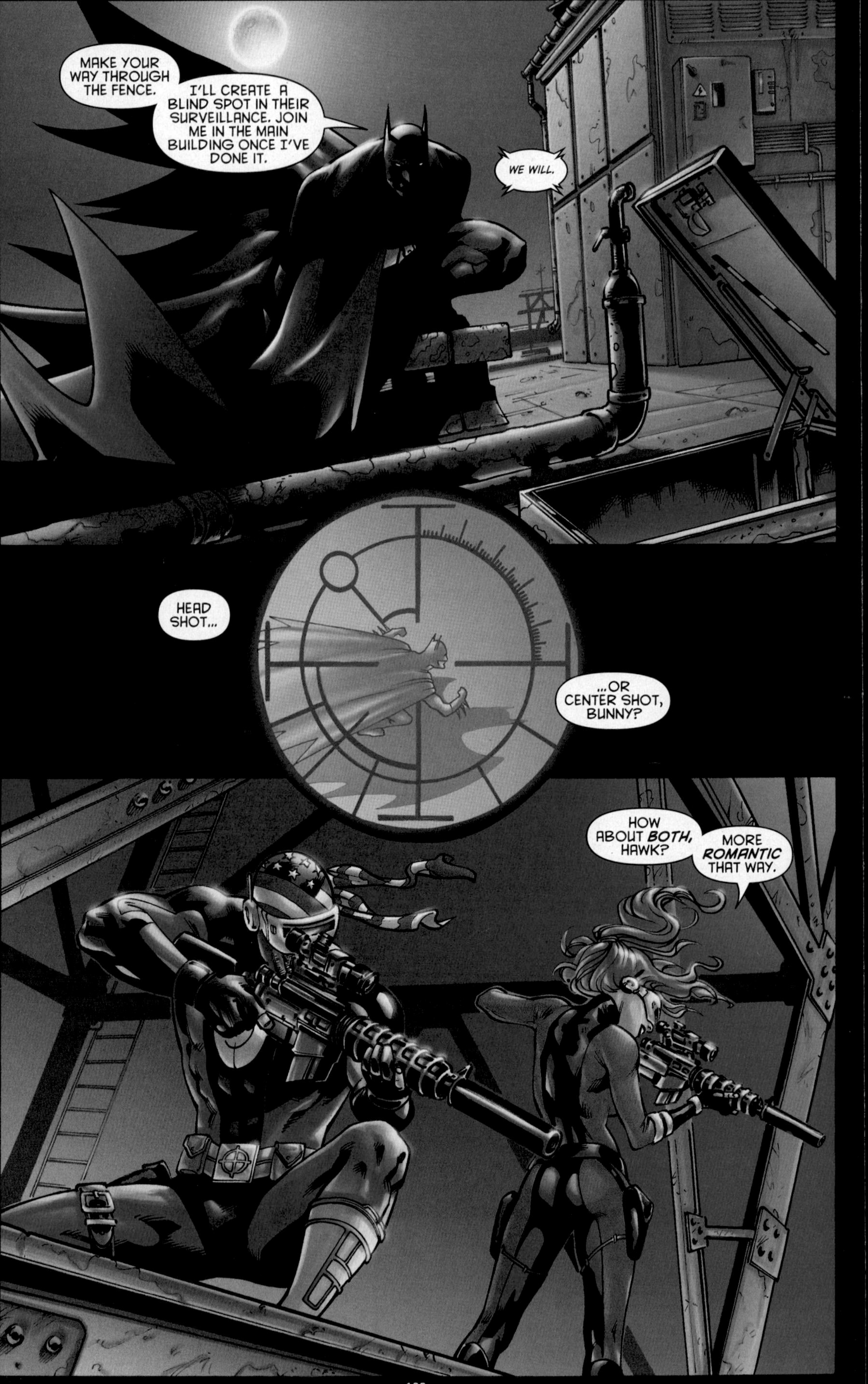
MAKE YOUR WAY THROUGH THE FENCE.
I'LL CREATE A BLIND SPOT IN THEIR SURVEILLANCE. JOIN ME IN THE MAIN BUILDING ONCE I'VE DONE IT.
WE WILL.
HEAD SHOT...
...OR CENTER SHOT, BUNNY?
HOW ABOUT **BOTH,** HAWK?
MORE **ROMANTIC** THAT WAY.

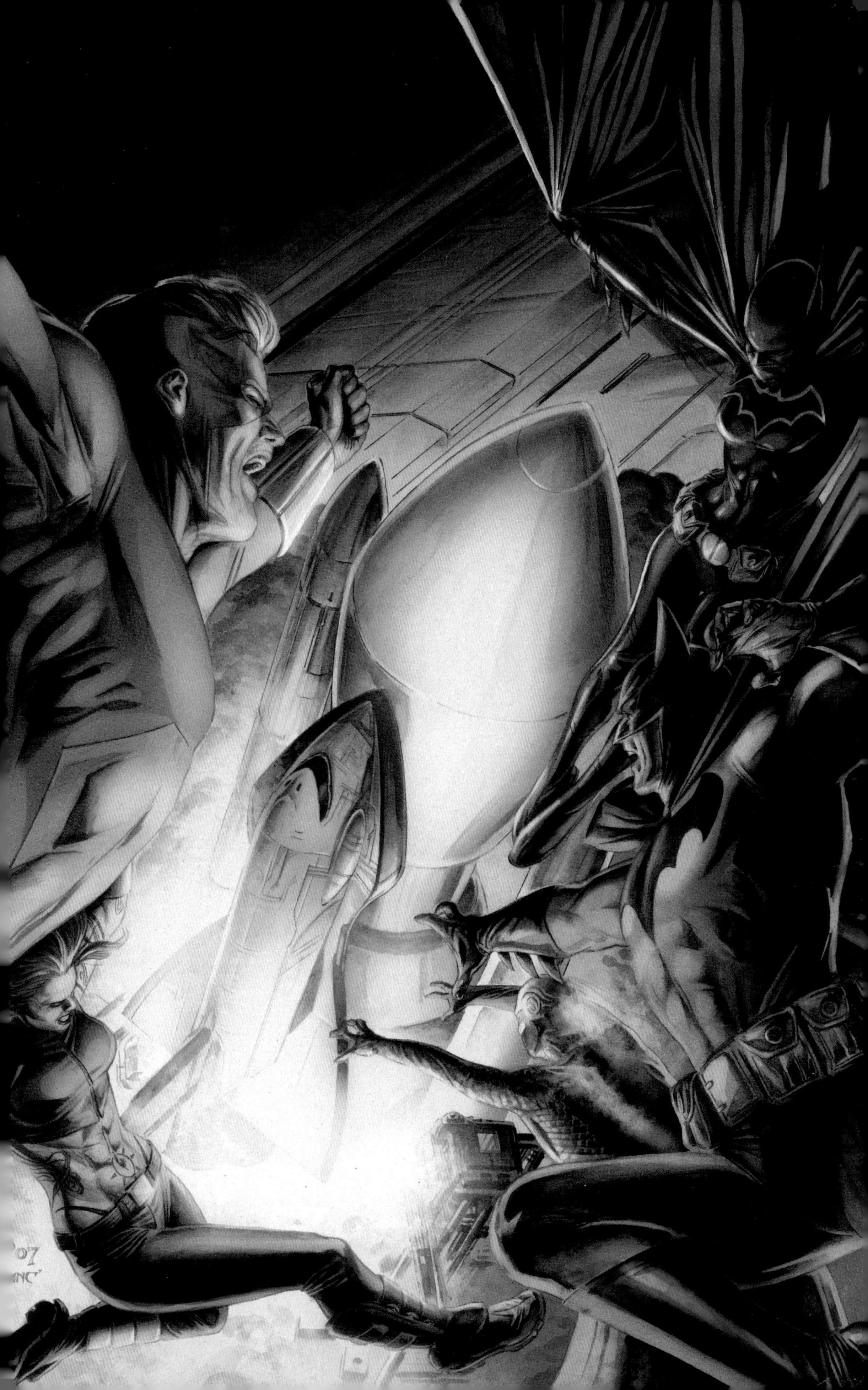

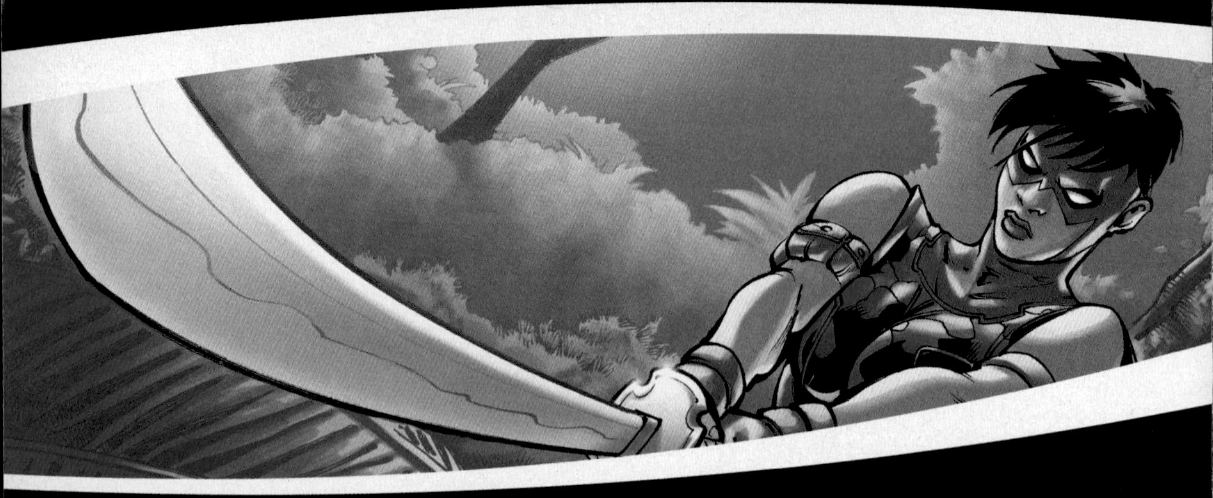

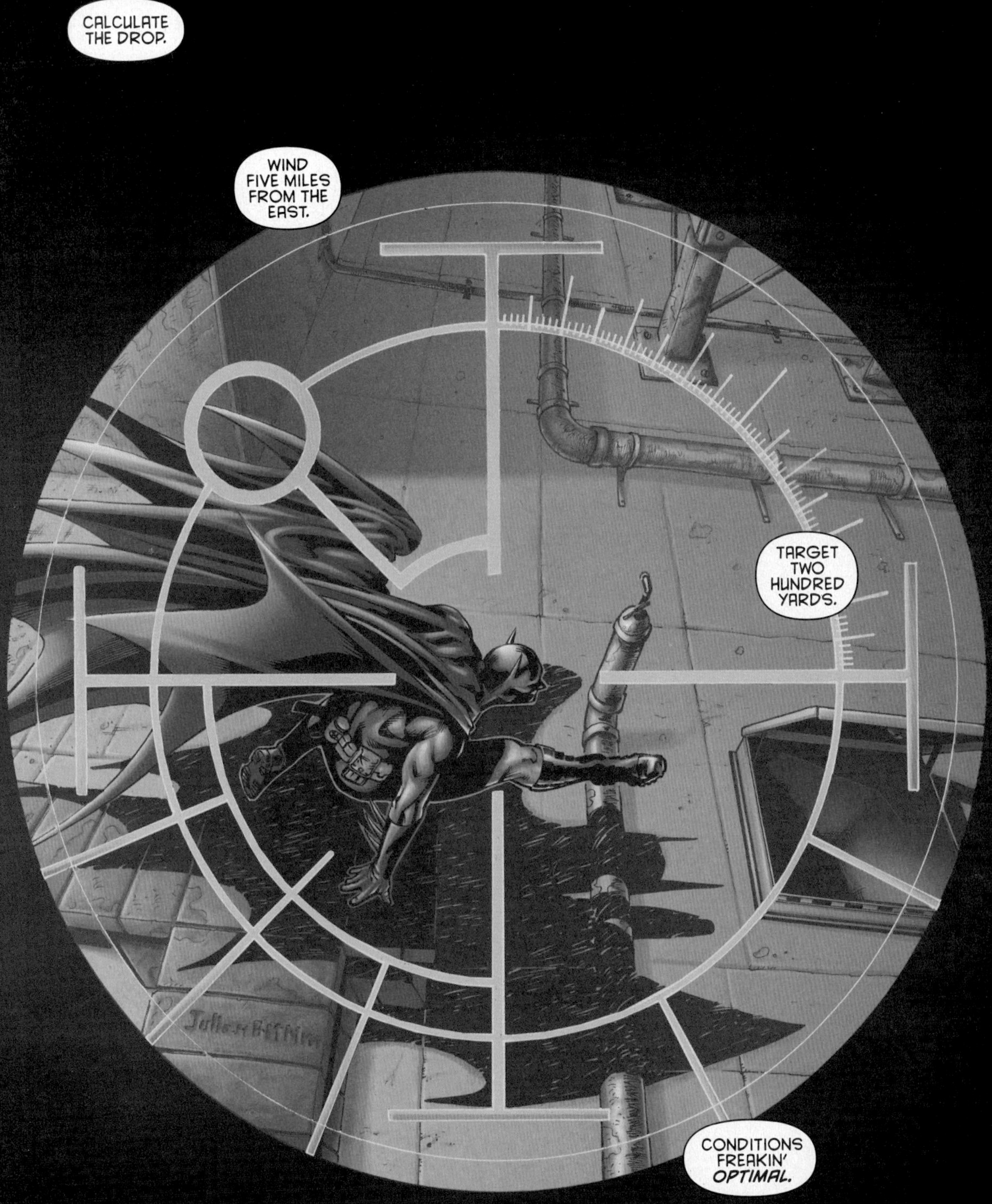
CALCULATE THE DROP.
WIND FIVE MILES FROM THE EAST.
TARGET TWO HUNDRED YARDS.
CONDITIONS FREAKIN' *OPTIMAL.*

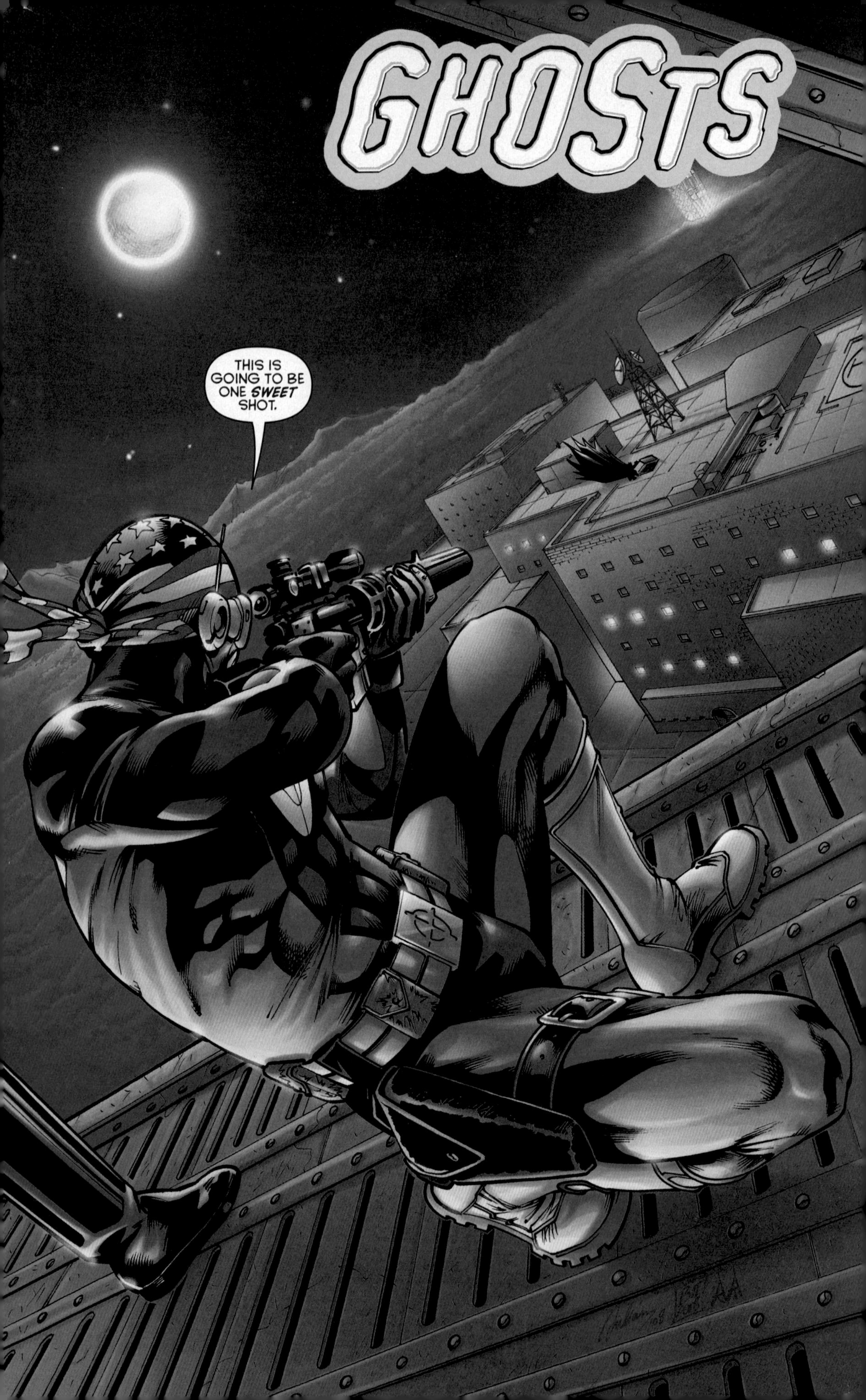
GHOSTS
THIS IS GOING TO BE ONE *SWEET* SHOT.

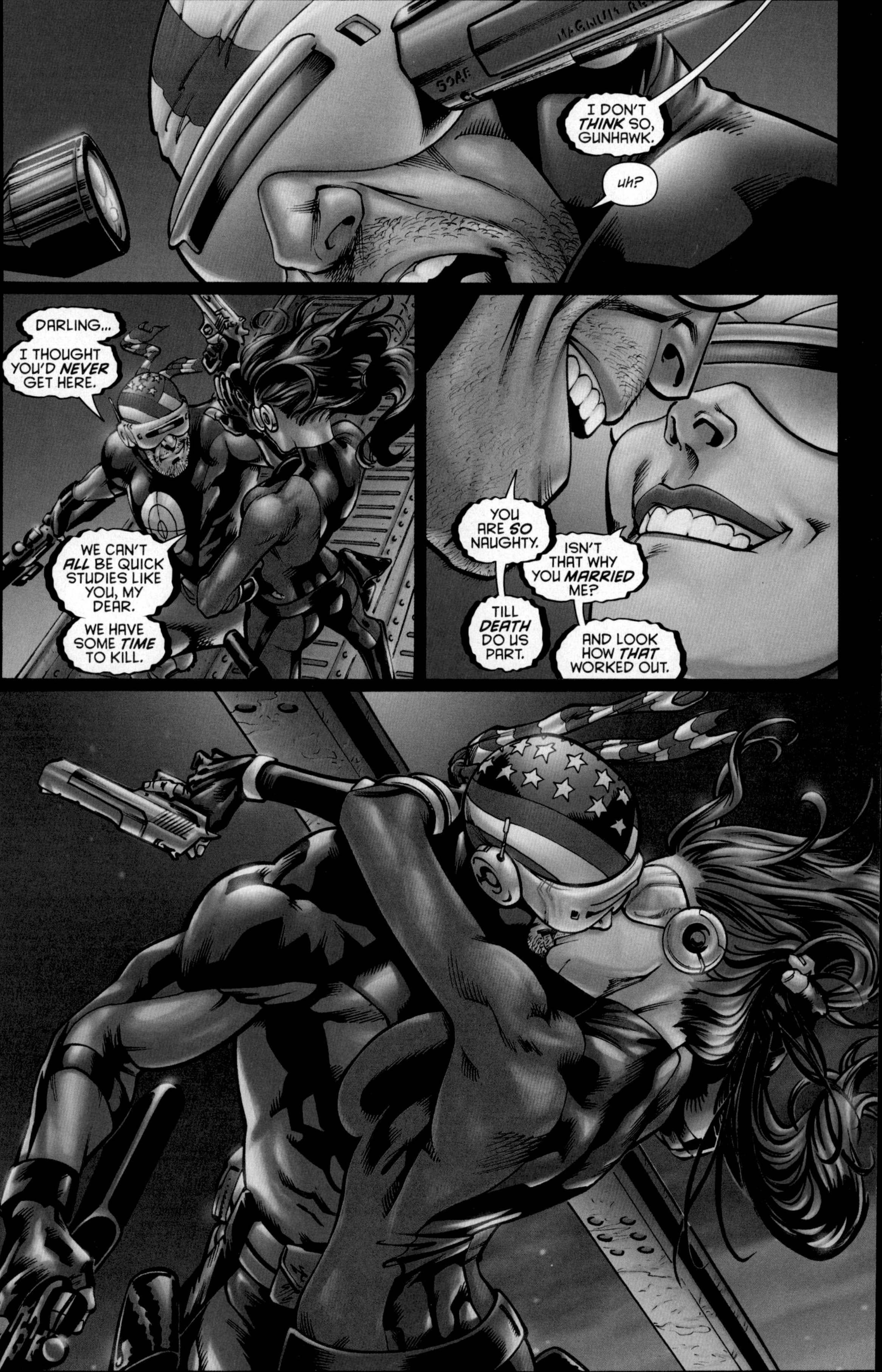
MAGNUM RE
50AE
I DON'T THINK SO, GUNHAWK.
uh?
DARLING...
I THOUGHT YOU'D NEVER GET HERE.
WE CAN'T ALL BE QUICK STUDIES LIKE YOU, MY DEAR.
WE HAVE SOME TIME TO KILL.
YOU ARE SO NAUGHTY.
ISN'T THAT WHY YOU MARRIED ME?
TILL DEATH DO US PART.
AND LOOK HOW THAT WORKED OUT.

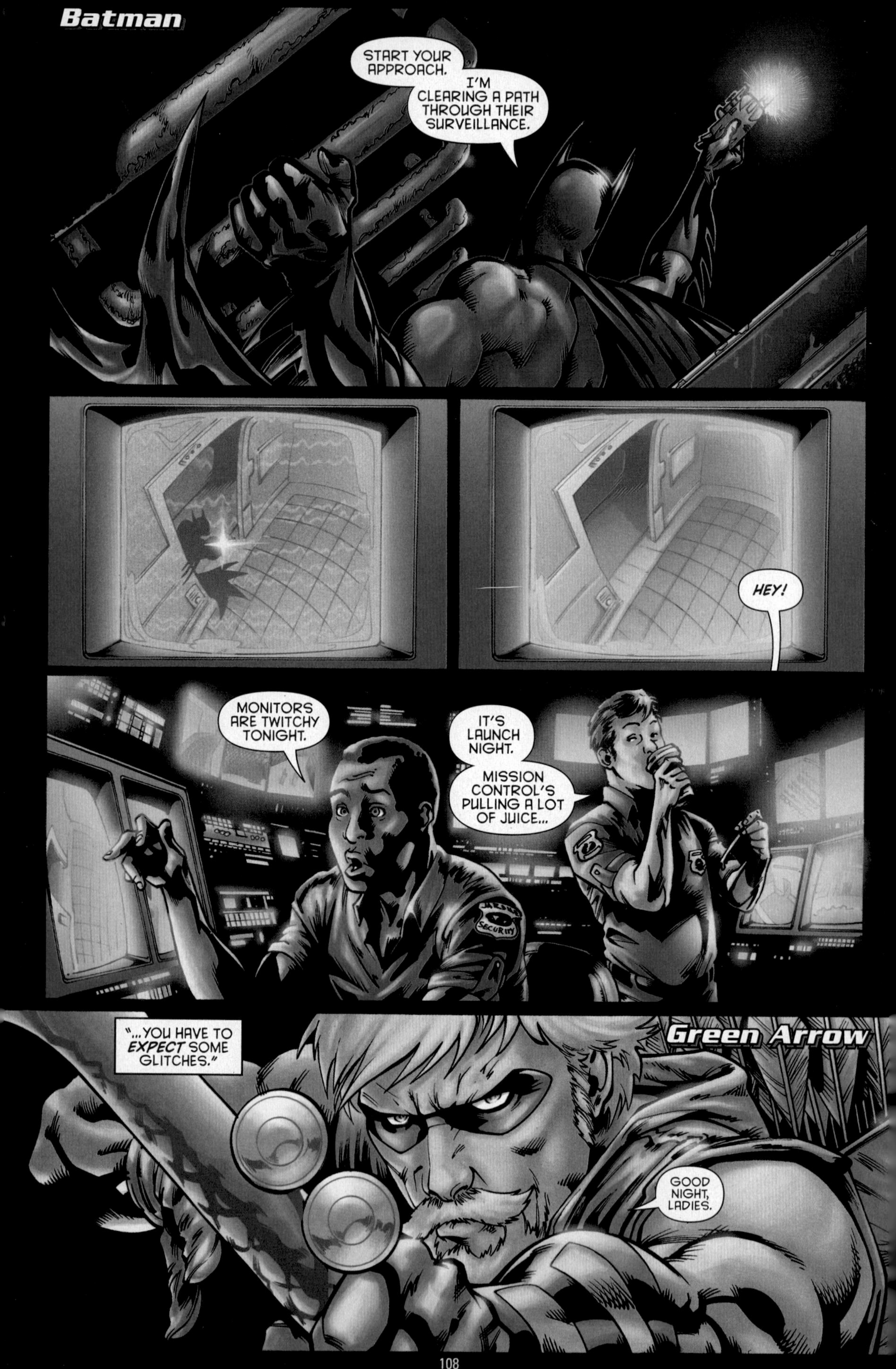
Batman
START YOUR APPROACH.
I'M CLEARING A PATH THROUGH THEIR SURVEILLANCE.
HEY!
MONITORS ARE TWITCHY TONIGHT.
IT'S LAUNCH NIGHT.
MISSION CONTROL'S PULLING A LOT OF JUICE...
"...YOU HAVE TO EXPECT SOME GLITCHES."
Green Arrow
GOOD NIGHT, LADIES.

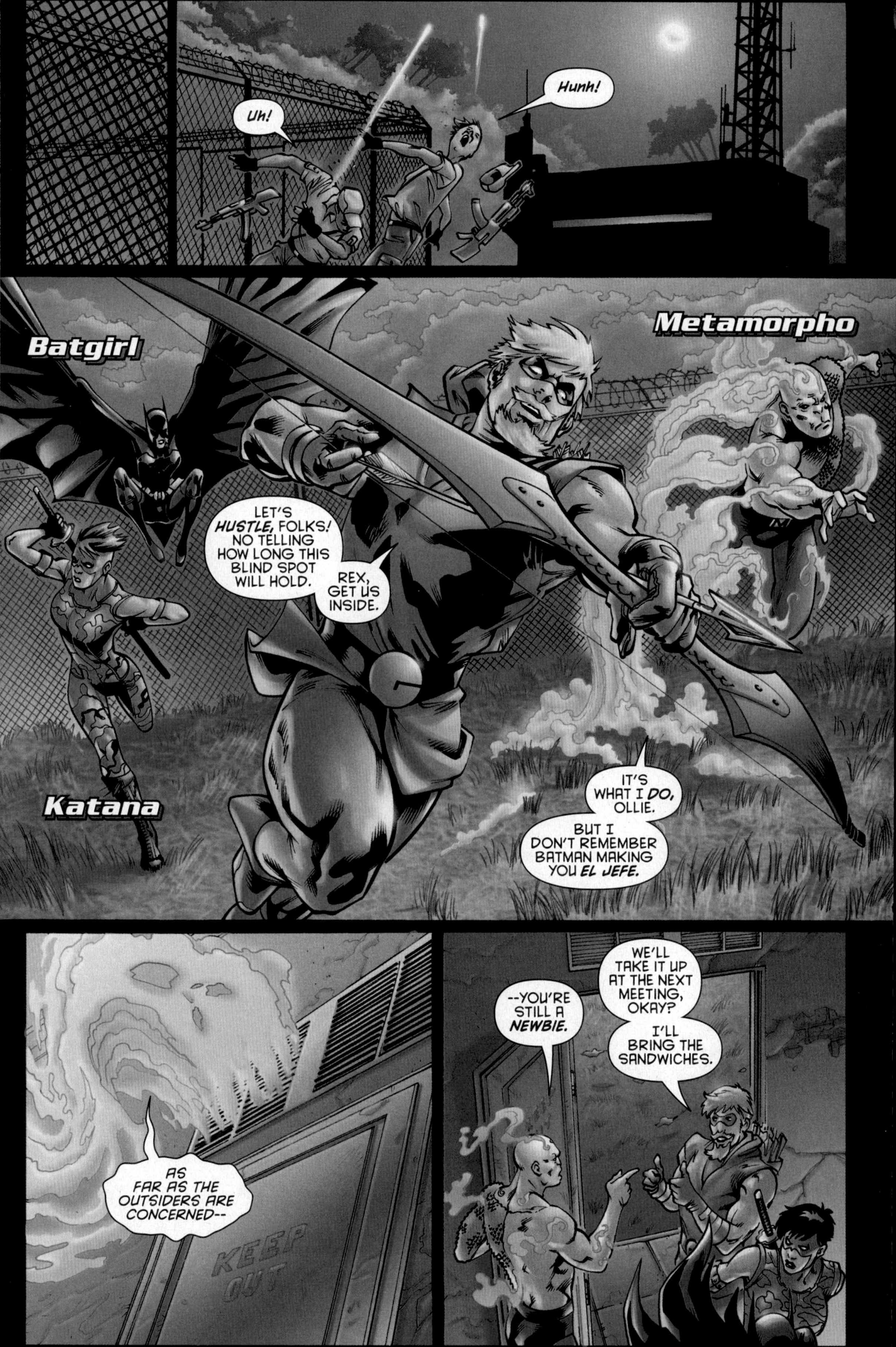

Uh!
Hunh!
Batgirl
Metamorpho
Katana
LET'S HUSTLE, FOLKS! NO TELLING HOW LONG THIS BLIND SPOT WILL HOLD.
REX, GET US INSIDE.
IT'S WHAT I DO, OLLIE.
BUT I DON'T REMEMBER BATMAN MAKING YOU EL JEFE.
AS FAR AS THE OUTSIDERS ARE CONCERNED--
KEEP OUT
--YOU'RE STILL A NEWBIE.
WE'LL TAKE IT UP AT THE NEXT MEETING, OKAY?
I'LL BRING THE SANDWICHES.

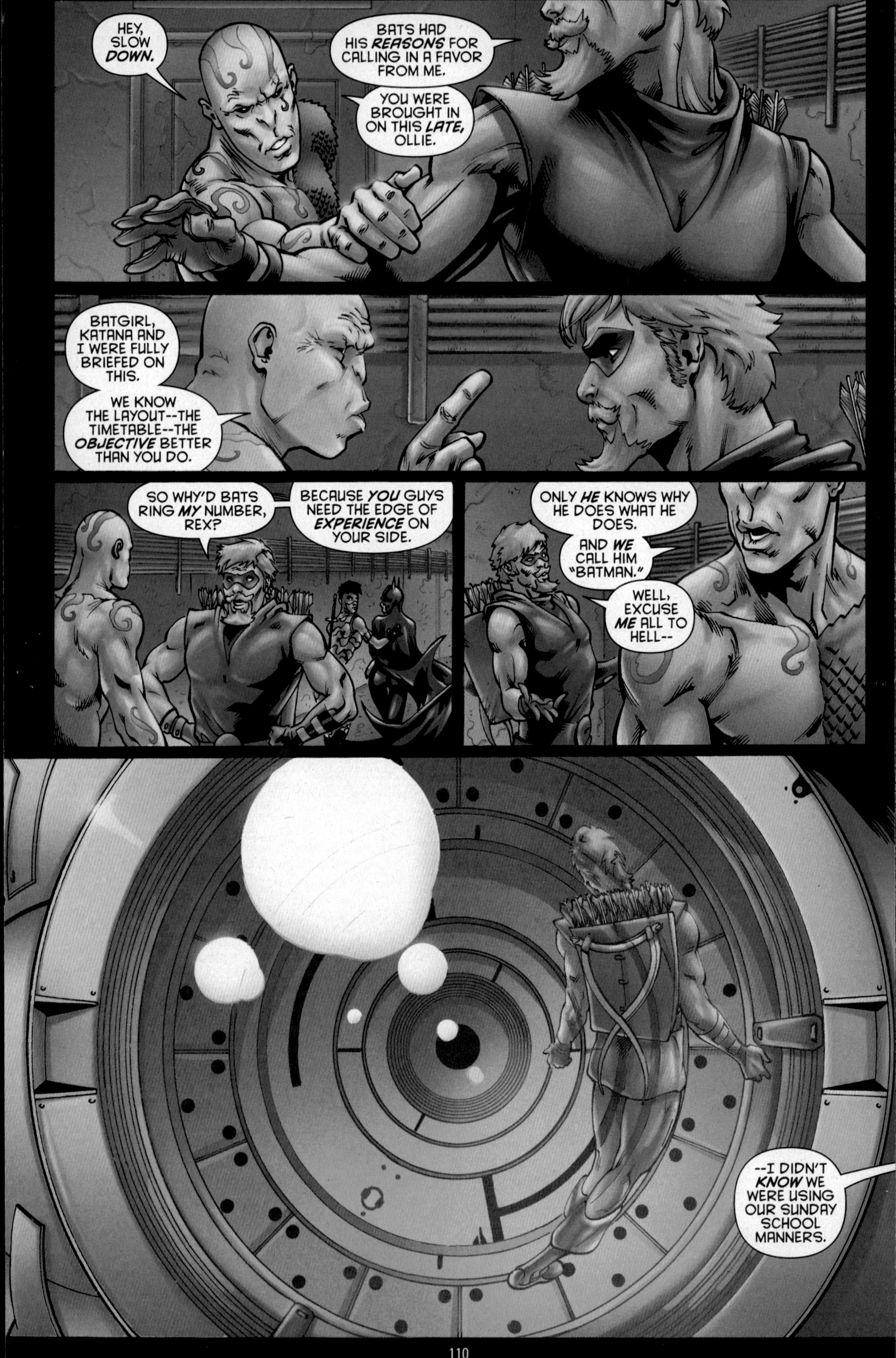
HEY, SLOW DOWN.
BATS HAD HIS REASONS FOR CALLING IN A FAVOR FROM ME.
YOU WERE BROUGHT IN ON THIS LATE, OLLIE.
BATGIRL, KATANA AND I WERE FULLY BRIEFED ON THIS.
WE KNOW THE LAYOUT--THE TIMETABLE--THE OBJECTIVE BETTER THAN YOU DO.
SO WHY'D BATS RING MY NUMBER, REX?
BECAUSE YOU GUYS NEED THE EDGE OF EXPERIENCE ON YOUR SIDE.
ONLY HE KNOWS WHY HE DOES WHAT HE DOES.
AND WE CALL HIM "BATMAN."
WELL, EXCUSE ME ALL TO HELL--
--I DIDN'T KNOW WE WERE USING OUR SUNDAY SCHOOL MANNERS.

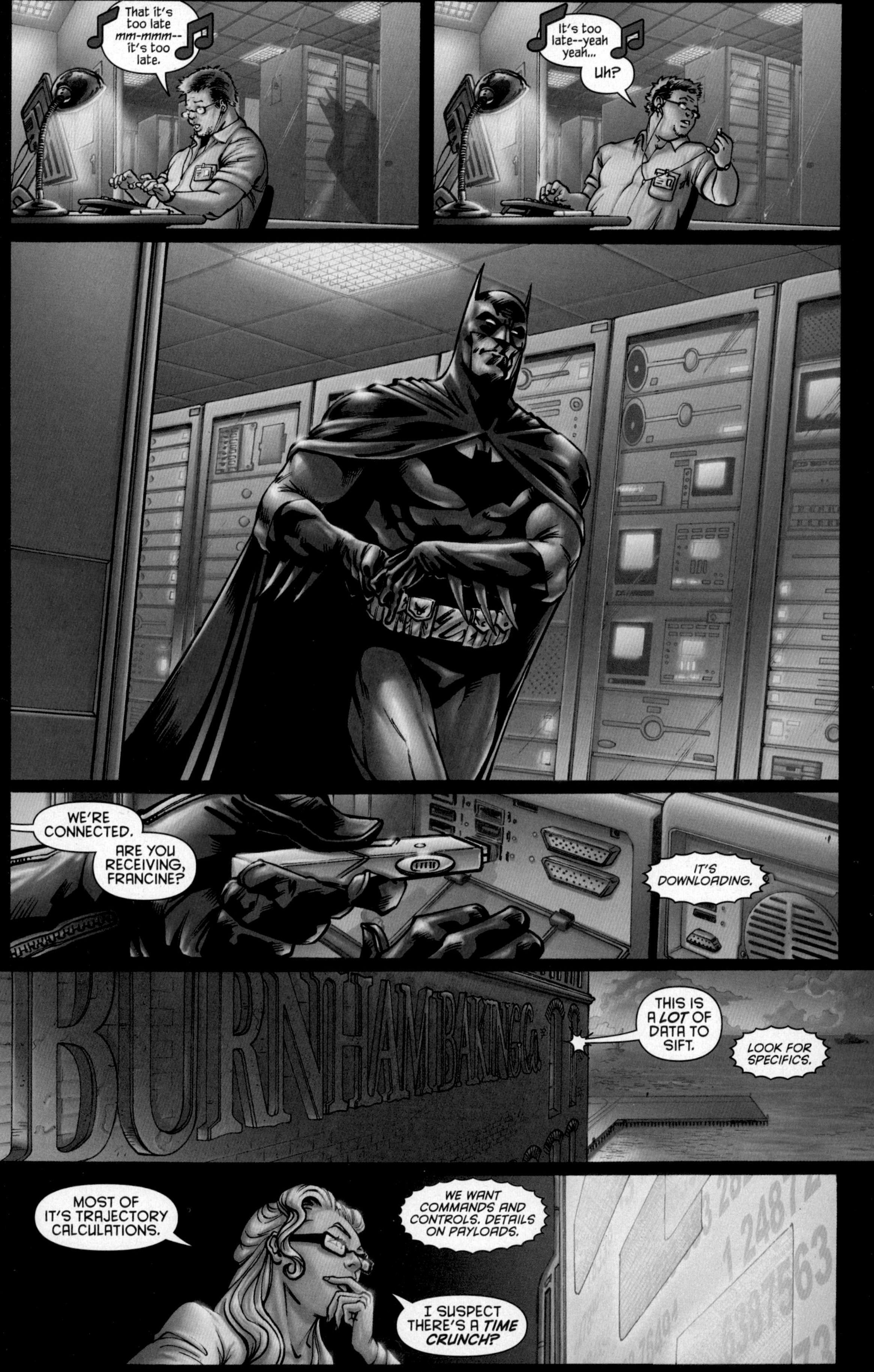
That it's too late mm-mmm-- it's too late.
It's too late--yeah yeah...
Uh?
WE'RE CONNECTED.
ARE YOU RECEIVING, FRANCINE?
IT'S DOWNLOADING.
BURNHAM BAKING CO.
THIS IS A LOT OF DATA TO SIFT.
LOOK FOR SPECIFICS.
MOST OF IT'S TRAJECTORY CALCULATIONS.
WE WANT COMMANDS AND CONTROLS. DETAILS ON PAYLOADS.
I SUSPECT THERE'S A TIME CRUNCH?

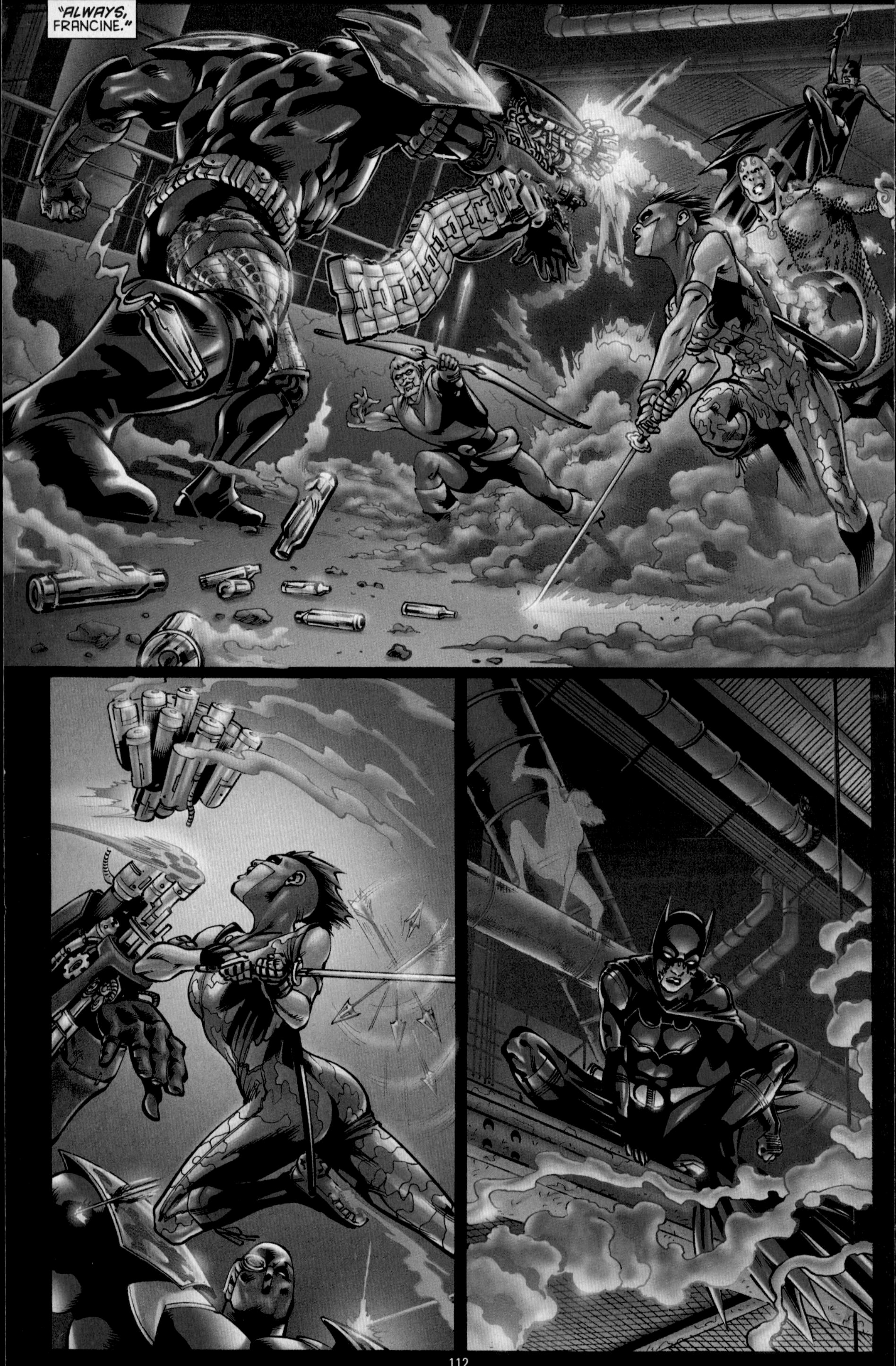
"ALWAYS,
FRANCINE."

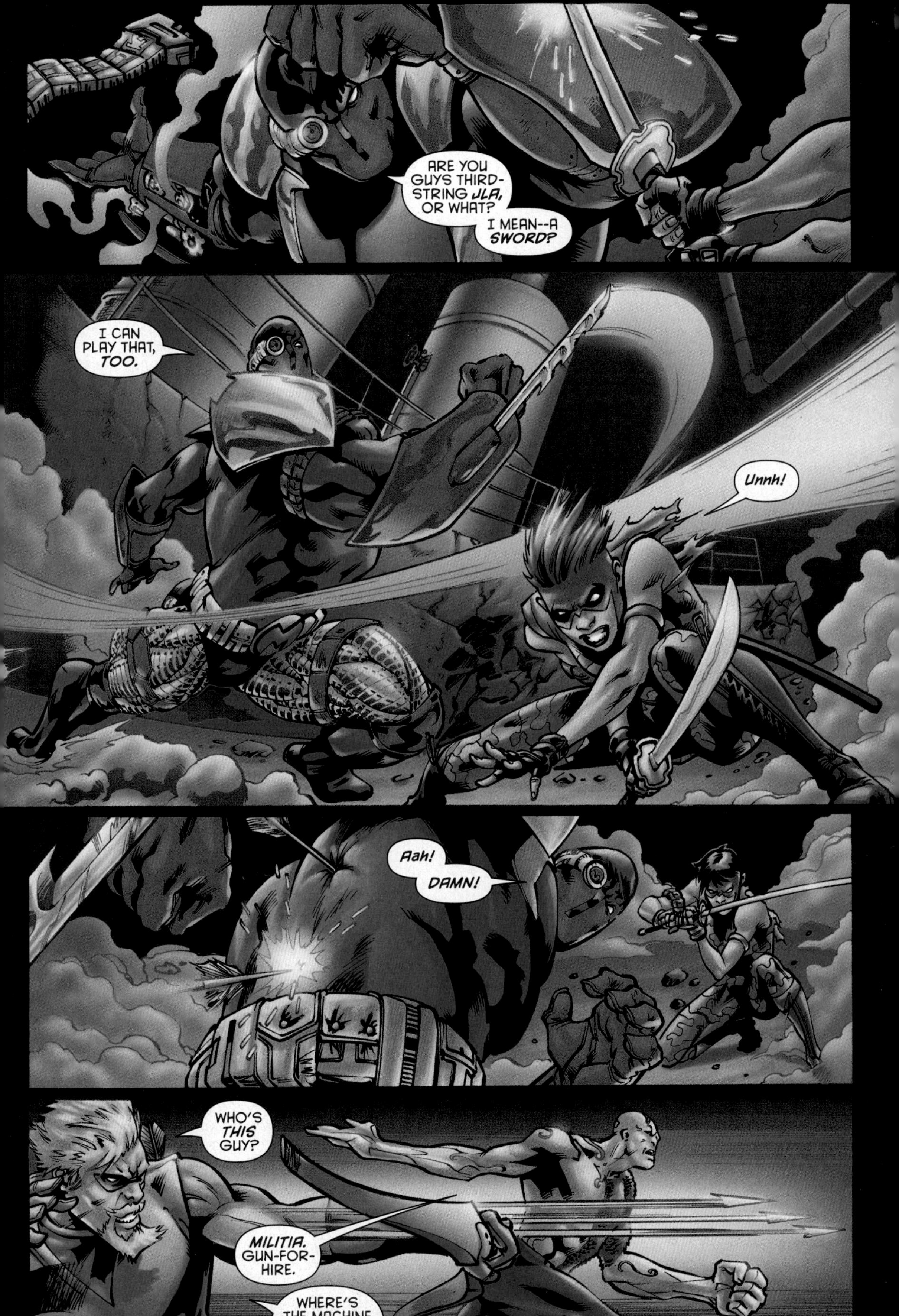
ARE YOU GUYS THIRD-STRING JLA, OR WHAT?
I MEAN--A SWORD?
I CAN PLAY THAT, TOO.
Unnh!
Aah!
DAMN!
WHO'S THIS GUY?
MILITIA. GUN-FOR-HIRE.
WHERE'S THE MACHINE END AND THE MAN BEGIN?

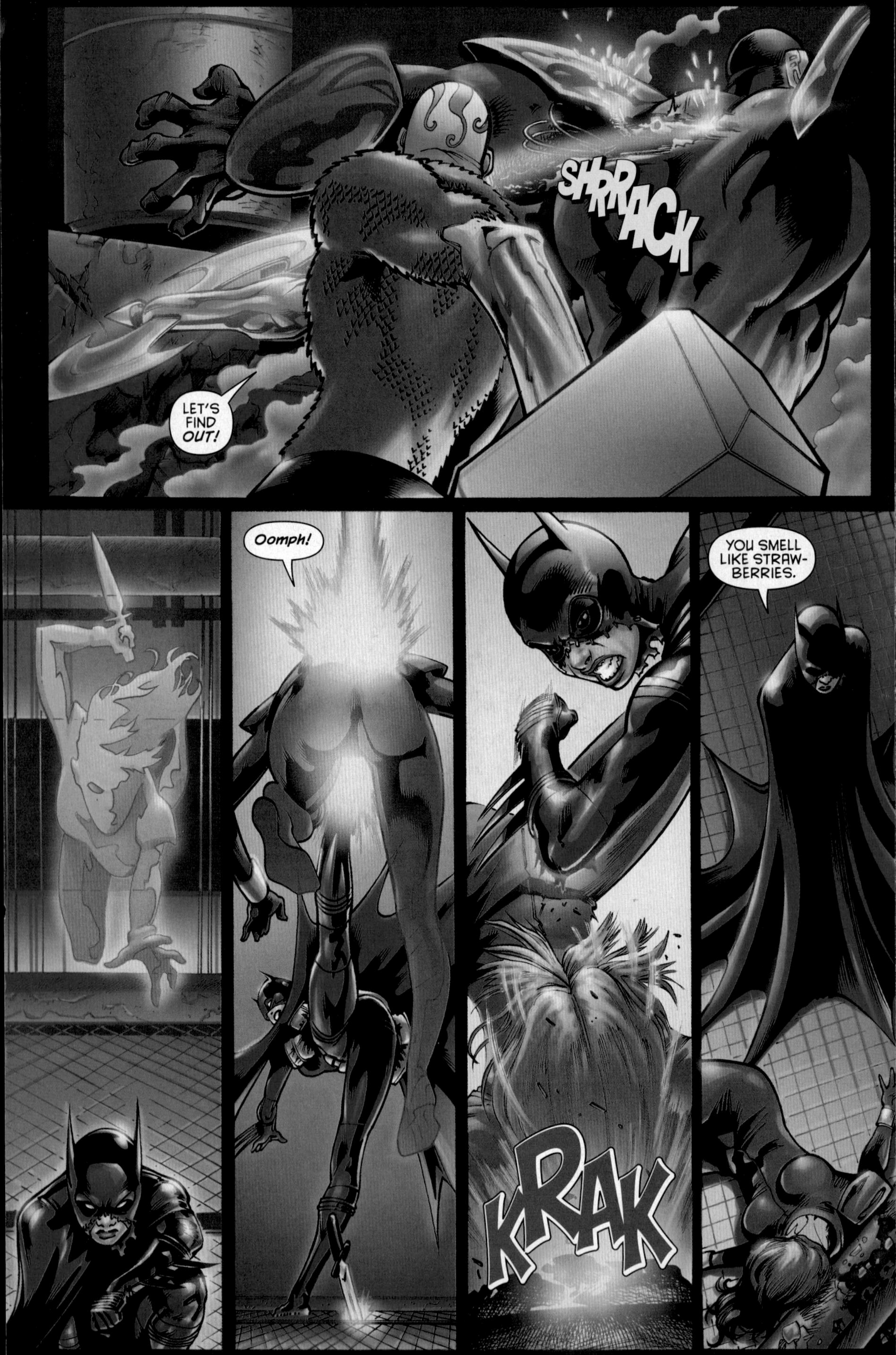
SHRRACK
LET'S FIND OUT!
Oomph!
KRAK
YOU SMELL LIKE STRAW-BERRIES.

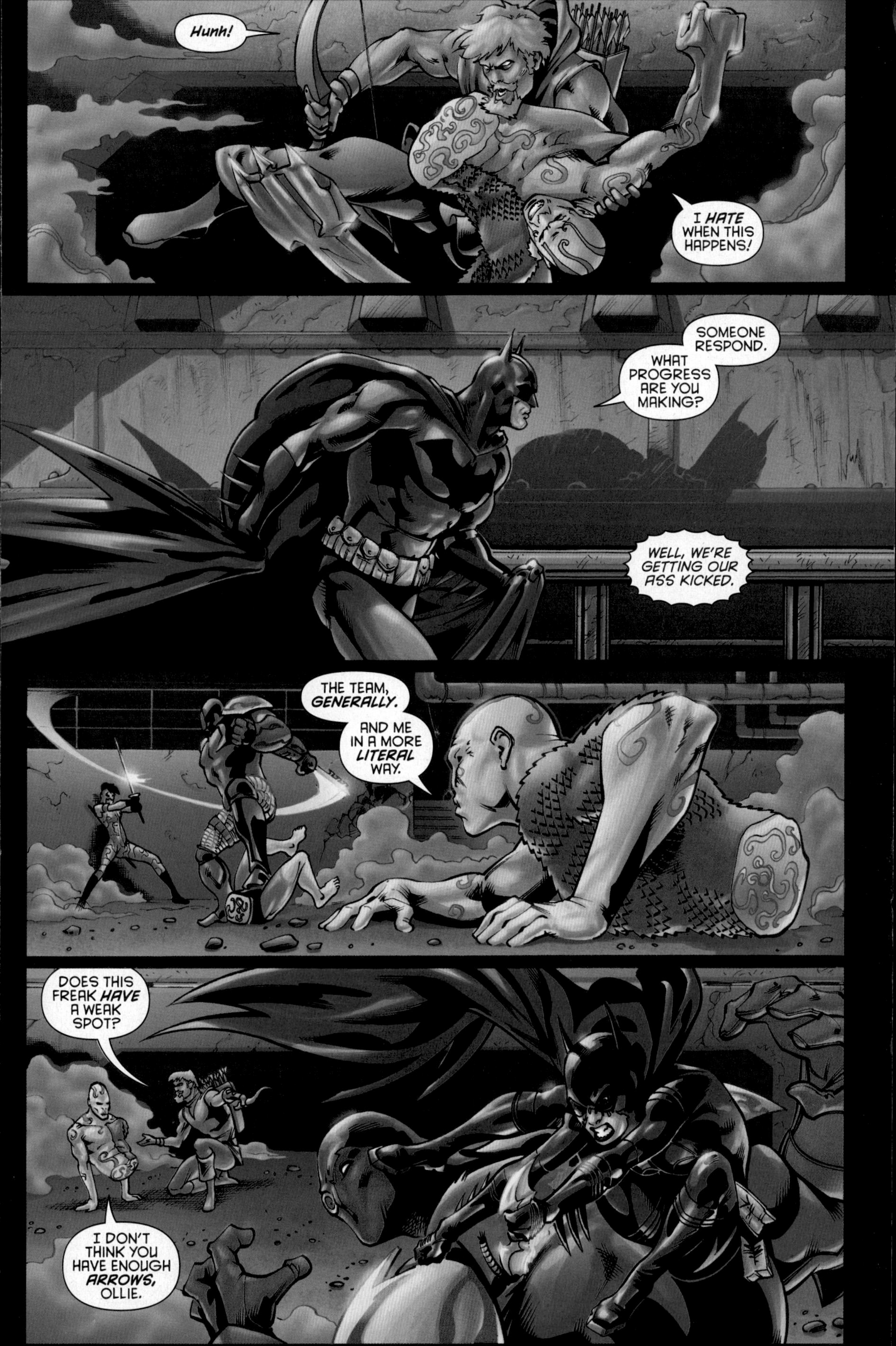
Hunh!
I *HATE* WHEN THIS HAPPENS!
SOMEONE RESPOND.
WHAT PROGRESS ARE YOU MAKING?
WELL, WE'RE GETTING OUR ASS KICKED.
THE TEAM, *GENERALLY.*
AND ME IN A MORE *LITERAL* WAY.
DOES THIS FREAK *HAVE* A WEAK SPOT?
I DON'T THINK YOU HAVE ENOUGH *ARROWS,* OLLIE.

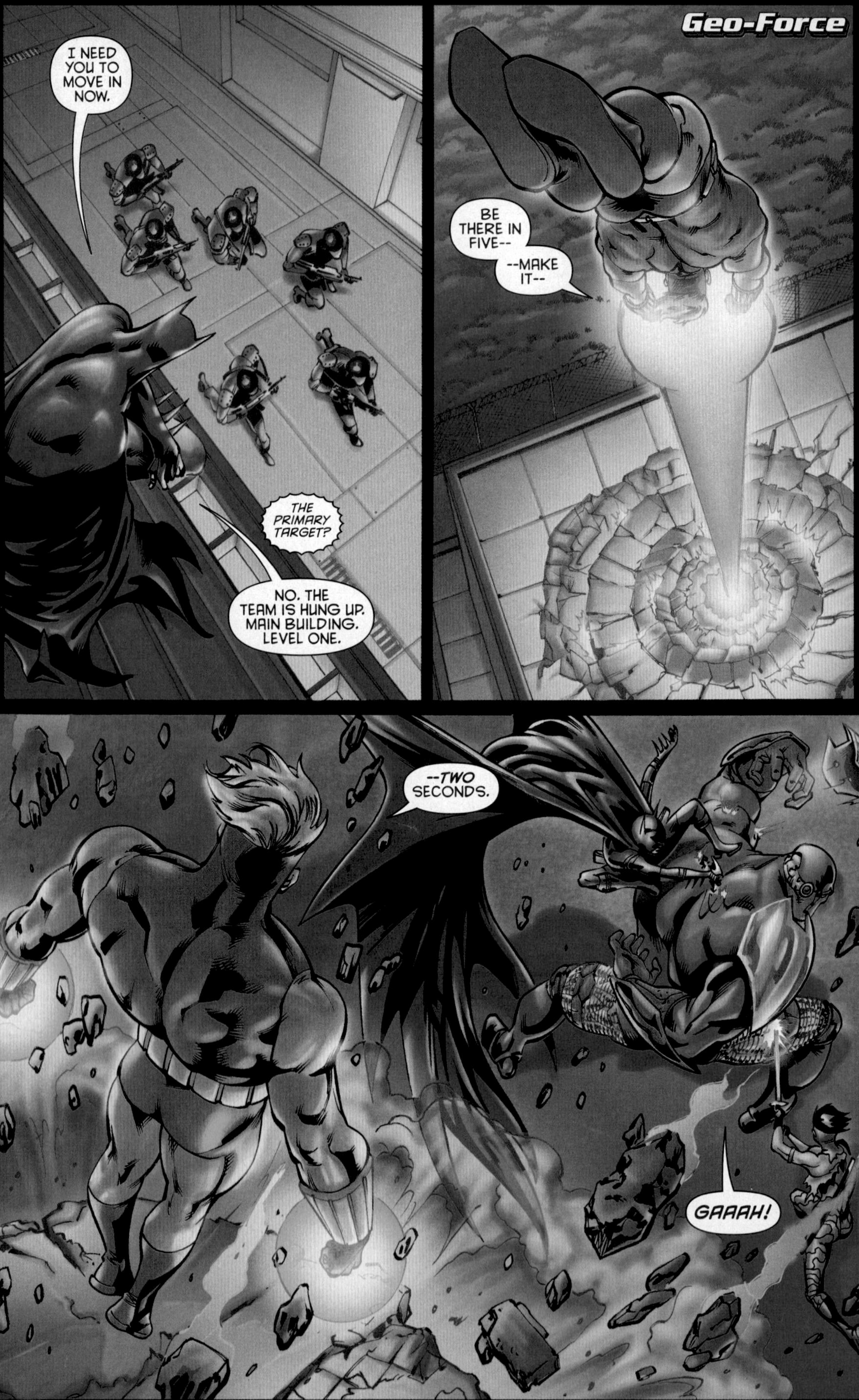
I NEED YOU TO MOVE IN NOW.
THE PRIMARY TARGET?
NO. THE TEAM IS HUNG UP. MAIN BUILDING. LEVEL ONE.
Geo-Force
BE THERE IN FIVE--
--MAKE IT--
--TWO SECONDS.
GAAAH!

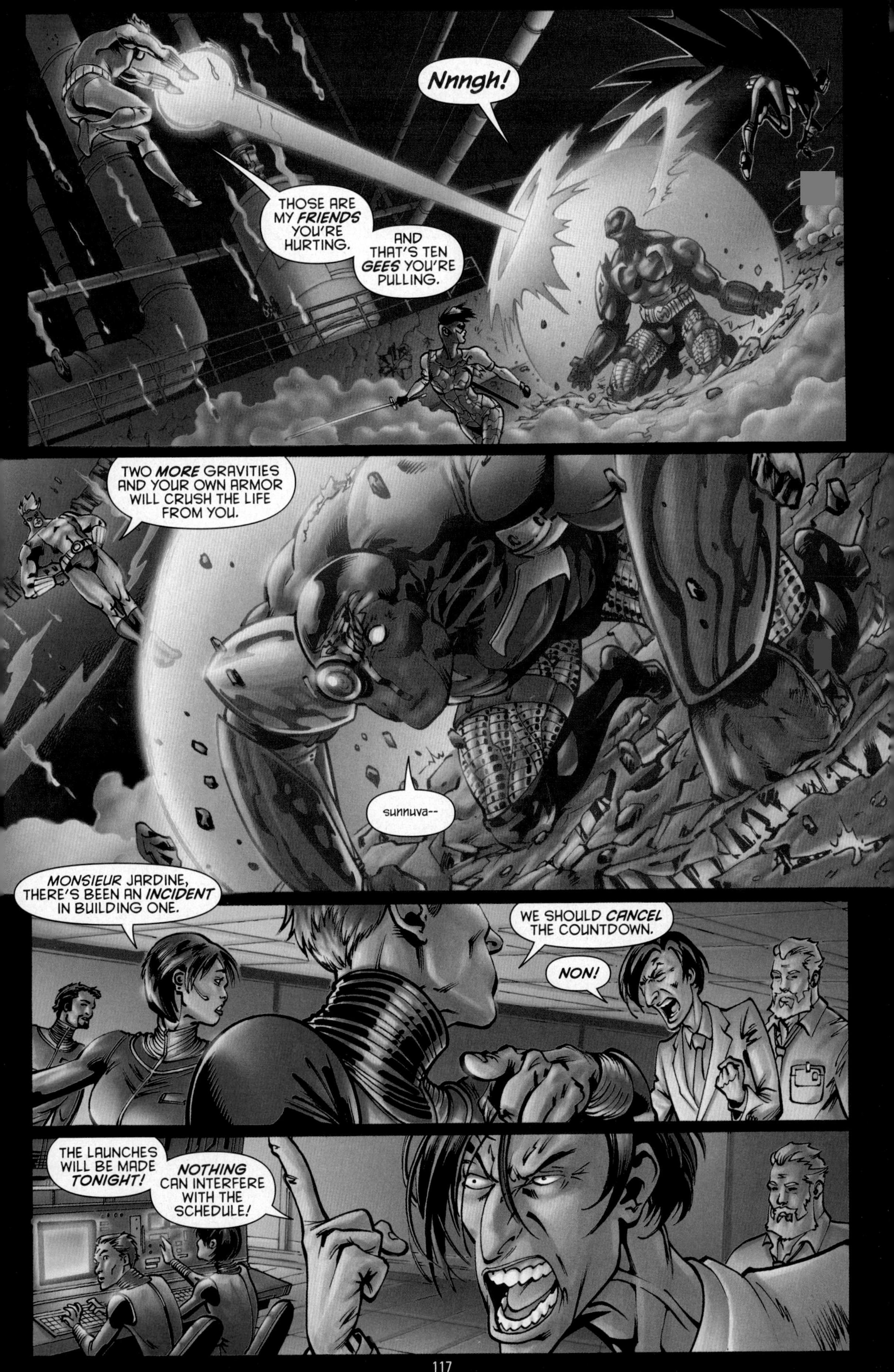
Nnngh!
THOSE ARE MY FRIENDS YOU'RE HURTING.
AND THAT'S TEN GEES YOU'RE PULLING.
TWO MORE GRAVITIES AND YOUR OWN ARMOR WILL CRUSH THE LIFE FROM YOU.
sunnuva--
MONSIEUR JARDINE, THERE'S BEEN AN INCIDENT IN BUILDING ONE.
WE SHOULD CANCEL THE COUNTDOWN.
NON!
THE LAUNCHES WILL BE MADE TONIGHT!
NOTHING CAN INTERFERE WITH THE SCHEDULE!

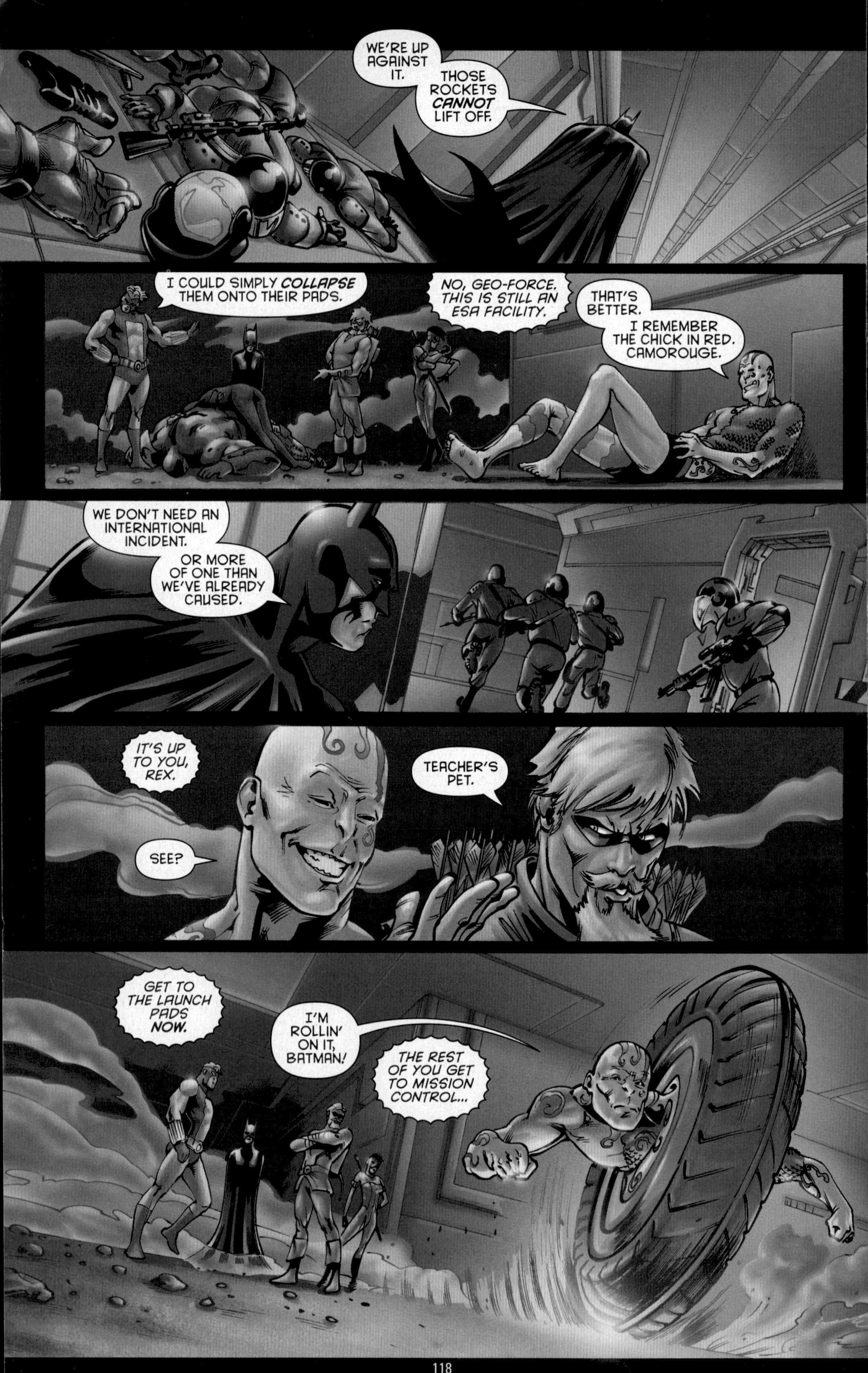
WE'RE UP AGAINST IT.
THOSE ROCKETS CANNOT LIFT OFF.
I COULD SIMPLY COLLAPSE THEM ONTO THEIR PADS.
NO, GEO-FORCE. THIS IS STILL AN ESA FACILITY.
THAT'S BETTER.
I REMEMBER THE CHICK IN RED. CAMOROUGE.
WE DON'T NEED AN INTERNATIONAL INCIDENT.
OR MORE OF ONE THAN WE'VE ALREADY CAUSED.
IT'S UP TO YOU, REX.
TEACHER'S PET.
SEE?
GET TO THE LAUNCH PADS NOW.
I'M ROLLIN' ON IT, BATMAN!
THE REST OF YOU GET TO MISSION CONTROL...

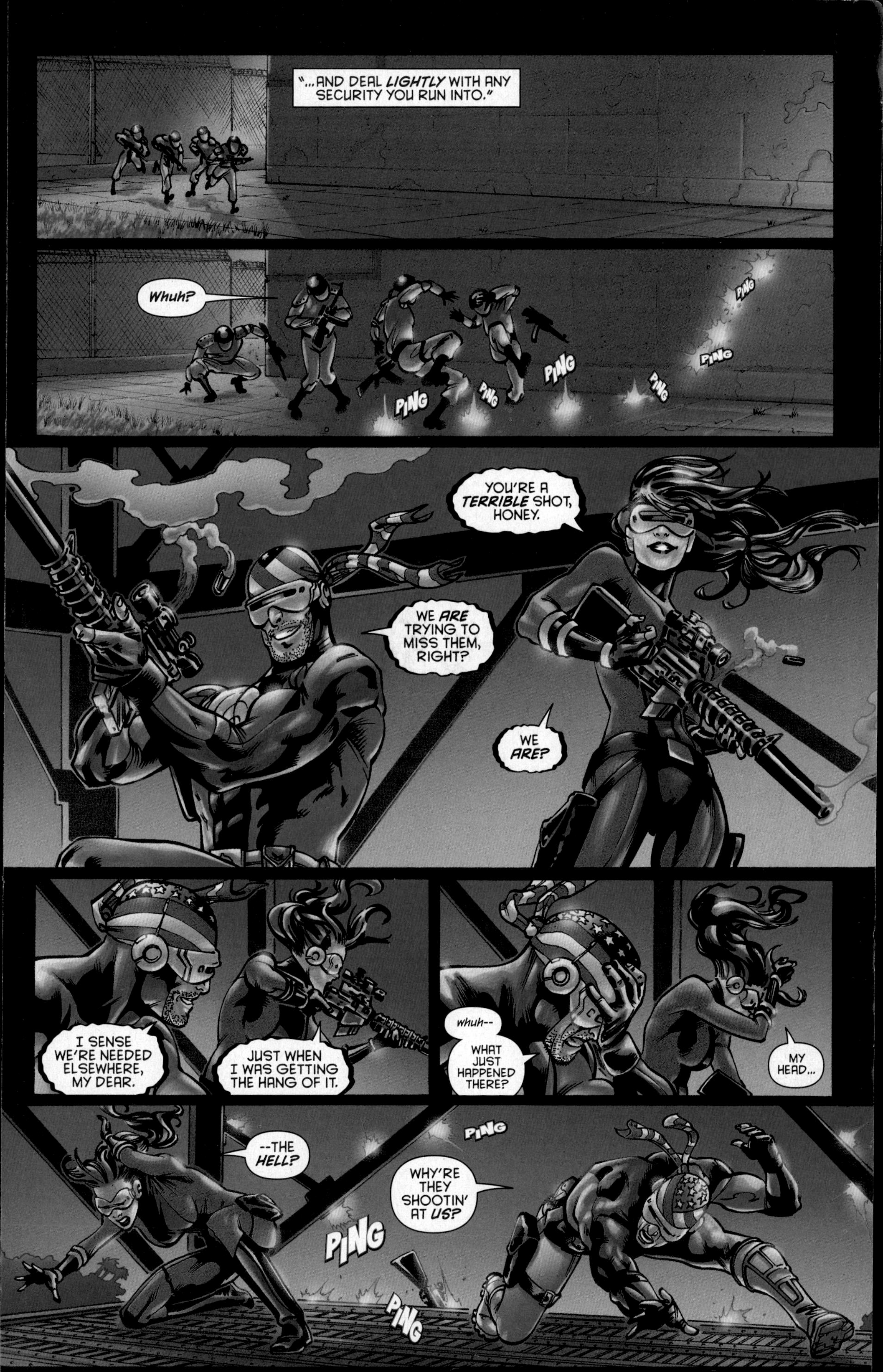
"...AND DEAL LIGHTLY WITH ANY SECURITY YOU RUN INTO."
Whuh?
PING
PING
PING
PING
PING
PING
YOU'RE A TERRIBLE SHOT, HONEY.
WE ARE TRYING TO MISS THEM, RIGHT?
WE ARE?
I SENSE WE'RE NEEDED ELSEWHERE, MY DEAR.
JUST WHEN I WAS GETTING THE HANG OF IT.
whuh--
WHAT JUST HAPPENED THERE?
MY HEAD...
--THE HELL?
WHY'RE THEY SHOOTIN' AT US?
PING
PING
PING

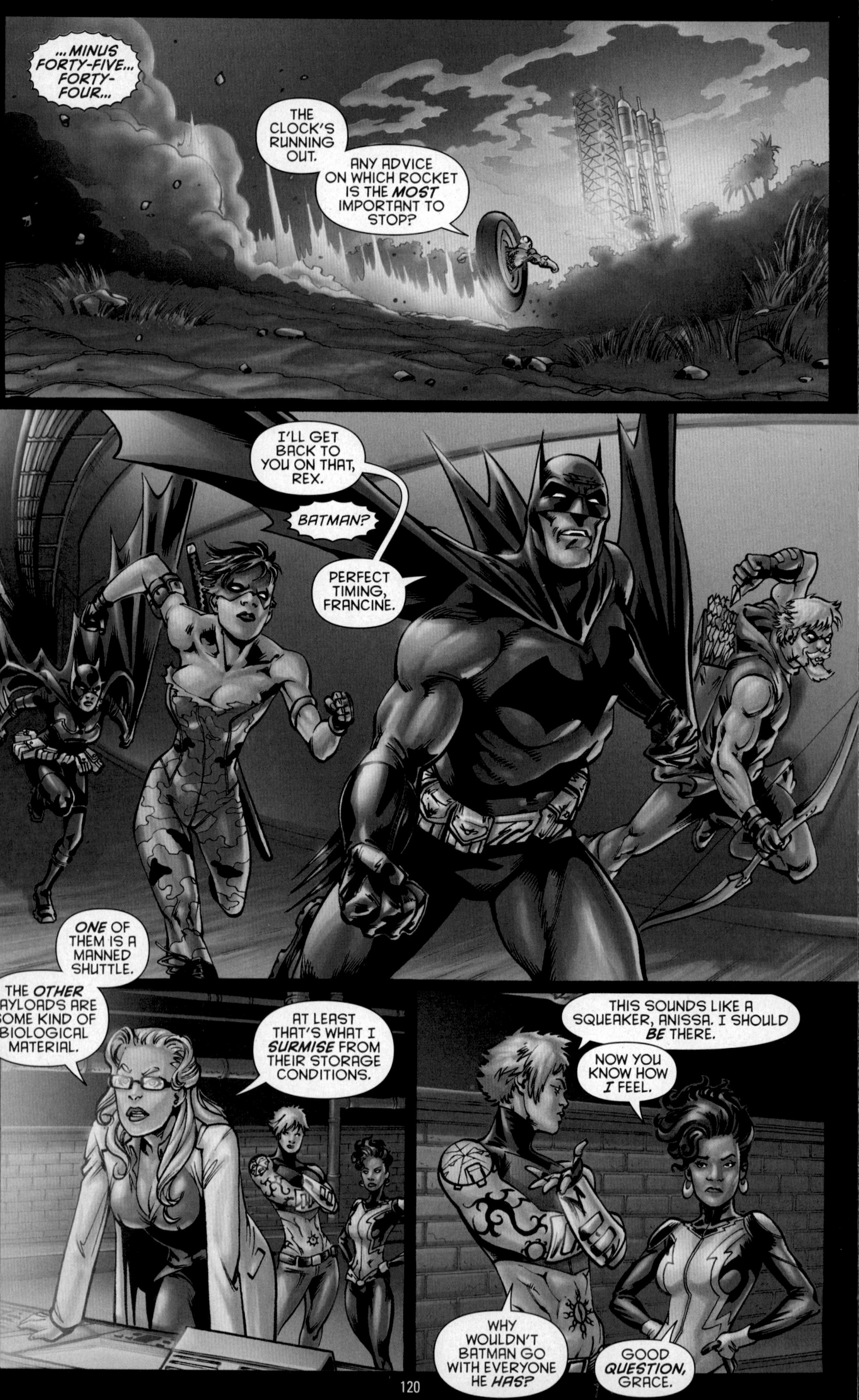
...MINUS FORTY-FIVE... FORTY-FOUR...
THE CLOCK'S RUNNING OUT.
ANY ADVICE ON WHICH ROCKET IS THE *MOST* IMPORTANT TO STOP?
I'LL GET BACK TO YOU ON THAT, REX.
BATMAN?
PERFECT TIMING, FRANCINE.
ONE OF THEM IS A MANNED SHUTTLE.
THE *OTHER* PAYLOADS ARE SOME KIND OF BIOLOGICAL MATERIAL.
AT LEAST THAT'S WHAT I *SURMISE* FROM THEIR STORAGE CONDITIONS.
THIS SOUNDS LIKE A SQUEAKER, ANISSA. I SHOULD *BE* THERE.
NOW YOU KNOW HOW *I* FEEL.
WHY WOULDN'T BATMAN GO WITH EVERYONE HE *HAS?*
GOOD *QUESTION,* GRACE.

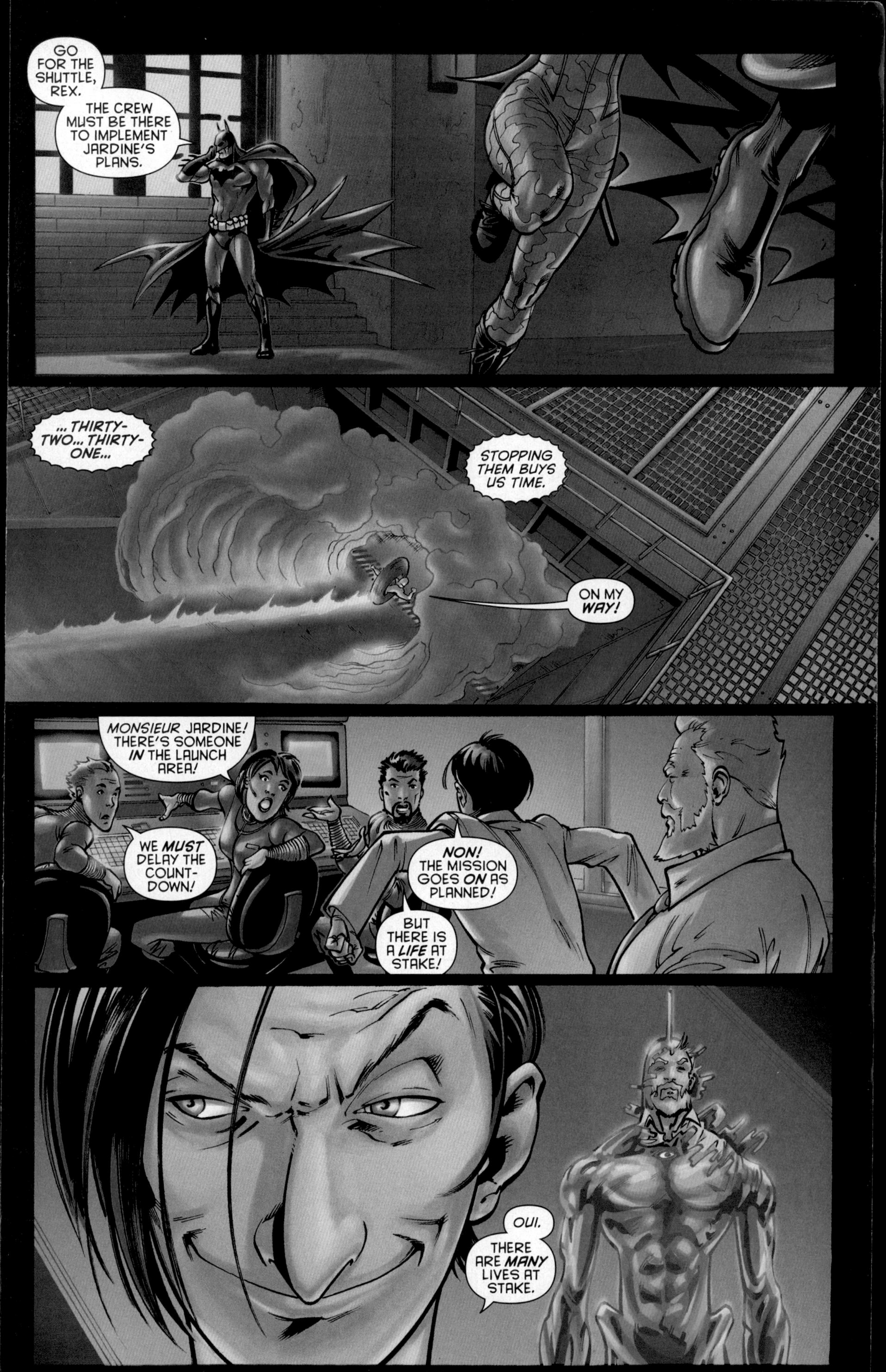

GO FOR THE SHUTTLE, REX.
THE CREW MUST BE THERE TO IMPLEMENT JARDINE'S PLANS.
...THIRTY-TWO...THIRTY-ONE...
STOPPING THEM BUYS US TIME.
ON MY WAY!
MONSIEUR JARDINE! THERE'S SOMEONE IN THE LAUNCH AREA!
WE MUST DELAY THE COUNT-DOWN!
NON! THE MISSION GOES ON AS PLANNED!
BUT THERE IS A LIFE AT STAKE!
OUI.
THERE ARE MANY LIVES AT STAKE.

...MINUS TWENTY... NINETEEN... EIGHTEEN...

--JUST ONCE I WISH WE COULD BE EARLY--

STOP THE COUNTDOWN. RIGHT NOW.

I THINK NOT.

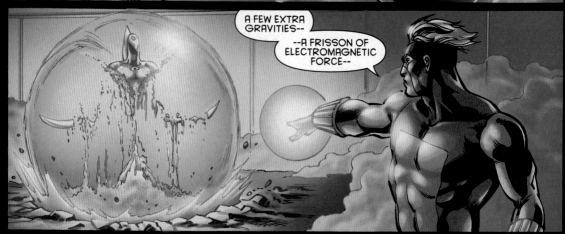

A FEW EXTRA GRAVITIES-- --A FRISSON OF ELECTROMAGNETIC FORCE--

--AND WE HAVE A PILE OF DISINCORPORATED NANITES.

REX...

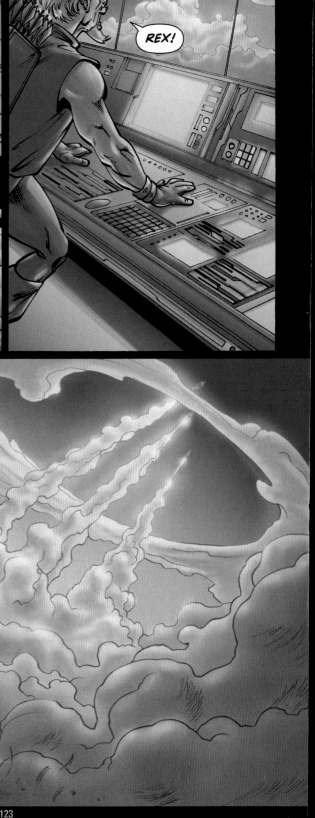

REX!

OLIVER... NO.

DON'T *WORRY*, OLLIE.

QUE?

HE'LL *PAY* FOR WHAT HE'S DONE.

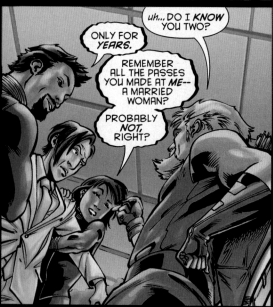

uh...DO I KNOW YOU TWO?

ONLY FOR *YEARS*.

REMEMBER ALL THE PASSES YOU MADE AT *ME*-- A MARRIED WOMAN?

PROBABLY *NOT*, RIGHT?

RALPH?

SUE?

THE *DIBNYS*.

GUILTY AS CHARGED.

BUT I THOUGHT YOU BOTH--

DIED? YEP. DEAD AS DEAD CAN *BE*.

BUT *THAT* DOESN'T STOP MY HUBBY FROM PURSUING HIS FAVORITE PASTIME.

--AS *GHOSTS?*

WE PREFER "SPIRITS".

BOO.

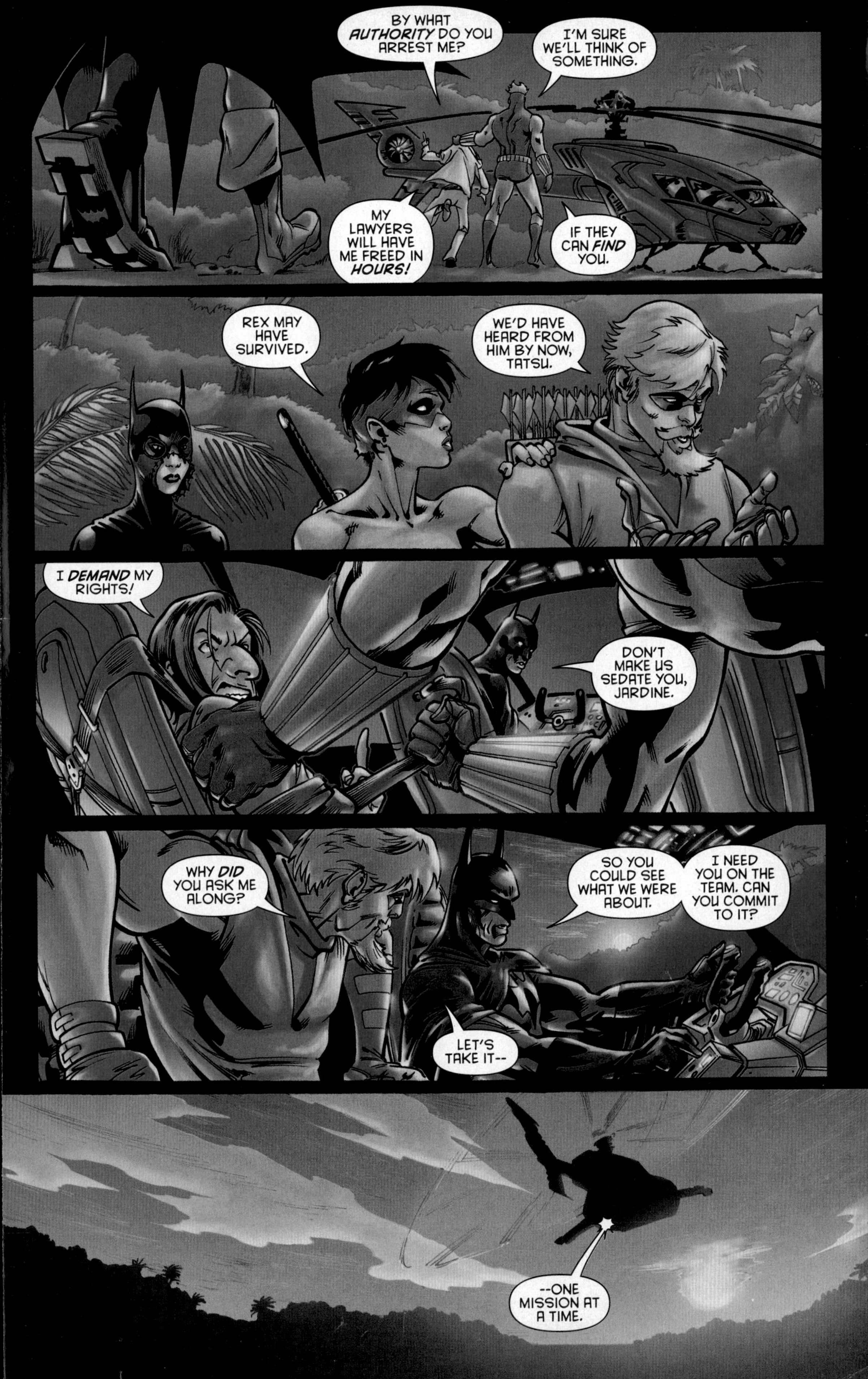
BY WHAT AUTHORITY DO YOU ARREST ME?
I'M SURE WE'LL THINK OF SOMETHING.
MY LAWYERS WILL HAVE ME FREED IN HOURS!
IF THEY CAN FIND YOU.
REX MAY HAVE SURVIVED.
WE'D HAVE HEARD FROM HIM BY NOW, TATSU.
I DEMAND MY RIGHTS!
DON'T MAKE US SEDATE YOU, JARDINE.
WHY DID YOU ASK ME ALONG?
SO YOU COULD SEE WHAT WE WERE ABOUT.
I NEED YOU ON THE TEAM. CAN YOU COMMIT TO IT?
LET'S TAKE IT--
--ONE MISSION AT A TIME.

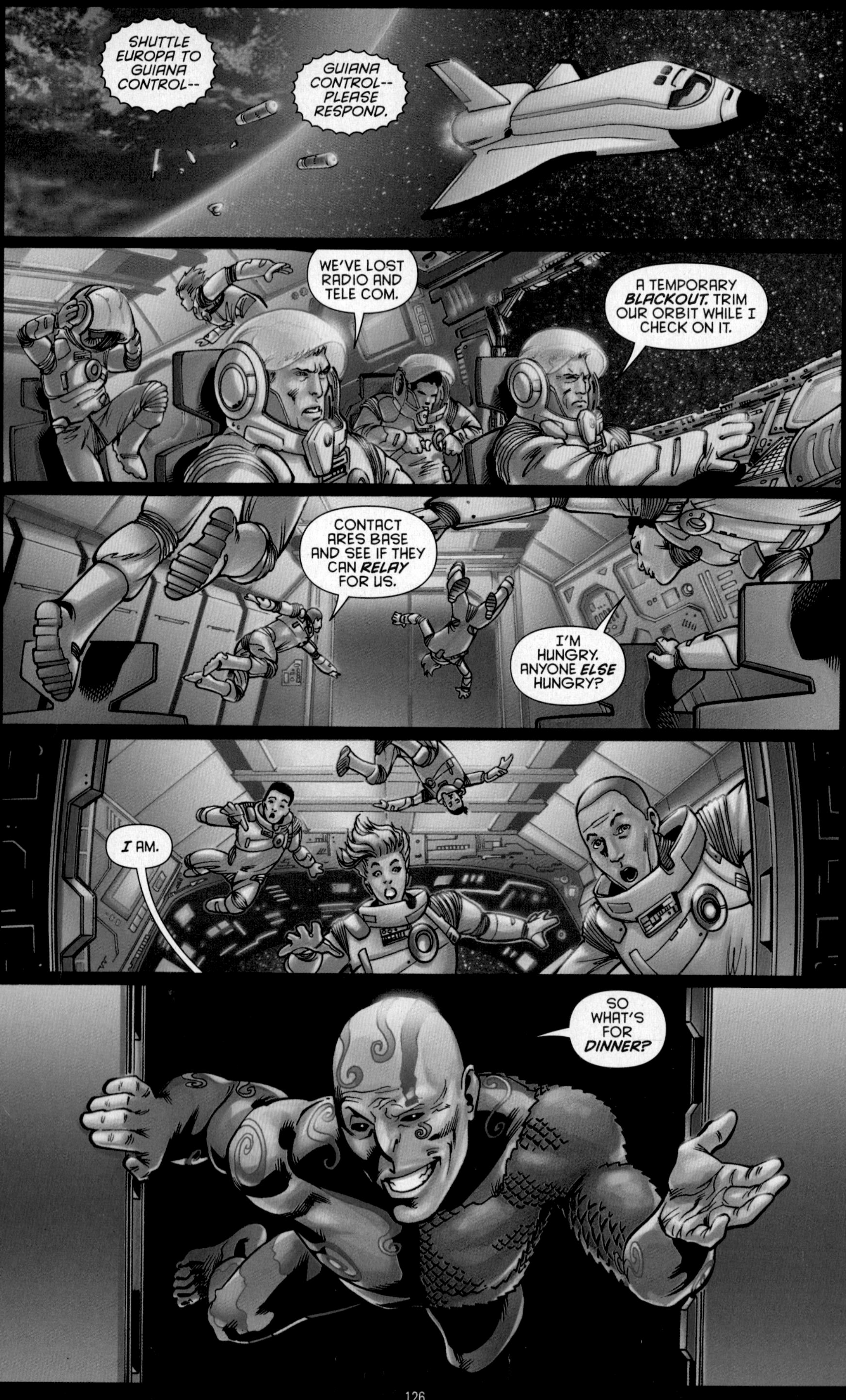
SHUTTLE EUROPA TO GUIANA CONTROL--
GUIANA CONTROL-- PLEASE RESPOND.
WE'VE LOST RADIO AND TELE COM.
A TEMPORARY BLACKOUT. TRIM OUR ORBIT WHILE I CHECK ON IT.
CONTACT ARES BASE AND SEE IF THEY CAN RELAY FOR US.
I'M HUNGRY. ANYONE ELSE HUNGRY?
I AM.
SO WHAT'S FOR DINNER?

READ MORE OF THE DARK KNIGHT DETECTIVE'S ADVENTURES IN THESE COLLECTIONS FROM DC COMICS:

BATMAN

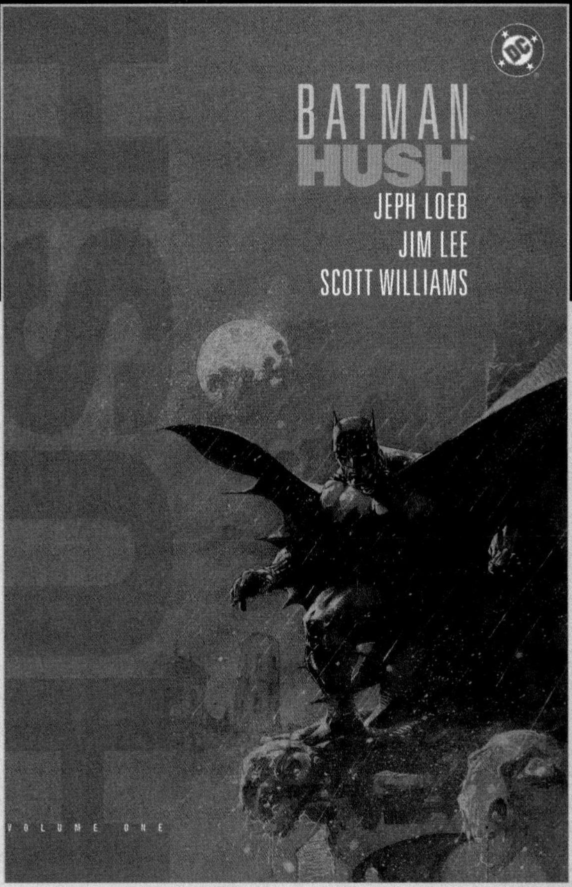
BATMAN
HUSH
JEPH LOEB
JIM LEE
SCOTT WILLIAMS
VOLUME ONE

BATMAN: HUSH VOLUME 1

Jeph Loeb, Jim Lee and **Scott Williams** tell an epic tale of friendship, trust and betrayal, in the first volume of a tale that spans a lifetime of the Dark Knight.

"THE ACTION IS EXCITING AND THE DETAIL IS METICULOUS."
— CRITIQUES ON INFINITE EARTHS

BATMAN:
THE DARK KNIGHT RETURNS

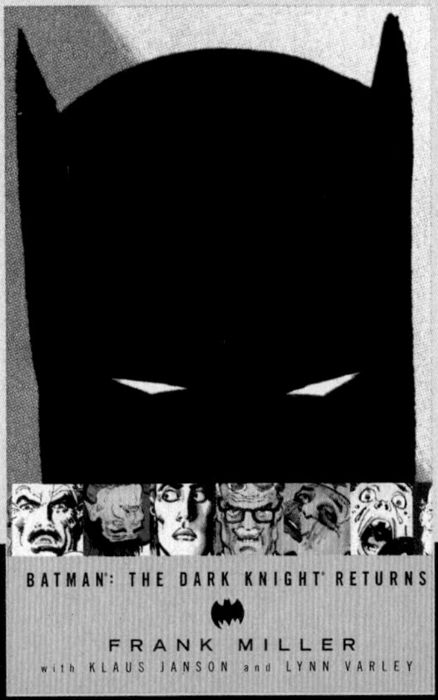
BATMAN: THE DARK KNIGHT RETURNS
FRANK MILLER
with KLAUS JANSON and LYNN VARLEY

FRANK MILLER
KLAUS JANSON
LYNN VARLEY

BATMAN:
THE LONG HALLOWEEN

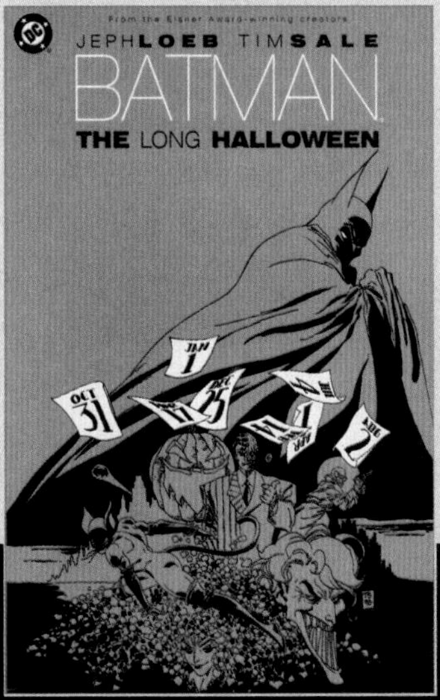
JEPH LOEB TIM SALE
BATMAN
THE LONG HALLOWEEN

JEPH LOEB
TIM SALE

BATMAN:
YEAR ONE

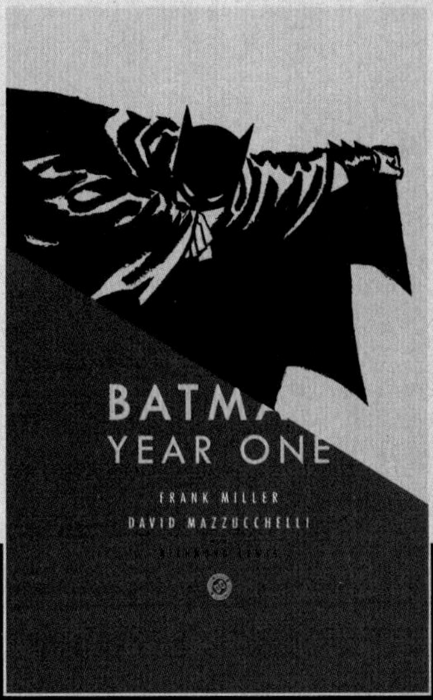
YEAR ONE
FRANK MILLER
DAVID MAZZUCCHELLI

FRANK MILLER
DAVID MAZZUCCHELLI

AND DON'T MISS THESE OTHER GREAT TITLES FEATURING **BATMAN!**

BATMAN: WAR GAMES ACT ONE

**BILL WILLINGHAM
ED BRUBAKER
PETE WOODS**

THE BATMAN CHRONICLES VOLUME 1

**BOB KANE
BILL FINGER**

BATMAN: THE DARK KNIGHT STRIKES AGAIN

**FRANK MILLER
LYNN VARLEY**

BATMAN: DARK VICTORY

**JEPH LOEB
TIM SALE**

BATMAN: HUSH VOLUME 2

**JEPH LOEB
JIM LEE
SCOTT WILLIAMS**

BATMAN: THE GREATEST STORIES EVER TOLD

**BOB KANE
NEAL ADAMS
FRANK MILLER**

SEARCH THE GRAPHIC NOVELS SECTION OF

www. DCCOMICS.com

FOR ART AND INFORMATION ON ALL OF OUR BOOKS!